Investigating Hard Disks, File and Operating Systems

EC-Council | Press

Volume 2 of 5 mapping to

C|HFI™

Computer | Hacking Forensic INVESTIGATOR

Certification

COURSE TECHNOLOGY
CENGAGE Learning™

Australia • Brazil • Japan • Korea • Mexico • Singapore • Spain • United Kingdom • United States

Investigating Hard Disks, File and Operating Systems: EC-Council | Press

Course Technology/Cengage Learning Staff:

Vice President, Career and Professional Editorial: Dave Garza

Director of Learning Solutions: Matthew Kane

Executive Editor: Stephen Helba

Managing Editor: Marah Bellegarde

Editorial Assistant: Meghan Orvis

Vice President, Career and Professional Marketing: Jennifer Ann Baker

Marketing Director: Deborah Yarnell

Marketing Manager: Erin Coffin

Marketing Coordinator: Shanna Gibbs

Production Director: Carolyn Miller

Production Manager: Andrew Crouth

Content Project Manager: Brooke Greenhouse

Senior Art Director: Jack Pendleton

EC-Council:

President | EC-Council: Sanjay Bavisi

Sr. Director US | EC-Council: Steven Graham

For product information and technology assistance, contact us at **Cengage Learning Customer & Sales Support, 1-800-354-9706**

For permission to use material from this text or product, submit all requests online at **www.cengage.com/permissions**. Further permissions questions can be e-mailed to **permissionrequest@cengage.com**

Library of Congress Control Number: 2009933548

ISBN- 13: 978-1-4354-8350-7

ISBN-10: 1-4354-8350-2

Cengage Learning
5 Maxwell Drive
Clifton Park, NY 12065-2919
USA

Cengage Learning is a leading provider of customized learning solutions with office locations around the globe, including Singapore, the United Kingdom, Australia, Mexico, Brazil, and Japan. Locate your local office at: **international.cengage.com/region**

Cengage Learning products are represented in Canada by Nelson Education, Ltd.

For more learning solutions, please visit our corporate website at **www.cengage.com**

NOTICE TO THE READER

Cengage Learning and EC-Council do not warrant or guarantee any of the products described herein or perform any independent analysis in connection with any of the product information contained herein. Cengage Learning and EC-Council do not assume, and expressly disclaim, any obligation to obtain and include information other than that provided to it by the manufacturer. The reader is expressly warned to consider and adopt all safety precautions that might be indicated by the activities described herein and to avoid all potential hazards. By following the instructions contained herein, the reader willingly assumes all risks in connection with such instructions. Cengage Learning and EC-Council make no representations or warranties of any kind, including but not limited to, the warranties of fitness for particular purpose or merchantability, nor are any such representations implied with respect to the material set forth herein, and Cengage Learning and EC-Council take no responsibility with respect to such material. Cengage Learning and EC-Council shall not be liable for any special, consequential, or exemplary damages resulting, in whole or part, from the readers' use of, or reliance upon, this material.

Printed in the United States of America
1 2 3 4 5 6 7 12 11 10 09

Brief Table of Contents

Table of Contents

Hacking and electronic crimes sophistication has grown at an exponential rate in recent years. In fact, recent reports have indicated that cyber crime already surpasses the illegal drug trade! Unethical hackers, better known as *black hats,* are preying on information systems of government, corporate, public, and private networks and are constantly testing the security mechanisms of these organizations to the limit with the sole aim of exploiting them and profiting from the exercise. High-profile crimes have proven that the traditional approach to computer security is simply not sufficient, even with the strongest perimeter, properly configured defense mechanisms such as firewalls, intrusion detection, and prevention systems, strong end-to-end encryption standards, and anti-virus software. Hackers have proven their dedication and ability to systematically penetrate networks all over the world. In some cases, black hats may be able to execute attacks so flawlessly that they can compromise a system, steal everything of value, and completely erase their tracks in less than 20 minutes!

The EC-Council Press is dedicated to stopping hackers in their tracks.

About EC-Council

The International Council of Electronic Commerce Consultants, better known as EC-Council, was founded in late 2001 to address the need for well-educated and certified information security and e-business practitioners. EC-Council is a global, member-based organization comprised of industry and subject matter experts all working together to set the standards and raise the bar in information security certification and education.

EC-Council first developed the *Certified Ethical Hacker* (C|EH) program. The goal of this program is to teach the methodologies, tools, and techniques used by hackers. Leveraging the collective knowledge from hundreds of subject matter experts, the C|EH program has rapidly gained popularity around the globe and is now delivered in more than 70 countries by more than 450 authorized training centers. More than 60,000 information security practitioners have been trained.

C|EH is the benchmark for many government entities and major corporations around the world. Shortly after C|EH was launched, EC-Council developed the *Certified Security Analyst* (E|CSA). The goal of the E|CSA program is to teach groundbreaking analysis methods that must be applied while conducting advanced penetration testing. The E|CSA program leads to the *Licensed Penetration Tester* (L|PT) status. The *Computer Hacking Forensic Investigator* (C|HFI) was formed with the same design methodologies and has become a global standard in certification for computer forensics. EC-Council, through its impervious network of professionals and huge industry following, has developed various other programs in information security and e-business. EC-Council certifications are viewed as the essential certifications needed when standard configuration and security policy courses fall short. Providing a true, hands-on, tactical approach to security, individuals armed with the knowledge disseminated by EC-Council programs are securing networks around the world and beating the hackers at their own game.

About the EC-Council | Press

The EC-Council | Press was formed in late 2008 as a result of a cutting-edge partnership between global information security certification leader, EC-Council and leading global academic publisher, Cengage Learning. This partnership marks a revolution in academic textbooks and courses of study in information security, computer forensics, disaster recovery, and end-user security. By identifying the essential topics and content of EC-Council professional certification programs, and repurposing this world-class content to fit academic programs, the EC-Council | Press was formed. The academic community is now able to incorporate this powerful cutting-edge content into new and existing information security programs. By closing the gap between academic study and professional certification, students and instructors are able to leverage the power of rigorous academic focus and high demand industry certification. The EC-Council | Press is set to revolutionize global information security programs and ultimately create a new breed of practitioners capable of combating the growing epidemic of cybercrime and the rising threat of cyber-war.

Computer Forensics Series

The EC-Council | Press *Computer Forensics* series, preparing learners for C|HFI certification, is intended for those studying to become police investigators and other law enforcement personnel, defense and military personnel, e-business security professionals, systems administrators, legal professionals, banking, insurance and other professionals, government agencies, and IT managers. The content of this program is designed to expose the learner to the process of detecting attacks and collecting evidence in a forensically sound manner with the intent to report crime and prevent future attacks. Advanced techniques in computer investigation and analysis with interest in generating potential legal evidence are included. In full, this series prepares the learner to identify evidence in computer-related crime and abuse cases as well as track the intrusive hacker's path through client system.

Books in Series
- *Computer Forensics: Investigation Procedures and Response*/1435483499
- *Computer Forensics: Investigating Hard Disks, File and Operating Systems*/1435483502
- *Computer Forensics: Investigating Data and Image Files*/1435483510
- *Computer Forensics: Investigating Network Intrusions and Cybercrime*/1435483529
- *Computer Forensics: Investigating Wireless Networks and Devices*/1435483537

Investigating Hard Disks, File and Operating Systems

Investigating Hard Disks, File and Operating Systems provides a basic understanding of file systems, hard disks and digital media devices. Boot processes, Windows and Linux Forensics and application of password crackers are all discussed.

Chapter Contents

Chapter 1, *Understanding File Systems and Hard Disks,* provides an overview of disk drives and then delves deeper into hard disks. Coverage also includes physical data storage and various file systems in use on computer systems. Chapter 2, *Understanding Digital Media Devices,* focuses on the different types of data that can be stored on digital media devices, including older digital media such as magnetic tapes and floppy disks to new digital media such as CDs, DVDs, digital audio players, and flash drives. Chapter 3, *Windows, Linux, and Macintosh Boot Processes,* covers basic information about the boot process for various operating systems including MS-DOS, Windows, Linux, and Mac OS. Chapter 4, *Windows Forensics I,* covers the different types of volatile and nonvolatile information an investigator can collect from a Windows system including detail about collecting and analyzing data in memory, the registry, and files. Chapter 5, *Windows Forensics II,* continues the discussion from Chapter 4 by covering events and event logs, password and authentication issues, and various popular Window forensic tools. Chapter 6, *Linux Forensics,* explains not only how to perform forensics with a Linux system as a target, but also why it can be beneficial to use a Linux system in other investigations. Chapter 7, *Application Password Crackers,* covers tools used in password recovery, ways to bypass BIOS passwords, methods for removing CMOS batteries, and Windows XP/2000/NT keys.

Chapter Features

Many features are included in each chapter and all are designed to enhance the learner's learning experience. Features include:

- *Objectives* begin each chapter and focus the learner on the most important concepts in the chapter.
- *Key Terms* are designed to familiarize the learner with terms that will be used within the chapter.
- *Case Examples,* found throughout the chapter, present short scenarios followed by questions that challenge the learner to arrive at an answer or solution to the problem presented.
- *Chapter Summary,* at the end of each chapter, serves as a review of the key concepts covered in the chapter.
- *Review Questions* allow learners to test their comprehension of the chapter content.
- *Hands-On Projects* encourage learners to apply the knowledge they have gained after finishing the chapter. Files for the *Hands-On Projects* can be found on the Student Resource Center. Note: You will need your access code provided in your book to enter the site. Visit *www.cengage.com/community/eccouncil* for a link to the Student Resource Center.

Student Resource Center

The Student Resource Center contains all the files you need to complete the Hands-On Projects found at the end of the chapters. Access the Student Resource Center with the access code provided in your book. Visit *www.cengage.com/community/eccouncil* for a link to the Student Resource Center.

Additional Instructor Resources

Free to all instructors who adopt the *Investigating Hard Disks, File and Operating Systems* book for their courses is a complete package of instructor resources. These resources are available from the Course Technology Web site, *www.cengage.com/coursetechnology*, by going to the product page for this book in the online catalog, and choosing "Instructor Downloads."

Resources include:

- *Instructor Manual* : This manual includes course objectives and additional information to help your instruction.

- *Examview Testbank*: This Windows-based testing software helps instructors design and administer tests and pre-tests. In addition to generating tests that can be printed and administered, this full-featured program has an online testing component that allows students to take tests at the computer and have their exams automatically graded.

- *PowerPoint Presentations*: This book comes with a set of Microsoft PowerPoint slides for each chapter. These slides are meant to be used as teaching aids for classroom presentations, to be made available to students for chapter reviews, or to be printed for classroom distribution. Instructors are also at liberty to add their own slides.

- *Labs*: These are additional hands-on activities to provide additional practice for your students.

- *Assessment Activities*: These are additional assessment opportunities including discussion questions, writing assignments, Internet research activities, and homework assignments along with a final cumulative project.

- *Final Exam*: This exam provides a comprehensive assessment of *Investigating Hard Disks, File and Operating Systems* content.

Cengage Learning Information Security Community Site

Cengage Learning Information Security Community Site was created for learners and instructors to find out about the latest in information security news and technology.
Visit *community.cengage.com/infosec* to:

- Learn what's new in information security through live news feeds, videos and podcasts;

- Connect with your peers and security experts through blogs and forums;

- Browse our online catalog.

How to Become CIHFI Certified

Today's battles between corporations, governments, and countries are no longer fought only in the typical arenas of boardrooms or battlefields using physical force. Now the battlefield starts in the technical realm, which ties into most every facet of modern day life. The CIHFI certification focuses on the necessary skills to identify an intruder's footprints and to properly gather the necessary evidence to prosecute. The CIHFI certification is primarily targeted at police and other law enforcement personnel, defense and military personnel, e-business security professionals, systems administrators, legal professionals, banking, insurance and other professionals, government agencies, and IT managers. This certification will ensure that you have the knowledge and skills to identify, track, and prosecute the cyber-criminal.

CIHFI Certification exams are available through authorized Prometric testing centers. To finalize your certification after your training by taking the certification exam through a Prometric testing center, you must:

1. Apply for and purchase an exam voucher by visiting the EC-Council Press community site: *www.cengage.com/community/eccouncil*, if one was not purchased with your book.

2. Once you have your exam voucher, visit *www.prometric.com* and schedule your exam, using the information on your voucher.

3. Take and pass the C|HFI certification examination with a score of 70% or better.

C|HFI certification exams are also available through Prometric Prime. To finalize your certification after your training by taking the certification exam through Prometric Prime, you must:

1. Purchase an exam voucher by visiting the EC-Council Press community site: *www.cengage.com/community/eccouncil*, if one was not purchased with your book.

2. Speak with your instructor about scheduling an exam session, or visit the EC-Council community site referenced above for more information.

3. Take and pass the C|HFI certification examination with a score of 70% or better.

About Our Other EC-Council | Press Products

Ethical Hacking and Countermeasures Series

The EC-Council | Press *Ethical Hacking and Countermeasures* series is intended for those studying to become security officers, auditors, security professionals, site administrators, and anyone who is concerned about or responsible for the integrity of the network infrastructure. The series includes a broad base of topics in offensive network security, ethical hacking, as well as network defense and countermeasures. The content of this series is designed to immerse the learner into an interactive environment where they will be shown how to scan, test, hack, and secure information systems. A wide variety of tools, viruses, and malware is presented in these books, providing a complete understanding of the tactics and tools used by hackers. By gaining a thorough understanding of how hackers operate, ethical hackers are able to set up strong countermeasures and defensive systems to protect their organization's critical infrastructure and information. The series, when used in its entirety, helps prepare readers to take and succeed on the C|EH certification exam from EC-Council.

Books in Series
- *Ethical Hacking and Countermeasures: Attack Phases*/143548360X
- *Ethical Hacking and Countermeasures: Threats and Defense Mechanisms*/1435483618
- *Ethical Hacking and Countermeasures: Web Applications and Data Servers*/1435483626
- *Ethical Hacking and Countermeasures: Linux, Macintosh and Mobile Systems*/1435483642
- *Ethical Hacking and Countermeasures: Secure Network Infrastructures*/1435483650

Network Security Administrator Series

The EC-Council | Press *Network Administrator* series, preparing learners for E|NSA certification, is intended for those studying to become system administrators, network administrators, and anyone who is interested in network security technologies. This series is designed to educate learners, from a vendor neutral standpoint, how to defend the networks they manage. This series covers the fundamental skills in evaluating internal and external threats to network security, design, and how to enforce network level security policies, and ultimately protect an organization's information. Covering a broad range of topics from secure network fundamentals, protocols and analysis, standards and policy, hardening infrastructure, to configuring IPS, IDS and firewalls, bastion host and honeypots, among many other topics, learners completing this series will have a full understanding of defensive measures taken to secure their organizations information. The series, when used in its entirety, helps prepare readers to take and succeed on the E|NSA, Network Security Administrator certification exam from EC-Council.

Books in Series
- *Network Defense: Fundamentals and Protocols*/1435483553
- *Network Defense: Security Policy and Threats*/1435483561
- *Network Defense: Perimeter Defense Mechanisms*/143548357X
- *Network Defense: Securing and Troubleshooting Network Operating Systems*/1435483588
- *Network Defense: Security and Vulnerability Assessment*/1435483596

Security Analyst Series

The EC-Council | Press *Security Analyst/Licensed Penetration Tester* series, preparing learners for E|CSA/LPT certification, is intended for those studying to become network server administrators, firewall administrators, security testers, system administrators, and risk assessment professionals. This series covers a broad base of topics in advanced penetration testing and security analysis. The content of this program is designed to expose the learner to groundbreaking methodologies in conducting thorough security analysis, as well as advanced penetration testing techniques. Armed with the knowledge from the *Security Analyst* series, learners will be able to perform the intensive assessments required to effectively identify and mitigate risks to the security of the organizations infrastructure. The series, when used in its entirety, helps prepare readers to take and succeed on the E|CSA, Certified Security Analyst, and L|PT, License Penetration Tester certification exam from EC-Council.

Books in Series
- *Certified Security Analyst: Security Analysis and Advanced Tools*/1435483669
- *Certified Security Analyst: Customer Agreements and Reporting Procedures in Security Analysis*/1435483677
- *Certified Security Analyst: Penetration Testing Methodologies in Security Analysis*/1435483685
- *Certified Security Analyst: Network and Communication Testing Procedures in Security Analysis*/1435483693
- *Certified Security Analyst: Network Threat Testing Procedures in Security Analysis*/1435483707

Cyber Safety/1435483715

Cyber Safety is designed for anyone who is interested in learning computer networking and security basics. This product provides information cyber crime; security procedures; how to recognize security threats and attacks, incident response, and how to secure Internet access. This book gives individuals the basic security literacy skills to begin high-end IT programs. The book also prepares readers to take and succeed on the Security|5 certification exam from EC-Council.

Wireless Safety/1435483766

Wireless Safety introduces the learner to the basics of wireless technologies and its practical adaptation. *Wireless|5* is tailored to cater to any individual's desire to learn more about wireless technology. It requires no pre-requisite knowledge and aims to educate the learner in simple applications of these technologies. Topics include wireless signal propagation, IEEE and ETSI wireless standards, WLANs and operation, wireless protocols and communication languages, wireless devices, and wireless security networks. The book also prepares readers to take and succeed on the Wireless|5 certification exam from EC-Council.

Network Safety/1435483774

Network Safety provides the basic core knowledge on how infrastructure enables a working environment. Intended for those in office environments and for home users who want to optimize resource utilization, share infrastructure and make the best of technology and the convenience it offers. Topics include foundations of networks, networking components, wireless networks, basic hardware components, the networking environment and connectivity as well as troubleshooting. The book also prepares readers to take and succeed on the Network|5 certification exam from EC-Council.

Disaster Recovery Professional

The *Disaster Recovery Professional Series,* preparing the reader for E|DRP certification, introduces the methods employed in identifying vulnerabilities and how to take the appropriate countermeasures to prevent and mitigate failure risks for an organization. It also provides a foundation in disaster recovery principles, including preparation of a disaster recovery plan, assessment of risks in the enterprise, development of policies, and procedures, and understanding of the roles and relationships of various members of an organization, implementation of the plan, and recovering from a disaster. Students will learn how to create a secure network by putting policies and procedures in place, and how to restore a network in the event of a disaster. The series, when used in its entirety, helps prepare readers to take and succeed on the E|DRP, Disaster Recovery Professional certification exam from EC-Council.

Books in Series
- *Disaster Recovery*/1435488709
- *Business Continuity*/1435488695

Acknowledgements

Michael H. Goldner is the Chair of the School of Information Technology for ITT Technical Institute in Norfolk Virginia, and also teaches bachelor level courses in computer network and information security systems. Michael has served on and chaired ITT Educational Services Inc. National Curriculum Committee on Information Security. He received his Juris Doctorate from Stetson University College of Law, his undergraduate degree from Miami University and has been working for more than 15 years in the area of Information Technology. He is an active member of the American Bar Association, and has served on that organization's cyber law committee. He is a member of IEEE, ACM, and ISSA, and is the holder of a number of industrially recognized certifications including, CISSP, CEH, CHFI, CEI, MCT, MCSE/Security, Security +, Network +, and A+. Michael recently completed the design and creation of a computer forensic program for ITT Technical Institute and has worked closely with both EC-Council and Delmar/Cengage Learning in the creation of this EC-Council Press series.

Understanding File Systems and Hard Disks

Objectives

After completing this chapter, you should be able to:

- Understand disk drives, hard disks, and hard disk interfaces
- Understand disk partitions
- Understand the master boot record
- Understand different types of file systems
- Enumerate and explain popular Linux file systems
- Understand the Sun Solaris 10 file system ZFS
- Understand the Mac OS X file system
- Understand the UFS (Unix File System)
- Understand the various Windows file systems, including FAT and NTFS
- Understand the EFS recovery key agent
- Understand CD-ROM and DVD file systems
- Examine registry data
- Enumerate Windows XP system files

Key Terms

Bad sector   an area of a disk that has become unusable

Boot sector   the first sector of a data storage device that contains the code for bootstrapping a system

Bootstrapping   the process by which a small program actually initializes the operating system installed on a computer

Cluster   the smallest logical storage unit on a hard disk

Disk drive   a mechanism that reads data from a disk and writes data onto a disk

Disk file system   a type of file system used for storing and recovering the files on a storage device, such as a hard disk, that is directly or indirectly connected to a computer

Disk platter   a round, flat, magnetic metal or ceramic disk in a hard disk that holds the actual data

Endianness   the way bytes are ordered in a system

FAT32   a 32-bit version of the FAT file system using smaller clusters, which results in a more efficient storage capacity

Floppy disk   a portable magnetic disk with a shell made of either flexible or rigid plastic material

IDE (integrated drive electronics)   a type of interface used to connect a disk drive to a computer, in which the controller is built into the drive itself

Lost cluster   a FAT file system error that results from how the FAT file system allocates space and chains files together

Master boot record (MBR)   the first sector of a data storage device such as a hard disk

Network file system   a type of file system that provides access to files on other computers on a network

NTFS (New Technology File System)   a type of file system used on Windows operating systems that provides features, such as security and file compression, that FAT does not provide

Parallel ATA   a type of interface that offers a connection between a hard drive and a computer, in which communication can only flow in one direction at a time

Partitioning   the creation of logical drives on a disk

Registry Checker   a part of the Windows 98 operating system that is used to backup and restore the registry and fix errors in the registry

Registry Monitor   a program that can be used to monitor changes to the registry as they occur

Sector   the basic physical unit of hard drive data storage; a series of predefined sectors form a circle on the hard drive platter called a track

Serial ATA   a type of interface that offers a point-to-point connection between a hard drive and a computer, in which communication can flow both ways at the same time

Special purpose file system   a file system where the files are organized by software during runtime

USB (Universal Serial Bus)   a type of interface used to connect peripherals such as hard drives, modems, printers, scanners, and digitizers to a computer

ZFS (Zettabyte File System)   a self-managing, general-purpose file system used in Sun's Solaris 10 operating system

Introduction to File Systems and Hard Disks

This chapter describes file systems and hard disks, two important aspects of data storage. The chapter begins by giving a general overview of disk drives and then delves deeper into hard disks. The chapter then turns away from the discussion of physical data storage and discusses the various file systems in use on computer systems.

Disk Drive Overview

A *disk drive* is a mechanism that reads data from a disk and writes data onto a disk. The disk in the disk drive rotates at very high speeds, and heads in the disk drive are used to read and write data.

Different types of disk drives use different types of disks. For example, a hard disk drive (HDD) accesses hard disks, and a floppy disk drive (FDD) accesses floppy disks. An optical disc drive (ODD) reads and writes the data from optical discs.

Types of Disk Drives

Disk drives are categorized into the following types:

- *Fixed*: These are drives like hard disks, which use media that are not removable.
- *Removable*: These are drives that use media that are removable. A few examples of removable storage devices are:
    - *Floppy disk*: This type of drive uses media that are portable magnetic disks on which data and programs can be stored. *Floppy disks* are disks that are made of either flexible or rigid plastic material. The storage capacity of a floppy disk varies, but typically floppies can hold very little.

- *CD-ROM*: This type of drive uses optical discs. These discs are sturdier than floppy disks, and they can hold more data. Lasers are used to write data to the disc and read data from it. Although CD-ROM discs can only be written to once, other varieties of this optical format can be written to multiple times.

- *DVD*: DVD is an acronym for digital versatile disc. It is a type of optical disc that holds far more information than a CD-ROM. A DVD can hold a minimum of 4.7 GB of data to a maximum of 17 GB.

- *Zip disk*: Zip disks are used to hold data that requires more storage than a floppy disk can provide. Zip disks are used to back up disks and larger documents. Like floppy disks, Zip disks can be written to multiple times.

Hard Disks

Data is organized on a hard disk in a method similar to that of a filing cabinet. The user can easily access the data and programs. When a computer uses a program or data, the program or data is copied from its location to a temporary location. When a user makes changes to a file, the computer saves the file by replacing the older file with the new file. Data is recorded magnetically onto a hard disk. A rapidly spinning platter is used as the recording medium. Heads just above the surface of the platter are used to read data from and write data to the platter. A standard interface connects a hard disk to a computer. Two common interfaces are IDE and SCSI.

Characteristics

Some characteristics that people use to differentiate the various kinds of hard disks include:

- Capacity of the hard disk
- Interface used
- Speed in rotations per minute
- Seek time
- Access time
- Transfer time

Once damaged, a hard disk usually cannot be repaired. When a disk fails, recovering data from it is possible only after installing a new hard disk and accessing the damaged disk as a secondary drive.

Physical Makeup

A hard disk is a sealed unit containing a number of platters in a stack. It can be mounted in a horizontal or vertical position. Electromagnetic read/write heads are positioned above and below each platter. As the platters spin, the drive heads move in toward the center surface and out toward the edge. In this way, the drive heads reach the entire surface of every platter.

On every hard disk, data is stored in thin, concentric bands, called tracks. A drive head reads from or writes to a circular ring called a track. On a 3.5-inch hard disk, there could be a thousand tracks. Tracks consist of sectors, the smallest physical storage units on a hard disk. A sector is almost always 512 bytes (0.5 kilobyte) in size. Figure 1-1 shows the parts of a hard disk.

Zoned Bit Recording

Data is recorded onto a hard disk using a method called zoned bit recording. Zoned bit recording is also known as multiple zone recording (zone recording). In this technique, tracks are combined together into zones depending on their distance from the center of the disk. Each zone is assigned a number of sectors per track.

There are three types of data densities on a hard disk:

- *Track density*: Space between tracks on a disk
- *Area density*: Number of bits per square inch on a platter
- *Bit density*: The bits per unit length of track

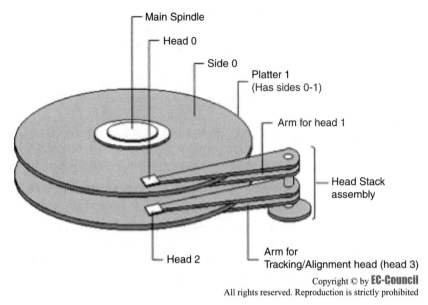

Figure 1-1   A hard disk platter has two sides, and there is a read/write head for each side.

Hard Disk Interfaces

The following are the types of hard disk interfaces:

- *Small computer system interface (SCSI)*: Allows a user to connect 15 peripheral devices to one PCI board known as a SCSI host adapter, which is plugged into the motherboard.
- ***Integrated drive electronics/enhanced IDE (IDE/EIDE)***: Connects hard disk drives, optical disc drives, and tape drives to personal computers. With this type of interface, the drive controller is built into the drive itself.
- ***Universal Serial Bus (USB)***: Connects peripheral devices such as hard disks, modems, printers, digitizers, and data gloves to a computer.
- *Advanced technology attachment (ATA)*: This type of interface comes in two forms:
  - ***Serial ATA***: This provides a point-to-point channel between the motherboard and the drive.
  - ***Parallel ATA***: This provides a communications channel between the drive and the computer on which data can travel only one way at a time.
- *Fiber Channel*: A point-to-point bidirectional serial interface that supports up to 1.0625 Gbps transfer rates. This interface comes in two forms:
  - *Fiber Channel electrical interface*: This uses ECL (emitter-coupled logic) signaling levels over an unbalanced 75 W or balanced 150 W line.
  - *Fiber Channel optical interface*: This uses a long-wave laser light source that can carry data at 1 Gbps over a distance of up to 10 km. It uses a long-wave laser (LL), a short-wave laser (SL), and a light-emitting diode (LED).
    - LL: long-wave laser (1300 nm)
    - SL: short-wave laser (780 nm)
    - LED: light-emitting diode (1300 nm)

SCSI

SCSI (small computer system interface) is a set of ANSI standard electronic interfaces used for communication between computers and peripheral devices such as hard drives, CD-ROM drives, and scanners. The SCSIs

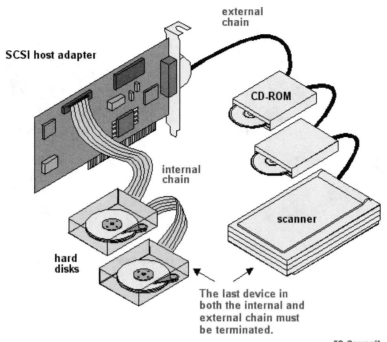

Figure 1-2   This shows a typical SCSI chain.

Technology Name	Maximum Cable Length (meters)	Maximum Speed (Mbps)	Maximum Number of Devices
SCSI-1	6	5	8
SCSI-2	6	5–10	8 or 16
Fast SCSI-2	3	10–20	8
Wide SCSI-2	3	20	16
Fast Wide SCSI-2	3	20	16
Ultra SCSI-3, 8-bit	1.5	20	8
Ultra SCSI-3, 16-bit	1.5	40	16
Ultra-2 SCSI	12	40	8
Wide Ultra-2 SCSI	12	80	16
Ultra-3 (Ultra160/m) SCSI	12	160	16

Table 1-1   **This table shows the current SCSI standards**

currently in use are parallel interfaces. SCSI devices are supported by all major operating systems, including Linux, Mac OS, and Windows. Figure 1-2 shows a typical SCSI chain.

SCSI supports high-speed data transfers. Ultra-2 SCSI for a 16-bit bus can transfer data at a rate of up to 80 Mbps. SCSI is also very versatile. A user can attach up to 7 or 15 devices (depending on the bus width) to a single SCSI port in a chain. This makes SCSI an ideal choice for desktop computers and laptops alike, as only one slot is used up when connecting many devices.

Table 1-1 summarizes the current SCSI standards.

IDE/EIDE

IDE (integrated drive electronics) is a standard electronic interface used between a computer motherboard's data paths or bus and the computer's disk storage devices. The IDE interface is based on the IBM PC Industry Standard Architecture (ISA) 16-bit bus standard, but it is also used in computers that use other bus standards. Most computers sold today use either an enhanced version of IDE called enhanced integrated drive electronics (EIDE) or serial ATA (SATA). IDE drives are connected to PCs with the help of IDE host adapter cards. In today's computers, the IDE and SATA controllers are often built into the motherboard.

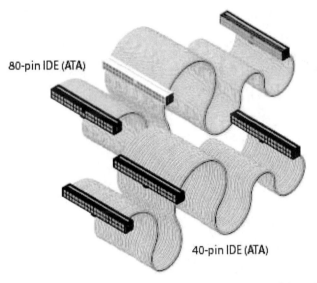

80-pin IDE (ATA)

40-pin IDE (ATA)

Figure 1-3   IDE cables come in both 40-pin and 80-pin versions.

Figure 1-4   The DupliDisk PCI card provides fault tolerance.

Two types of enhanced IDE sockets are built into motherboards. Each socket connects two drives; 40-pin ribbon cables connect CD-ROM drives and older hard disks to computers, and 80-pin cables connect fast hard disks to computers. Figure 1-3 shows the 80-pin and 40-pin IDE cables.

IDE drives are configured as master and slave. Jumper pins on the drive itself are used to set up the first drive on the cable as the master and the second one, if present, as the slave.

Fault Tolerance for IDE Drives   The DupliDisk PCI card (Figure 1-4) provides fault tolerance for IDE drives. An IDE cable connects the card to the motherboard, and two other cables connect the card to primary and secondary drives. When the computer tries to write data to a drive, the DupliDisk card passes the command to both drives. In this way, the two drives contain the exact same information.

USB

Universal Serial Bus (USB), developed by Intel, was first released in 1995 with a maximum speed of 12 Mbps. Currently available USB supports data transfer speeds up to 480 Mbps. USB allows external peripheral devices like disks, modems, printers, digitizers, and data gloves to connect to a computer.

Some of the features of USB are:

- Ease of use
- Expandability
- Speed for the end user
- High performance and ubiquity
- Easy connection of peripherals outside the PC
- Automatic configuration of devices by most operating systems
- Usefulness in PC telephony and videoconferencing

ATA

There are two different types of ATA interfaces: serial ATA (SATA) and parallel ATA (PATA).

Serial ATA   Serial ATA (SATA) offers a point-to-point channel between the motherboard and the drive. SATA cables (Figure 1-5) are shorter in length when compared to PATA cables (Figure 1-6), with a maximum length of one meter. The cables consist of four wires and are shielded. SATA connectors are smaller in size when compared to PATA connectors.

Figure 1-5   An SATA cable is thinner than a PATA cable.

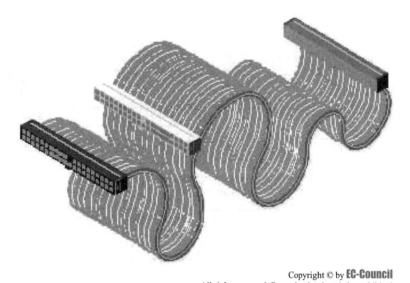

Figure 1-6   A PATA cable is longer than an SATA cable.

Some of the features of SATA are:

- Fast operating speed
- Upgradeable storage devices
- Ease of configuration
- Transfer speeds of 1.5 or 3 Gbps

An SATA RAID controller (Figure 1-7) supports four SATA drives in a RAID 0, 1, 5, or 10 configuration.

Parallel ATA   Parallel ATA (PATA) provides a controller on the disk drive itself and thereby eliminates the need for a separate adapter card.

Some of the features of PATA are:

- Low relative cost
- Ease of configuration
- Look-ahead caching

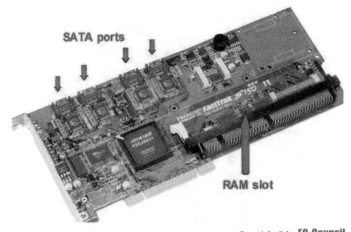

Figure 1-7   This shows an SATA RAID controller.

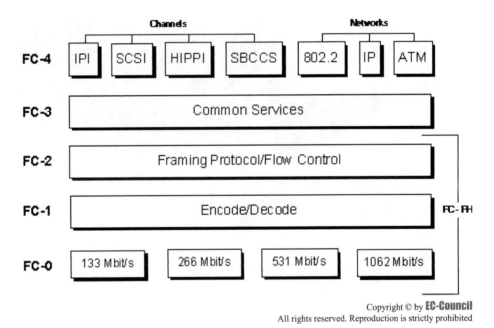

Figure 1-8   This shows a typical Fiber Channel interface.

Fiber Channel

Fiber Channel is a point-to-point bidirectional serial interface that supports up to 1.0625 Gbps transfer rates. The American National Standards Institute (ANSI) developed this interface. Figure 1-8 shows the structure of a Fiber Channel interface.

Some of the features of Fiber Channel are:

- Low costs
- Support of higher data transfer rates between workstations, mainframes, supercomputers, desktop computers, storage devices, displays, and other peripherals

The protocols that support Fiber Channel are:

- SCSI
- IP
- ATM
- HIPPI
- IEEE 802.2

Disk Platters

Disk platters are the round, flat, magnetic metal or ceramic disks in a hard disk that hold the actual data. They are made of two components: a substrate material and a magnetic media coating.

Substrate Material

The substrate material gives the platter structure and rigidity. The platters must be extremely smooth and flat, as they spin with the read/write heads very close to them. The gap between the heads and platters is minimized so that the heads can speedily read and write data. If the surface is uneven, a head crash can result. Previously, an aluminum alloy was used as the substrate material. To lower the chance of an uneven surface, manufacturers now use glass, glass composites, and magnesium alloys.

Magnetic Media Coating

Platters are coated with magnetic media that holds the magnetic impulses that represent the data. They are coated with iron oxide or a cobalt alloy. These media are inexpensive to use.

Various techniques are used to deposit the media material on the platters. One of the techniques used is electroplating, in which the material is deposited on the platters using electrolysis. The other process is vapor deposition, in which a very thin magnetic layer is deposited on the surface using a technique called sputtering. Vapor deposition provides a more uniform coating and thus results in a flatter surface than electroplating does.

The amount of data that can be stored on a given amount of a hard disk platter is called area density, also known as bit density.

Platter Organization

For the organized storage and retrieval of data, platters are divided into specific structures. Both sides of a platter can hold large chunks of data that allow for easier and faster access to information. Each platter has two read/write heads, one on the top of the platter and one on the bottom, so a hard disk with five platters has ten surfaces and ten total heads. Platters are further divided into tracks. Tracks are concentric circles that logically partition platters. Tracks are divided into smaller pieces called sectors. Each sector holds 512 bytes of information.

Platter Size

The size of the platters is one of the important factors in determining the structure of a hard disk. This is called the drive's form factor. Hard disks are generally referred to by their size, such as a 5.25-inch or 3.5-inch hard disk. The platters in a particular disk are usually the same in diameter. For instance, the diameter of a platter in a 5.25-inch disk is usually 5.12 inches, and the diameter of a platter in a 3.5-inch disk is usually 3.74 inches. As technology improves, manufacturers are able to make smaller and smaller hard disks with greater capacities.

Number of Platters

The number of platters in a hard disk may vary from one to dozens. As the number of platters increases, storage capacity rises, but the space between each platter becomes smaller. This makes hard disks with a large number of platters more sensitive to vibrations, flaws in the surface of a platter, and head misalignment. Therefore, the trend is to increase the area density of a hard drive and thus require a smaller number of platters.

Tracks

Tracks are the concentric circles on platters where all the information is stored. A modern hard disk contains tens of thousands of tracks on each platter. Every platter in a hard disk has the same track density. The track density refers to the compactness of the track circles. Manufacturers try to increase track density so that the maximum number of bits can be placed within each unit area on the surface of a platter. Track density determines the amount of information that can be placed on a hard disk. It is a component of area density.

Track Numbering Tracks are typically numbered from 0 at the outer edge to 1023 at the center. The read/ write heads on both surfaces of a platter are tightly packed and locked together on an assembly of head arms. The arms move in and out together so that all heads remain physically located at the same track number. Therefore, a track location is often referred to by a cylinder number rather than a track number. A cylinder is the set of tracks that can be accessed by all the heads when the heads are in a particular position. One cylinder represents a set of tracks on all the platters in a hard disk.

Sectors

Tracks are divided into sectors. A *sector* is the basic physical unit of hard drive data storage. Each sector holds 512 bytes of data and some additional bytes used for internal drive control, drive management, error detection and correction, and sector identification.

The contents of a sector are as follows:

- *ID information*: This contains the sector number and location that identify the sector on the disk. It also contains status information about the sector.
- *Synchronization fields*: This helps the drive controller guide the read process.
- *Data*: This is the actual data in the sector.
- *ECC*: This is error-correcting code that ensures data integrity.
- *Gaps*: Spaces are provided to give the drive controller time to continue the read process.

Sector Organization and Overhead The contents of a sector that aren't user data constitute sector overhead. This overhead must be minimized for greater efficiency. Data is stored on a disk in a contiguous series of sectors. For example, a 900-byte file is stored in two 512-byte sectors. The track number and the sector number can be used to refer to the address of any data on a hard disk.

Bad Sectors **Bad sectors** are areas of a disk that have become unusable. Bad sectors can be caused by configuration problems or physical disturbances. Some of the more common causes are excessive read/write operations, sudden voltage surges, certain viruses, and corrupted boot records. If data is in a sector that becomes bad, then it might not be recoverable. Users can try to recover the data using software tools such as ScanDisk and Chkdsk. Once a bad sector is identified, it is marked as bad and cannot be used again. This is called defect mapping. Modern hard disks contain reserved sectors that are used in place of bad sectors. When the drive controller receives a read or write command for a bad sector, it substitutes one of the sectors from the pool of reserves. This is called spare sectoring. Bad sectors are cleverly hidden and are never seen by the operating system.

Cluster

Clusters are the smallest logical storage units on a hard disk. The file system divides the storage on a disk volume into discreet chunks of data for efficient disk usage and performance. These chunks are called clusters. A file is allocated a certain number of clusters.

Cluster Organization Cluster entries are maintained by the file system running on the computer. In the FAT file system, an entry is made in the FAT (file allocation table).

Clusters are chained to each other and are ordered on a disk using continuous numbers, so an entire file does not have to be stored in one continuous block on the disk. This cluster chaining is invisible to the operating system.

Cluster Size The size of a cluster is determined when the disk volume is partitioned. Larger volumes use larger cluster sizes. For hard disk volumes, each cluster ranges in size from 4 sectors (2,048 bytes) to 64 sectors (32,768 bytes). In some situations, 128-sector clusters may be used (65,536 bytes per cluster). The sectors in a cluster are continuous, so each cluster is a continuous block of space on a disk. In a cluster, any remaining space is wasted. This space is known as slack space. If the cluster size is large, there will be less fragmentation, but there will be more wasted space.

Slack Space Slack space is the area of a disk cluster between the end of the file and the end of the cluster. If the size of a file is less than the cluster size, a full cluster is still assigned to that file. The remaining space remains unused and is called slack space.

When a greater number of files are stored on a disk with a large cluster size, a lot of the disk space is wasted as slack space. DOS and Windows file systems use fixed-size clusters. DOS and older Windows versions use a 16-bit file allocation table (FAT16) that results in a large cluster size for large partitions. For example, if the partition size is 4 GB, each cluster will be 32 KB. Even if a file requires only 10 KB, the entire 32 KB will be allocated, resulting in 22 KB of slack space. The 32-bit file allocation table (FAT32) used in later versions of Windows helps alleviate this problem.

Lost Clusters   A *lost cluster* is a FAT file system error that results from how the FAT file system allocates space and chains files together. It is mainly the result of a logical structure error and not a physical disk error. They usually occur because of interrupted file activities; thus, the clusters involved never get correctly linked to a file. Operating systems mark these clusters as being used in the FAT, even though they are not assigned to any file. Disk-checking programs can scan an entire disk volume for lost clusters. The programs can then either clear the lost clusters or save them as files. In the latter case, artificial files are generated and linked to these clusters. These newly formed files are considered damaged, but some orphaned data can be seen and recovered.

Disk-checking programs, such as ScanDisk, can find lost clusters using the following procedure:

- Create a memory copy of the FAT, noting all of the clusters marked as being in use.
- Trace the clusters starting from the root directory, and mark each cluster used by a file as being accounted for. Continue through all of the directories on the disk.
- When the scanning process is finished, any clusters that are in use but not accounted for are orphans, or lost clusters.

Disk Partition

Partitioning is the creation of logical drives on a disk. A partition is a logical drive that holds data.
A partition can be one of two types:

- *Primary partition*: This type of partition holds information regarding the operating system and system area, as well as other information required for booting.
- *Extended partition*: This partition holds the data and files that are stored on the disk.

Data can be hidden on a hard disk by creating hidden partitions on the disk drive. That is, partitions can be created from the unused space between the primary partition and the first logical partition. The space between the primary partition and the secondary partition is known as the interpartition gap. If data is hidden in the interpartition gap, investigators can find the data using disk editor utilities like Norton Disk Edit.

There are various tools for examining disk partitions. A few of the disk editor tools are Disk Edit, WinHex, and Hex Workshop. A user can use these tools to view the file headers and other important information about the file.

Master Boot Record

The *master boot record (MBR)* is the first sector of a data storage device such as a hard disk.

The MBR is also called the partition sector or the master partition table because it includes a table that contains information about each partition that the hard disk has been formatted into. In addition to this table, the MBR also includes a program that reads the boot sector record of the partition containing the operating system into RAM. The *boot sector* is the sector of a storage device that contains the code for bootstrapping a system. *Bootstrapping* is the process by which a small program actually initializes the operating system installed on a computer. Information about the files present on the disk, their location, and their size is contained in the master boot record file. In DOS and Windows systems, a user can create the MBR with the **fdisk/mbr** command. The MBR is used to:

- Bootstrap operating systems
- Hold disk partition tables

Many products replace the MBR file that is provided by Microsoft operating systems. A few third-party utility tools, such as PartitionMagic, allow a user to install two or more operating systems on a disk.

Backing up the MBR

In UNIX and Linux, **dd** can be used to backup and restore the MBR. To backup the MBR, the command is **dd if=/dev/xxx of=mbr.backup bs=512 count=1.** To restore the MBR, the command is **dd if=mbr.backup of=/dev/xxx bs=512 count=1.**

Hard Disk Tools

Computer forensic investigators use various software tools for analyzing and recovering data on hard disks. These tools allow investigators to perform the following tasks:

- Search the text on hard disks in file space, slack space, and unallocated space.
- Find and recover data from files that have been deleted.
- Find data in encrypted files.
- Repair FATs, partition tables, and boot records.
- Concatenate and split files.
- Analyze and compare files.
- Clone hard disks.
- Make drive images and backups.
- Erase confidential files securely.
- Edit files using a hex editor.

Disk Capacity Calculation

Consider a hard disk drive with the following attributes:

- 16,384 cylinders
- 80 heads
- 63 sectors per track

Assume a sector has 512 bytes. What is the capacity of such a disk?
The conversion factors appropriate to this hard disk are:

- 16,384 cylinders/disk
- 80 heads/cylinder
- 63 sectors/track
- 512 bytes/sector

The total capacity for this disk = 1 disk * (16,384 cylinders/disk) * (80 heads/cylinder) * (1 track/head) * (63 sectors/track) * (512 bytes/sector) = 42,278,584,320 bytes.
Here are some useful definitions:

- 1 kilobyte (KB) = 2^{10} bytes = 1,024 bytes
- 1 megabyte (MB) = 2^{20} bytes = 1,048,576 bytes = 1,024 KB
- 1 gigabyte (GB) = 2^{30} bytes = 1,073,741,824 bytes = 1,048,576 KB = 1,024 MB
- 1 terabyte (TB) = 2^{40} bytes = 1,099,511,627,776 bytes = 1,073,741,824 KB = 1,048,576 MB = 1,024 GB

Using these definitions, the result of the example above can be expressed in GB as 39.375 GB.

Understanding File Systems

A file system is a type of system that is used to most effectively store, organize, and access data on a computer. Data storage devices like hard disks, CD-ROMs, flash memory devices, and floppy disks use file systems to store data.

A file system provides the following:

- Storage
- Hierarchical categorization
- Management
- Navigation
- Access
- Data recovery features

Users can access the files using a graphical user interface (GUI) or a command line interface (CLI). File systems are organized in the form of tree-structured directories. Directories generally require access authorization.

Types of File Systems

File systems are classified into the following four categories:

- *Disk file system*: A *disk file system* is used for storing and recovering the files on a storage device, such as a hard disk, that is directly or indirectly connected to a computer. A few examples of disk file systems are FAT16, FAT32, NTFS, ext2, ISO 9660, ODS-5, and UDF. Table 1-2 lists many different types of disk file systems used in the past and today.

- *Network file system*: A *network file system* is a type of file system that provides access to files on other computers on a network. The file system is transparent to the user. A few examples of network file systems are NFS, CIFS, and GFS. Table 1-3 lists different types of network file systems.

- *Database file system*: Earlier file systems use a hierarchical management structure, but in the database file system, files are identified by their characteristics, like the name, type, topic, and author of the file, or similar metadata. Therefore, a file can be easily searched using SQL queries or text searches. For example, if a user needs to find the documents written by ABC, then the search string "documents written by ABC" will show the results.

- *Special purpose file system*: A *special purpose file system* is a file system where the files are organized by software during runtime. This type of file system is used for various purposes, such as communication between computer processes or temporary file space. Special purpose file systems are used by file-centric operating systems such as UNIX. One example in UNIX is the /proc file system, which can be used to access information about processes and other operating system features. Table 1-4 lists different types of special purpose file systems.

File System	Acronym Meaning	Features
ADFS	Advanced Disc Filing System	It was introduced as an add-on to the Disc Filing System (DFS).
		The length of file names was increased from 7 to 10 letters, and this increased the number of files in a directory to 77.
		ADFS uses a flat directory structure, which uses characters to represent the current directory; the default character is $.
BFS	Be File System	It is the file system that is used in BeOS.
		It can support extended file attributes by providing indexing and querying functionality similar to a relational database.
		It is case sensitive, and it can be used on any physical memory device. However, it is not advisable to use BFS for small removable media because the system header occupies more space than is available.

Table 1-2   **Many different types of disk file systems have been used in the past and are still in use today**   *(continues)*

File System	Acronym Meaning	Features
EFS	Encrypting File System	This file system stores the files in an encrypted form on NTFS to ensure the confidentiality of data.
		Public key encryption is used to encrypt the files. This encryption makes it practically impossible to decrypt the file without the correct key.
		The file and folders are encrypted with an attribute. When the files are copied to other file systems, the encrypted files are decrypted and copied.
EFS	Extent File System	EFS has been superseded by XFS.
ext	Extended File System	This file system was specifically designed to overcome the few limitations of the Minix file system, but it has been quickly replaced by the ext2 file system, which is the second version of the extended file system.
		The two major problems that were solved by ext are increasing the maximum partition size and increasing the file name length to 14 characters.
ext2	Second Extended File System	This file system is the standard file system that is used on the Linux operating system. The major disadvantage of using this file system is that it is not a journaling file system.
		This file system was introduced to solve problems like separate access, inode modification, and modification time stamps.
ext3	Third Extended File System	The following are features that were added to ext2: • A journal file system • H-tree directory indexes • In-directory file types It doesn't support transparent compression.
FAT	File Allocation Table	Every partition of the physical medium is divided into clusters. The size of the clusters depends on the size of the FAT and the size of the partition.
		FAT maintains the list of entries that are connected to every cluster in the partition. Every entry has the following: • The address of the next cluster in a chain. • A character that indicates the end of file (EOF). • A special character to indicate a bad cluster. • A special character to denote a reserved cluster. • A zero to indicate that the cluster is not used.
FFS (Amiga)	Amiga Fast File System	It is used to remove superfluous information. Data blocks contain only data; this allows the file system to manage the large pieces of data directly from the adapter to the destination.
Files-11		Files-11 is the term for a set of five different file systems. Every file system is supported by an ancillary control process (ACP), one for every ODS level (i.e., from ODS-1 through ODS-5).
		This hierarchical file system supports the following features: • Access control lists • Record-oriented I/O • Remote network access • File versioning
HFS	Hierarchical File System	Apple Computer developed HFS for computers using Mac OS.
		A few of the features of HFS that are not present in the existing Macintosh operating system are: • It can support file names up to 31 characters in length. • It supports metadata. • It supports dual-forked files. (Dual forks are those forks with separate data and resource forks per file.) One of the disadvantages of HFS is that it cannot be used for booting.
HFS Plus	Hierarchical File System Plus	HFS Plus is a file system that was developed to replace HFS.
		A few of the features that were added to the HFS Plus are: • HFS Plus uses B-trees to store data. • It permits file names of 255 characters in length. • It uses a 32-bit allocation mapping table.
HFSX	Hierarchical File System	HFSX is an updated version of Apple's HFS Plus file system.
		HFSX allows the use of case-sensitive file names and directory names.
		HFSX volumes are identified by the entries in the volume header. The two entries are the signature field and the version field.

Table 1-2   Many different types of disk file systems have been used in the past and are still in use today

File System	Acronym Meaning	Features
HPFS	High Performance File System	This file system was developed to cover the limitations of the FAT. The following are the features of HPFS: • It supports longer file names (up to 256 characters) of mixed case. • It manages disk space in an efficient way. • It has separate time stamps for last modification, last access, and creation. • It supports a B-tree structure for directories. • It has a centrally located root directory.
ISO 9660		ISO 9660 is a standard published by the International Organization for Standardization. It describes a file system for CD-ROMs and DVDs that supports different operating systems for the easy exchange of data.
JFS	Journaled File System	IBM created this file system. It was released with the first version of AIX. The goals of creating this file system were: • To provide scalability • To support computers that have more than one processor • To have a more portable file system • To provide the capability of running multiple operating systems
LFS	Log-structured File System	The following features of LFS are borrowed from UFS: • Indirect paths • Inodes • Directory formats LFS divides the disk into smaller segments; the segments are filled from the bottom to the top. Every segment contains a header called a summary block. When there is a change in a file, LFS does the following: • Adds raw file data to the log head • Updates indirect blocks to the log file • Updates inodes • Updates the inode map block
MFS	Macintosh File System	Apple created MFS for floppy disks. MFS introduced a resource fork to store data as well as metadata, which are required to support the GUI of Mac OS.
Minix		The features of Minix are similar to those of the UNIX operating system. The Minix file system has six components: • *Boot block*: Loads and runs the operating system • *Superblock*: Stores the data and helps the operating system in managing and understanding the file structure • *Inode block*: Maps the tracks in use and the ones that are free • *Zone bitmap*: Works in a similar way as the inode block but tracks the zones • *Inode area*: Records the metadata • *Data area*: Actual files and directories where data is stored
NTFS	New Technology File System	Microsoft designed this specifically for Windows NT and higher versions. The main advantages of this file system are: • Easy file recovery • Very large storage areas • Long file names It supports object-oriented applications by treating all files as objects with user-defined and system-defined attributes.
NSS	Novell Storage Services	It is a 64-bit journaling file system with a balanced tree algorithm for the directory structure.
OFS	Old File System	This file system is a predecessor of the Amiga Fast File System for Amiga OS. It uses 512-byte blocks. A small portion of each block is used for metadata, leaving an irregular data block with a real capacity of only 488 bytes.

Table 1-2 Many different types of disk file systems have been used in the past and are still in use today *(continues)*

File System	Acronym Meaning	Features
PFS	Professional File System	This file system was developed for the Amiga. It consists of two sections: • Metadata, which consists of a root block • A generic array of blocks that can be allocated to store metadata It stores the data in the form of a tree of single blocks of metadata. It is very useful for storing files that are unfragmented.
ReiserFS	Reiser File System	It is a general-purpose file system that was developed for the Linux operating system. The features of the ReiserFS are: • Metadata-only journaling • Online resizing (only to increase the size) • Tail packing (to reduce internal file fragmentation)
Reiser4	Reiser4 File System	This file system is the successor to ResierFS. It provides the following features: • Efficient journaling • Efficient support of small files in terms of disk space and speed • Effective handling of a large number of files • Flexible plug-in infrastructure • Atomic file system modification • Dynamically optimized disk layout through allocate-on-flush
SFS	Smart File System	The main features of SFS are: • Performance is enhanced by grouping multiple directory entries into a block and by grouping metadata files into clusters. • Keeping track of the amount of free space available enhances scalability, and extents are arranged into a B+ tree structure. • Integrity is maintained by rolling back the logs for changes that are made to metadata. • The file system can defragment itself when it is still in use or when the files are locked.
Sprite		The main features of the Sprite file system are: • It has many utilities, which makes it appear as a time-sharing system. • It has a process migration feature, which can be used to swap processes between computers.
UDF	Universal Disk Format	It is used mainly for optical disc media, such as DVDs, CD-Rs, and CD-RWs. It supports larger files, larger disk capacities, and more information about individual files and folders. It supports special file properties, such as Apple's file types, resource forks, and other operating system data.
UFS	UNIX File System	It uses a special structure called an inverted branching-tree file structure. It provides access control at both the file level and the directory level. It provides a flexible file system that presents devices as file systems. It requires minimum administration of the multitasking environment.
UMSDOS		UMSDOS is a file system that was developed for Linux. It has access attributes and longer file names. It provides some Linux semantics to a FAT system. It can be used without repartitioning the hard disk. The major disadvantages are that it is slower than the ext file system and that it can be corrupted from within DOS or Windows.
VxFS	Veritas File System	It is the first commercial journaling file system built by Veritas Software. It is the primary file system of the HP-UX operating system. It supports file systems up to 32 terabytes in size. It supports individual files up to 2 terabytes in size.
VSAM	Virtual Storage Access Method	It is the scheme for IBM and is used in the S/370 and for virtual storage. VSAM comprises three access methods: • Keyed Sequential Data Set (KSDS) • Relative Record Data Set (RRDS) • Entry Sequenced Data Set (ESDS)

Table 1-2 Many different types of disk file systems have been used in the past and are still in use today

File System	Acronym Meaning	Features
XFS		XFS is a high-performance journaling file system with the following features: • Metadata-only journaling • Online resizing (only increasing the size) • Striped allocation • Online defragmentation • A real-time I/O API • Allocate-on-flush
ZFS	Zettabyte File System	It integrates logical volume management features into the file system. It is compatible with little-endian and big-endian systems. It offers data integrity and checks for data corruption. It frees empty spaces in files or blocks used by small files.

Table 1-2 Many different types of disk file systems have been used in the past and are still in use today

File System	Acronym Meaning	Features
AFS	Andrew File System	It uses Kerberos for authentication and uses access control lists on directories for users and groups. Local clients cache files, improving the performance of the file system. When a locally cached file is closed, the modifications are written to the server. Cache consistency is maintained through a mechanism called callback.
AppleShare		AppleShare is a product that provides a range of network services. This product is mostly used for file servers, but it also provides print server, Web server, and mail server capabilities.
Coda		Coda provides a local caching system that allows a user to continue working on a file even if the server connection is lost. When the connection to the server is reestablished, modifications are integrated into the server copy. The security system is very similar to Kerberos, and the developers are in the process of integrating Kerberos support into the file system.
GFS	Global File System	This file system is a shared disk file system for Linux clusters. There are no clients and servers in GFS; every node in a cluster is a peer.
InterMezzo		It is a distributed file system that was developed for Linux. It is a high-availability file system because it operates even if the connection to the server is lost. It supports distributed file serving. It supports desktop workstations.
Lustre		Lustre is an open source file system for network-attached storage that is usually used for cluster computing. It was developed to cope with large nodes with large capacities without compromising speed and security.
NFS	Network File System	NFS was developed by Sun Microsystems. It is a file system that allows client computers to access files quickly and as easily as if the network storage devices were attached to the client locally. It has strong security. It was originally developed for UNIX, but it can also be used with other operating systems.
OpenAFS		It is an open source implementation of the Andrew File System (AFS). It supports various operating systems, such as AIX, Mac OS, Apple Darwin, Digital UNIX, HP-UX, Irix, Solaris, Linux, and Microsoft Windows.
SMB	Server Message Block	This protocol supports file sharing and interprocess communication. A server using SMB provides its files and printers to clients on the network. This file system is mainly used on Windows operating systems.

Table 1-3 Different operating systems use different network file systems

File System	Acronym Meaning	Features
cdfs	Compact Disc File System	It is also called ISO 9660. It was developed to provide a single common file system for all CD-ROM media on all operating systems.
davfs2	WebDAV Linux File System	It is a Linux file system driver that can be used to maintain a WebDAV server as a local disk drive. It uses the Coda file system to communicate with the kernel, and the neon WebDAV library to communicate with the Web server.
devfs	Device File System	It supports all UNIX-like operating systems. This file system treats every device as a different file. Managing these files can be a complex task, but devfs simplifies this through the automatic creation, deletion, and permission management of the files.
FUSE	Filesystem in Userspace	It has a simple library API. It can be installed easily. The implementation is very secure. It has an efficient kernel. It runs on UNIX-like operating systems. It allows nonprivileged users to create their own file systems.
lnfs	Long Name File System	It is used to enable long file names on file systems that do not support this feature.
ParFiSys	Parallel File System	This is an experimental file system that was designed to provide I/O services to scientific applications requiring high I/O bandwidth.
Plumber		This file system is used in the Plan 9 operating system to handle interprocess communication.
procfs	Process File System	It is a pseudo file system that is used on UNIX-like systems. It is used to get process information from the kernel. It does not consume any storage space.
wikifs	Wiki File System	It is a file system developed for the Plan 9 operating system. It allows wiki pages to be served as Web pages.

Table 1-4   There are different special purpose file systems that provide different resources

Popular Linux File Systems

The Linux operating system is a single hierarchical tree structure that represents the file system as one single entity. It supports many different file systems. It implements a basic set of common concepts that were actually developed for UNIX. Some of the Linux file system types are Minix, ISO 9660, UMSDOS, NFS, SMB, HPFS. Minix was Linux's first file system.

Some of the more popular file systems used with Linux are as follows:

- *ext (Extended File System)*: The ext file system was released in April 1992. It is an elaborate extension of the Minix file system. It has a maximum partition size of 2 GB and a maximum file name size of 255 characters. The ext file system removes the two major Minix limitations of a 64 MB partition size and short file names. The major limitation of this file system is that it doesn't support separate access, inode modification, and data modification time stamps. It keeps an unsorted list of free blocks and inodes, and the file system is also fragmented. It was soon replaced by the second extended file system.

- *ext2 (Second Extended File System)*: The ext2 file system was introduced in January 1993. It extends the features of ext. It uses improved algorithms, which greatly enhances its speed, and it maintains additional time stamps. It maintains a special field in the superblock that keeps track of the status of the file system and identifies it as either clean or dirty. A dirty file system will automatically scan itself for errors. The maximum file size in the ext2 file system is 4 TB (1 terabyte is 1,024 gigabytes). It is portable to other operating systems because drivers and other tools exist for accessing ext2 data. Its major shortcomings are that there is a risk of file system corruption when writing to ext2 and that it is not a journaling file system.

- *ext3 (Third Extended File System)*: The ext3 file system is a journaling version of the ext2 file system and is greatly used with the Linux operating system. It adds a journal, without which the file system is a valid ext2 file system. It can be mounted and used as an ext2 file system, and all the utilities of ext2 can be used on it.

Sun Solaris 10 File System: ZFS

ZFS (Zettabyte File System) is a dynamic file system in Sun's Solaris 10 operating system (Solaris OS). It is supported by both x86 and SPARC platforms. ZFS is endian-neutral. It supports moving disks from a SPARC server to an x86 server very easily. ZFS fulfills all the needs of a file system for everything from desktops to data centers. It is a self-managing, general-purpose file system.

ZFS supports almost unlimited scalability by refining the file system. It supports more storage, more file systems, more snapshots, more directory entries, and more files than can possibly be created in the foreseeable future. Without interrupting any services, it can dynamically grow and shrink the storage pool. Administrators can set quotas for users to limit space consumption and also to reserve space to guarantee future space availability.

Features

The following are some of the features of ZFS:

- *Copy on write*: Files are backed up immediately whenever they are written.
- *LVM*: ZFS integrates logical volume management features into the file system and manages expansion and shrinkage as needed.
- *Endianness*: **Endianness** is the way bytes are ordered in a system. This file system is portable between little-endian and big-endian systems.
- *Checksums*: ZFS provides data integrity features to detect and correct data corruption.
- *HA Storage+*: This supports cluster failover capabilities. This means that if any server in a cluster fails to perform a task due to an interruption, then only one server can write to a shared physical disk.
- *Clones*: At low cost, many copies of similar file systems can be made based on a single snapshot. Low cost means less consumption of space so that the performance of a file system is improved.
- *Compression*: This removes the small, unused memory chunks and space used by small files so that the space used by files is less than in other file systems.
- *ACLs (access control lists)*: The goal of ZFS's ACL implementation is to implement NFSv4 ACLs in a way that is compatible with Solaris. The ZFS ACL model is still in flux, but it is rapidly solidifying.

Mac OS X File Systems

HFS is a file system developed by Apple Computer for Mac OS. It was originally designed for use on floppy and hard disks, but it now also works on read-only media, such as CD-ROMs.

The Hierarchical File System divides a volume into logical blocks of 512 bytes. These logical blocks are then grouped together into allocation blocks, which can hold one or more logical blocks depending on the total size of the volume. HFS uses a 16-bit value to address allocation blocks, limiting the number of allocation blocks to 65,536.

There are five structures that make up an HFS volume:

- *Logical blocks 0 and 1*: These are the boot blocks, which include system startup information—for example, the names of the system and shell files, which are loaded at startup.
- *Logical block 2*: This contains the master directory block (MDB). The MDB defines a wide variety of data about the volume itself—for instance, date and time stamps for when the volume was created; the location of other volume structures, such as the volume bitmap; and the size of logical structures, such as allocation blocks. There is also a duplicate of the MDB called the alternate master directory block (alternate MDB) located at the opposite end of the volume in the second to last logical block. This is intended mainly for use by disk utilities and is only updated when either the catalog file or extent overflow file grow in size.
- *Logical block 3*: This is the starting block of the volume bitmap, which keeps track of which allocation blocks are in use and which are free. Each allocation block on the volume is represented by a bit in the map. If the bit is set, then the block is in use; if it is clear, then the block is free to be used. Since the volume bitmap must have a bit to represent each allocation block, its size is determined by the size of the volume itself.
- *The extent overflow file*: This is a B*-tree including extra extents that record which allocation blocks are allocated to which files, once the initial three extents in the catalog file are used up. Later versions also add the ability for the extent overflow file to store extents that record bad blocks, to prevent a machine from trying to write to them.

- *The catalog file*: This is a B*-tree that holds records for all the files and directories stored in the volume. It stores four types of records. Each file is made up of a file thread record and a file record, and each directory is made up of a directory thread record and a directory record. Files and directories in the catalog file are found using their unique catalog node ID.

UFS (Unix File System)

UFS is a file system utilized by many UNIX and UNIX-like operating systems. It is derived from the Berkeley Fast File System, which is an abstract of FS, the file system used in the first version of UNIX developed at Bell Labs.

UFS is composed of the following parts:

- A few blocks at the beginning of the partition reserved for boot blocks (which must be initialized separately from the file system)
- A superblock, including a magic number identifying this as a UFS file system, and some other vital numbers describing this file system's geometry, statistics, and behavioral tuning parameters
- A collection of cylinder groups, of which each cylinder group has the following components:
  - Backup copy of the superblock
  - Cylinder group header, with statistics, free lists, and other data about this cylinder group, similar to those in the superblock
  - Number of inodes, each containing file attributes
  - Number of data blocks

Windows and DOS File Systems

The main Windows and DOS file systems are the following:

- *FAT16 (File Allocation Table)*: The FAT file system is a 16-bit file system that was developed for DOS and further supported by other operating systems. It consumes little memory and is simple and reliable. File names are limited to 8 characters for the name and 3 characters for the extension. Its main shortcomings are that it supports a maximum of 64 KB allocation units and that it becomes less efficient on partitions larger than 32 MB. Due to its limitations, it is not suitable for file servers.
- *FAT12*: This is a version of FAT specifically designed for floppy disks.
- *FAT32*: This is a 32-bit version of the FAT file system using smaller clusters, which results in a more efficient storage capacity. It supports drive sizes up to 2 TB. It can relocate the root directory and use the backup copy instead of the default copy. One of the main features is that it can dynamically resize a partition.
- *NTFS (New Technology File System)*: NTFS is an entirely different file system from FAT. It provides enhanced security, file-by-file compression, quotas, and encryption. It is designed to quickly perform standard file operations such as read, write, search, and even advanced operations such as file-system recovery on very large hard disks. When a volume is formatted as an NTFS volume, the Master File Table (MFT) and several system files are created. The MFT is the first file on an NTFS volume and contains information about all the files and folders on the volume. The first information is about the partition boot sector, which starts at sector zero and can be up to 16 sectors long. NTFS has several versions:
  - *V1.2*: Found in Windows NT 3.51 and Windows NT 4
  - *V3.0 (sometimes called Version 5.0)*: Found in Windows 2000
  - *V3.1 (sometimes called Version 5.1)*: Found in Windows XP and Windows Server 2003
  - *Transactional NTFS (TxF)*: Found in Windows Vista

FAT File Systems

The FAT file system is the file system used with DOS, and it was the first file system used with the Windows operating system. Even the most recent versions of Windows still use the 32-bit version of FAT.

Boot Sector The first sector (512 bytes) of a FAT file system is the boot sector. In UNIX terminology, this would be called the superblock. It contains some general information.

Bytes	Content
0–2	Jump to bootstrap
3–10	OEM name/version
11–12	Number of bytes per sector
13	Number of sectors per cluster
14–15	Number of reserved sectors
16	Number of FATs
17–18	Number of root directory entries
19–20	Total number of sectors in the file system
21	Media descriptor type
22–23	Number of sectors per FAT
24–25	Number of sectors per track
26–27	Number of heads
28–29	Number of hidden sectors
30–509	Bootstrap
510–511	Signature

Table 1-5 The boot sector contains information about a disk

The following is an example of a boot sector:

0000000 eb 3f 90 49 42 4d 20 20 33 2e 33 00 02 01 01 00 0000020 02 e0 00 40 0b f0 09 00 12 00 02 00 00 00 00 00 0000040 00 00 00 00 00 00 00 00 00 00 00 00 70 00 ff ff 49 42 0000060 4d 42 49 4f 20 20 43 4f 4d 00 50 00 00 08 00 18 . . .

The two-byte numbers are stored little-endian. Table 1-5 describes the contents of the FAT12 version, which is similar to the FAT16 and FAT32 versions.

File Recovery When a file is deleted from a FAT volume, the operating system replaces the first letter of the file name with a lowercase Greek letter. The space is then made available for new files. These files can be recovered using forensic tools.

A few tools that can be used for forensics are:

- *WinHex*: Forensic investigators can use the hex editor, disk editor, and RAM editor, along with many other features like concatenating, separating, combining, and evaluating files; agile searching and substitution functions; data interpretation (accepts 19 data types); template editing; encryption; file editing; a highly developed backup mechanism; drive imaging; drive cloning; and printing. The disk editor maintains floppy disks, hard drives, and CD-ROM and DVD drives.

- *Undelete*: Undelete restores files that cannot be restored using the Recycle Bin. The following are the types of files that can be restored using Undelete:

  - Shared files on the network

  - Previous versions of Office files

  - Large files that do not fit in the Recycle Bin

  - Certain files that are created and deleted by applications

  - Files deleted from the command line

- *File Scavenger*: This tool retrieves digital photos from most media. It also retrieves files ruined by viruses and files deleted by mistake from Windows Explorer, the Recycle Bin, the DOS command line, or a network share. It can also recover formatted volumes, broken spanned volumes, broken RAID volumes, and disks with bad media areas.

NTFS

New Technology File System (NTFS) is one of the latest file systems supported by Windows. It is a high-performance file system that repairs itself. It supports several advanced features such as file-level security, compression, and auditing. It also supports large and powerful volume storage solutions such as self-recovering disks.

Features NTFS provides data security, as it has the capability to encrypt or decrypt data, files, or folders. NTFS uses a 16-bit Unicode character set to name files and folders. This attribute of NTFS lets users around the world manage their files in their native languages. It is a fault-tolerant file system. NTFS makes a note of modifications in a special log file. If a system crashes, NTFS can examine the log file and use it to restore the disk to a consistent state with minimal data loss.

NTFS volumes also contain a Master File Table. This table contains a record for every file and folder on the volume. The first 16 bytes of the table are reserved for metadata used to implement and maintain the file system structure. This metadata is stored in a set of system files (Table 1-6).

NTFS Partition Boot Sector When a volume is formatted as an NTFS volume, the format program allocates the first 16 sectors for the boot sector and the bootstrap code. Table 1-7 describes the boot sector of an NTFS volume.

NTFS Master File Table (MFT) NTFS file system contains a unique file called the Master File Table, or MFT. NTFS volumes have at least one entry stored in the MFT.

Information regarding file attributes like size, time and date stamps, and permissions is saved either with the MFT entries or in memory allocated outside the MFT that is described by MFT entries. When the number of files on an NTFS volume increases, the size of the MFT increases. When a file is deleted from an NTFS volume, the values in the MFT are marked as free, and that space can be reused.

File Name	System File	Record Position	Description
$MFT	MFT 1	0	This is the base file record for an NTFS volume.
$MftMirr	MFT 2	1	The first four records of MFT are stored here for restoration purposes.
$LogFile	Log File	2	Previous transactions are listed and stored, for restoration purposes.
$Volume	Volume	3	Information regarding the volume is stored in this table.
$AttrDef	Attribute definitions	4	This list contains attributes of files.
$	Root file name index	5	This is the root folder.
$Bitmap	Boot sector	6	This is a list that shows the availability and usage of the clusters.
$Boot	Boot sector	7	This is used to mount the NTFS volume during the bootstrap process.
$BadClus	Bad cluster file	8	This contains a list of the clusters that have unrecoverable errors.
$Secure	Security file	9	This access control list has the unique security descriptors for the files on the volume.
$Upcase	Upcase table	10	This is used to convert all uppercase characters to lowercase Unicode characters.
$Extend	NTFS extension file	11	Optional extensions like quotes and object identifiers are listed here.

Table 1-6   This table lists the NTFS system files

Byte Offset	Field Length	Field Name
0x00	3 bytes	Jump instruction
0x03	LONGLONG	OEM ID
0x0B	25 bytes	BPB
0x24	48 bytes	Extended BPB
0x54	426 bytes	Bootstrap Code
0x01FE	WORD	End of Sector Marker

Table 1-7   This is an example of a boot sector on a Windows 2000 NTFS volume

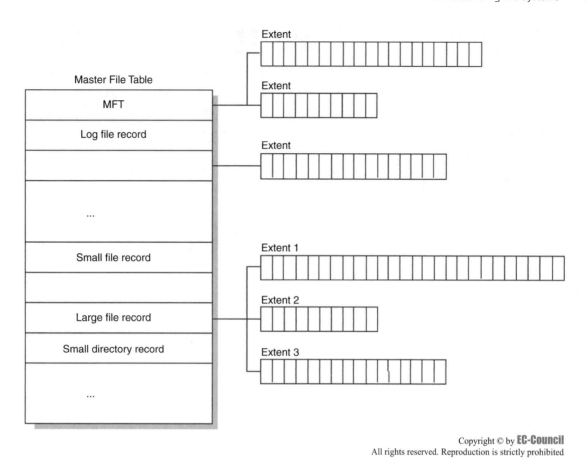

Figure 1-9 This is the structure of a Master File Table on an NTFS volume

The utilities that defragment NTFS volumes on Windows systems cannot move MFT entries, and as unnecessary fragmentation of the MFT breaks down the performance of the file system, NTFS reserves space for the MFT to maintain performance as it expands. The average file size and other variables are considered when allocating memory to the reserved MFT zone or the unreserved memory on the disk as the disk fills to its capacity.

Figure 1-9 shows the structure of a Master File Table.

NTFS Attributes The file attributes stored within an MFT record are called resident attributes, and those that lie outside the MFT are nonresident attributes. If the data attributes are small in size, then they can be stored within the MFT without the need for additional storage space on the NTFS volume. But if the attributes do not fit in the MFT, they are moved out of the MFT record as nonresident attributes. Table 1-8 lists the different types of attributes.

NTFS Data Streams A data stream is a unique set of file attributes. NTFS supports multiple data streams per file. A data stream can be created in an existing file on an NTFS volume using a command like the following: **C:\ECHO text_message > myfile.txt:stream1.** To display the contents of the data stream, the following command must be used: **C:\MORE < myfile.txt:stream1.**

A data stream does not appear when a file is opened in a text editor. The only way to see if a data stream is attached to a file is by examining the MFT entry for the file.

Figure 1-10 shows how to create and examine a data stream using the command line.

NTFS Compressed Files NTFS is capable of compressing individual files, all the files within a folder, and all the files within an NTFS volume. Compression is executed within NTFS, so any Windows-based program can read and write compressed files without considering the extent of compression of the file. When a compressed file is opened, only a part of the file is decompressed when being read. Data in memory, if uncompressed, does not hinder NTFS performance when it accesses data in memory. The modified or new data of the file is compressed when the data is written to disk.

Attribute Type	Purpose of the Attribute
Standard information	This lists the information regarding the time stamp data and link count information.
Attribute list	This is the list of attributes that are in the MFT. It also has a list of nonresident attributes.
File name	The file name is stored here and can be a long or short name. It stores up to 255 bytes.
Security descriptor	Ownership and access rights to the file are listed here.
Data	File data is stored here, and multiple data attributes are allowed for each file.
Object ID	The unique identifier that identifies the volume is listed here.
Logged tool stream	This attribute is used by the encrypted file system service that is used in Windows 2000 and Windows XP.
Reparse point	This lists volume mount points for installable file system filter drivers.
Index root	This is for the use of folders and files.
Index allocation	This is for the use of folders and files.
Bitmap	This is for the use of folders and files.
Volume information	This is where the version number of the volume is listed.
Volume name	The volume label is listed here.

Table 1-8   This table shows the different types of file attributes

NTFS compression algorithms support cluster sizes of up to 4 KB. To set the compression state of a volume:

1. In the **My Computer** or **Windows Explorer** window, right-click on the volume that is to be compressed.

2. Click **Properties** to show the **Properties** dialog box.

3. On the **General** tab, click **Advanced**.

4. In the **Advanced Attributes** dialog box, choose the **Compress drive to save disk space** check box, and then click **OK**.

5. In the **Confirm Attribute Changes** dialog box, choose an option. The compression can be applied to the entire volume or only to the root folder.

To set the compression state of a folder or file:

1. In the **My Computer** or **Windows Explorer** window, right-click on the file or folder that is to be compressed.

2. Click **Properties** to show the **Properties** dialog box.

3. On the **General** tab, click **Advanced**.

4. In the **Advanced Attributes** dialog box, choose the **Compress drive to save disk space** check box, and then click **OK**.

5. In the **Confirm Attribute Changes** dialog box, choose an option. This compression must be applied to the entire folder or file.

NTFS Encrypting File System (EFS)   To protect files from mishandling and to ensure their security, the files are encrypted. The Encrypting File System (EFS) was first introduced in NTFS. EFS uses symmetric key encryption technology with public key technology for encryption. The user is supplied with a digital certificate with a public key pair. A private key is not used for the users who are logged in to the local systems. Instead, an EFS key is used for users who are logged in to the local system.

This encryption technology maintains a level of transparency to the user who encrypted the file. There is no need for users to decrypt the file when they access it to make changes. After a user is done with the file, the encryption policy is automatically restored. When any unauthorized user tries to access an encrypted file, he or she is denied access.

To enable the encryption and decryption facilities, a user has to set the encryption attributes of the files and folders that he or she wants to encrypt or decrypt.

All the files and subfolders in a folder are automatically encrypted. To take the best advantage of the encryption capability, experts recommend that encryption should be done at the folder level. That means a particular encrypted file should not be kept in the same folder as other files that are not encrypted.

Encryption is done using the graphical user interface (GUI) in Windows, but a file or a folder can also be encrypted using a command line tool like Cipher.

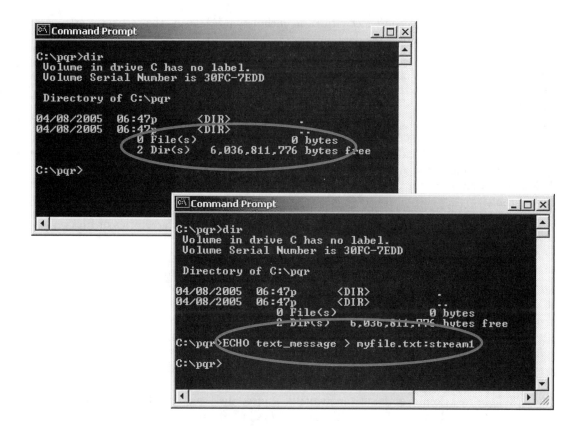

Figure 1-10   A user can create and examine data streams using the command line

A file encryption certificate is issued whenever a file is encrypted. If the person who encrypted the file loses that certificate and the associated private key, data recovery is performed through the recovery key agent.

In case of a Windows 2000 server-based network, which uses Active Directory, the recovery agent is assigned by default to the domain administrator. The recovery agent holds a special certificate and related private key.

The recovery certificate is issued by a certification authority (CA). Using the recovery certificate and its related private key, the agent can recover the data.

EFS Recovery Key Agent If there is a need to perform a recovery operation, the recovery certificate is first restored and associated with the private key in the agent's personal store by using the **Import** command in the Certificates snap-in.

After the data is recovered, it is deleted from the recovery certificate in the agent's personal store. The recovery agent's certificate is then deleted from the computer.

Stand-alone computers locally configure the default recovery policy. For computers on a network, the recovery policy can be configured at the domain, organizational unit, or individual computer level.

A Windows administrator can recover a lost key or encrypted data from the command prompt using the following tools:

- *CIPHER*: This tool is used to make changes to the encryption of directories or files on an NTFS partition.
  Syntax:
      CIPHER [/E | /D] [/S:dir] [/A] [/I] [/F] [/Q] [/H] [/K] [pathname [...]]
      CIPHER /W:directory
      CIPHER /X[:efsfile] [filename]
  Where:
/E	Encrypts the specified directories.
/D	Decrypts the specified directories.
/S	Performs operation on the given directory and all subdirectories.
/H	Displays files with hidden or system attributes.
/W	Removes data from available unused disk space on the entire volume.
/X	Backs up EFS certificate and keys into file name.

- *COPY*: This command is used to copy one or more files to other locations.
  Syntax:
      COPY [/V] [/N] [/Y | /-Y] [/Z] [/A | /B] source [/A | /B]
          [+ source [/A | /B] [+ ...]] [destination [/A | /B]]
  Where:
source	Specifies the file or files to be copied.
destination	Specifies the directory and/or filename for the new file(s).
/A	Indicates an ASCII text file.
/B	Indicates a binary file.
/V	Verifies that new files are written correctly.
/N	Uses short file names, if available, when copying a file with a non-8dot3 name.
/Y	Suppresses prompting to confirm overwriting an existing destination file.
/Z	Copies network files in restartable mode.

- *EFSRECVR*: This command helps the recovery agent recover encrypted files from the specified location.
  Syntax:
      EFSRECVR [/S[:dir]] [/I] [/Q] [filename [...]]
/S	Recovers the files from the respective directories and subdirectories.
/I	Recovers the file even after errors have occurred.
/Q	Reports only useful recovery keys from the list of recovery key identifications.

Deleting NTFS Files When a file is deleted in Windows Explorer, the file is moved into the Recycle Bin. This allows the user to restore the deleted file at a later time. The operating system takes the following steps when a file is deleted:

- Windows changes the name of the file and moves the file to the Recycle Bin with a unique identity.

- Windows stores the information about the original path and file name in an INFO2 file, which controls the Recycle Bin. This file contains ASCII data, Unicode data, and attributes like the date and time of deletion for each and every file or folder.

If a file is deleted from the command prompt, the file does not go into the Recycle Bin, but a part of the file or the complete file can be recovered using forensic tools. When a file is deleted at the command prompt or when a file is deleted from the Recycle Bin, then the following tasks are performed by the operating system:

- The clusters are made available for new data.
- The MFT attribute $BITMAP is updated.
- File attributes of the MFT are marked as available.
- Any connections to the inodes and VFN/LCN cluster locations are removed.
- The list of links to the cluster locations is deleted.

CD-ROM/DVD File Systems

Data stored on CD-ROM/DVDs is divided into sectors. These sectors contain both user data and error correction codes. Users don't need to worry about which data is stored in which sector, but users should have knowledge of the file structure of CD-ROM/DVDs.

ISO 9660

ISO 9660 (a standard defined by the International Organization for Standardization) defines a file system for CD-ROM/DVD media. Its aim is to support different computer operating systems, such as Microsoft Windows, Mac OS, and UNIX, to allow for the exchange of data between different operating systems.

ISO 9660 Specifications

There is a reserved area of 32,768 bytes at the beginning of the disk. This area's use is not specified in the ISO 9660 standard, but it is often used for boot information on bootable CD-ROM/DVDs.

Volume Descriptors Immediately afterward, a series of volume descriptors details the contents and the kind of information contained on the disk.

A volume descriptor describes the characteristics of the file system information present on a given CD-ROM/DVDs. It is divided into two parts: the type of volume descriptor and the characteristics of the descriptor.

A volume descriptor is constructed in this manner so that if a program reading the disk does not understand a particular descriptor, it can just skip over that descriptor until it finds one it recognizes, thus allowing the use of many different types of information on one CD-ROM/DVDs. Also, if an error were to render a descriptor unreadable, a subsequent redundant copy of a descriptor could then allow for fault recovery.

An ISO 9660 compliant disk contains at least a primary descriptor describing the ISO 9660 file system and a terminating descriptor indicating the end of the descriptor sequence. Joliet and UDF are examples of file systems adding more descriptors to this sequence.

The primary volume descriptor acts much like the superblock of the UNIX file system, providing details on the ISO 9660 compliant portion of the disk. Contained within the primary volume descriptor is the root directory record describing the location of the contiguous root directory. (As in UNIX, directories appear as files for the operating system's special use.) Directory entries are successively stored within this region. The root directory is stored as an extent, or sequential series of sectors, that contains each of the directory entries appearing in the root. In addition, since ISO 9660 works by segmenting the CD-ROM/DVD into logical blocks, the size of these blocks is found in the primary volume descriptor as well.

The first field in a volume descriptor is the volume descriptor type, which can have the following values:

- *Number 0*: This means that the volume descriptor is a boot record.
- *Number 1*: This means that the volume descriptor is a primary volume descriptor.
- *Number 2*: This means that the volume descriptor is a supplementary volume descriptor.
- *Number 3*: This means that the volume descriptor is a volume partition descriptor.
- *Number 255*: This means that the volume descriptor is a volume descriptor set terminator.

The second field is called the standard identifier and is set to CD001 for a CD-ROM compliant to the ISO 9660 standard.

Another interesting field is the volume space size, which contains the amount of data available on the CD-ROM.

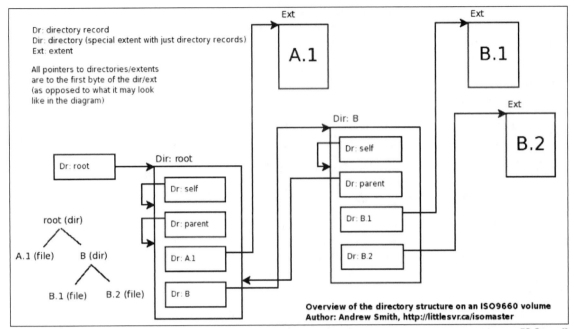

Overview of the directory structure on an ISO9660 volume
Author: Andrew Smith, http://littlesvr.ca/isomaster

Figure 1-11   This shows an overview of the ISO 9660 directory structure.

File attributes are very simple in ISO 9660. The most important file attribute determines whether the file is a directory or an ordinary file. File attributes for the file described by the directory entry are stored in the directory entry and, optionally, in the extended attribute record.

Figure 1-11 shows the directory structure specified in the ISO 9660 standard.

There are two ways to locate a file on an ISO 9660 file system:

- One way is to successively interpret the directory names and look through each directory's file structure to find the file (much the way MS-DOS and UNIX work to find a file).

- The other way is through the use of a precompiled table of paths, where all the entries are enumerated in the successive contents of a file with the corresponding entries.

Some systems do not have a mechanism for wandering through directories, so they obtain a match by consulting the table. While a large linear table seems a bit archaic, it can be of great value, as the system can quickly search without wandering across the disk (thus reducing seek time).

ISO 9660 Extensions   There are common extensions to ISO 9660 to deal with its limitations. The Rock Ridge Interchange Protocol allows for longer file names (up to 255 characters) in which any ASCII character can be used. It also supports deeper directory hierarchies and symbolic links. El Torito is an extension that allows machines to boot from a CD-ROM.

ISO/IEC 13490

ISO/IEC 13490 is the next version of ISO 9660 (level 3), intended to describe the file system of a CD-ROM. ISO 13490 has several improvements over its predecessor:

- It fully addresses the file name, POSIX attribute, and multibyte character issues that are not handled by ISO 9660.

- It is a more efficient format, and it permits incremental recording and both the ISO 9660 format and ISO/IEC 13490 format to coexist on the same media.

- It also specifies how to do multisession recording properly.

Comparison of File Systems

Table 1-9 provides a comparison of some of the file systems discussed in this chapter.

File System:	NTFS	FAT32	Mac OS X UFS	HFS+	ext2	ext3	ReiserFS	XFS	JFS	FFS	Be File System
Creator	Microsoft, Gary Kimura, Tom Miller	Microsoft	Apple	Apple	Rémy Card	Stephen Tweedie	Namesys	SGI	IBM	Marshall McKusick	Be Inc., D. Giampaolo, C. Meurillon
Original operating system	Windows NT	Windows 95	Mac OS X	Mac OS	Linux	Linux	Linux	IRIX	AIX	BSD	BeOS
Limits											
Maximum filename length	255 bytes	255 bytes	?	255 characters	255 bytes	255 bytes	4032 bytes/255 characters	255 bytes	?	?	?
Allowable filename characters	Space plus any printable except \ / : ? " " > < |	Space plus any printable except \ / : ? " " > < |	Any non-null except /	Any Unicode except:	Any non-null except /	Any non-null except /	Any non-null except /	Any non-null except /	?	Any non-null except /	?
Maximum pathname length	32767 bytes	At least 260 bytes	?	?	No limit defined	No limit defined	?	?	?	?	?
Maximum file size	16 EB	4 GB	?	8 EB	16 GB to 2 TB	16 GB to 2 TB	8 TB	9 EB	8 EB	8 TB	?
Maximum volume size	16 EB	2-STB	?	?	2 TB to 32 TB	2 TB to 32 TB	16 TB	9 EB	512 TB to 4 PB	?	?
Features											
File type metadata	None (file extensions)	None (file extensions)	Rich (type and creator)	Rich (type and creator)	None (file extensions or magic numbers)	None (file extensions or magic numbers)	?	Rich (extended attributes)	?	None (file extensions)	Rich
Stores file owner	Yes	No	Yes	Yes	Yes	Yes	Yes	Yes	Yes	Yes	Yes
POSIX file permissions	No	No	Yes	Yes	Yes	Yes	Yes	Yes	Yes	Yes	Yes
Access control lists	Yes	No	No	No	No	No	No	No	No	No	No
Hard links	Yes	No	Yes	Yes	Yes	Yes	Yes	Yes	Yes	Yes	Yes
Soft links	No	No	Yes	Yes	Yes	Yes	Yes	Yes	Yes	Yes	Yes
Alternate data stream/resource fork	Yes	No	No	Yes	No	No	No	No	No	No	Yes
Journaling	Yes	No	No	Yes	No	Yes	Yes	Yes	Yes	No	Yes
File system	NTFS	FAT32	Mac OS X UFS	HFS+	ext2	ext3	ReiserFS	XFS	JFS	FFS	Be file system

Table 1-9 This table compares different file systems and their features

Registry Data

The window registry contains a set of predefined keys:

- *HKEY_CURRENT_USER*: It is abbreviated HKCU and can be scanned for information about the configuration of the user currently logged in.
- *HKEY_USERS*: HKEY_CURRENT_USER is a subkey of HKEY_USERS. It can be checked for all the user profiles loaded on the computer.
- *HKEY_LOCAL_MACHINE*: It is abbreviated HKLM and can be searched for the configuration information of a particular computer.
- *HKEY_CLASSES_ROOT*: It is a subkey of HKEY_LOCAL_MACHINE\Software. The information stored in this key ensures that the correct program opens when a file is opened in Windows Explorer.
- *HKEY_CURRENT_CONFIG*: This key contains data about the hardware profile used by the local computer at start-up.

Examining Registry Data

A registry hive is defined as a set of keys, subkeys, and values in the Windows registry. The registry has a group of supporting files that contain backups of its data. The extensions and the file names of these files vary from operating system to operating system.

The various registry hives and their supporting files in Windows are listed below:

• HKEY_LOCAL_MACHINE\SAM	Sam, Sam.log, Sam.sav
• HKEY_LOCAL_MACHINE\Security	Security, Security.log, Security.sav
• HKEY_LOCAL_MACHINE\Software	Software, Software.log, Software.sav
• HKEY_LOCAL_MACHINE\System	System, System.alt, System.log, System.sav
• HKEY_CURRENT_CONFIG	System, System.alt, System.log, System.sav, Ntuser.dat, Ntuser.dat.log
• HKEY_USERS\DEFAULT	Default, Default.log, Default.sav

A user can examine the registry manually using the Registry Editor. There are two versions for Windows: REGEDIT (16-bit) and REGEDIT32 (32-bit). REGEDIT32 and REGEDIT are installed by default on a Windows computer. The following are the steps for opening the Registry Editor in any Windows version:

- To start the 32-bit Registry Editor:
  - Click **Start**.
  - Click **Run**.
  - Type **Regedt32** and click **OK**.
- To start the 16-bit Registry Editor:
  - Click **Start**.
  - Click **Run**.
  - Type **RegEdit** and click **OK**.

Other Registry Tools

There are other tools that a user can use to examine or monitor the registry:

- *Registry Monitor*: Registry Monitor is a program that can be used to monitor changes to the registry as they occur. It gives an idea of how the operating system and other applications use the registry. Windows Explorer can be monitored from the **Folder Options** dialog box to check where each program stores its option in the registry. The changes can be displayed by filtering the Registry Monitor's output from the setup program.
- *Registry Checker*: Registry Checker is a part of the Windows 98 operating system. This program can be used to:
  - Backup and restore the registry.
  - Scan and fix various errors in the registry.
  - Optimize the space that is unused in the registry.

Windows XP System Files

Table 1-10 describes the essential system files used by Windows XP.

File Name	Description
ntoskrnl.exe	The executable and kernel of Windows XP
ntkrnlpa.exe	Physical address support program
hal.dll	Used by kernel to communicate with computer's hardware
win32k.sys	Kernel mode for the Win32 subsystem
ntdll.dll	Supports internal functions and dispatches the stubs to executive functions
kernel32.dll	Win32 subsystem DLL file
advapi.dll	Win32 subsystem DLL file
user32.dll	Win32 subsystem DLL file
gdi32.dll	Win32 subsystem DLL file

Table 1-10   These are essential system files in Windows XP

Bootdisk.com

The Web site *www.bootdisk.com* provides boot disks for DOS, Linux, and Windows operating systems. It also offers drivers and utilities. The site also features tips and guides for maintaining hard disks and file systems.

Chapter Summary

- A hard disk is a sealed unit containing a number of platters in a stack. Hard disks may be mounted in a horizontal or a vertical position.

- A file system is a set of data types that is employed for storage, hierarchical categorization, management, navigation, access, and recovery of data.

- A registry is a hierarchical database.

- Every disk has a master boot record that contains information about partitions on the disk.

- EFS is the main file encryption technology used to store encrypted files in NTFS.

- MFT is a relational database that consists of information regarding files and file attributes.

- Windows continuously refers to the registry for information during the execution of applications.

Review Questions

1. Explain the difference between fixed and removable disk drives, and give at least one example of each.

   _____

   _____

2. Explain zoned bit recording.

   _____

   _____

3. Explain types of hard disk interfaces.

_____

_____

4. Explain the difference between serial ATA and parallel ATA.

_____

_____

5. Describe the composition of a hard disk platter.

_____

_____

6. List and describe the file systems most commonly used on Linux.

_____

_____

7. Explain the Master File Table (MFT) and its contents.

_____

_____

8. Describe the function of the EFS recovery key agent.

_____

_____

9. Explain what a partition is, including the different types of partitions.

_____

_____

10. List and describe the different tools used to examine the registry.

_____

_____

Hands-On Projects

1. Run a registry analyzer tool on your system and see the result.

2. Check which file system your computer has.

3. Download the tool Evidor from _www.x-ways.net/evidor/index.htm_. Run the tool and note the results.

4. Download the tool WinHex from _www.x-ways.net/winhex/index-m.html_ and run it.

5. Read about the various types of disk and network file systems.

Chapter 2

Understanding Digital Media Devices

Objectives

After completing this chapter, you should be able to:

- Understand magnetic tapes and their uses
- Understand the different types of floppy disks
- Understand the different types of compact discs (CDs)
- Understand the different types of digital versatile discs (DVDs)
- Understand HD DVD and Blu-ray
- Understand iPods and Zunes
- Understand the different types of flash memory cards
- Understand USB flash drives

Key Terms

Blu-ray   the next-generation optical medium patented by Sony

CD-ROM   a type of compact disc that holds data that a computer can read

Compact disc (CD)   an optical disc that is used to store different kinds of data

Digital versatile disc (DVD)   an optical disc that holds more data than a CD

Flash memory card   a solid-state electronic flash memory data storage device

HD DVD   a type of optical disc that is a successor to a standard DVD and holds more data

iPod   a portable digital audio player designed and marketed by Apple Computer

iTunes   a digital media player application that is typically used to interact with an iPod

Magnetic tape   a recording medium that consists of a thin plastic strip with a fine magnetic coating

Zune   a portable digital audio player designed and marketed by the Microsoft Corporation

Introduction to Understanding Digital Media Devices

This chapter focuses on the various types of digital media devices. Users can store different types of data on these devices, including pictures, videos, music, text, and applications. The chapter covers older digital media, such as magnetic tapes and floppy disks, before moving on to a discussion of optical discs, such as CDs and DVDs, and devices such as digital audio players and flash drives.

Magnetic Tapes

A *magnetic tape* is a recording medium that consists of a thin plastic strip with a coating of a fine magnetic material. It is generally used for recording audio, video, and digital data.

The magnetic layer consists of a magnetic pigment suspended within a polymer binder. As the name implies, the binder holds the magnetic particles and tape backing together.

Data is stored in frames across the width of a tape. The frames are grouped into blocks, or records, which are separated by gaps.

A magnetic tape is a serial access medium. If someone wants to find a particular piece of data on a tape, the tape drive has to start at the beginning of the tape and search until it finds that data. However, large amounts of information can be stored on a magnetic tape. This feature has made it an excellent choice for the regular backup of hard disks.

Floppy Disks

A floppy disk is a small, portable magnetic disk that is used to store and transfer computer data. It is also called a diskette or floppy. The access speed of a floppy disk is slow when compared to that of a hard disk. The storage capacity of a floppy disk is lower than that of a hard disk, but floppies are not as expensive as hard disks.

The following are the basic sizes of floppy disks:

- *8-inch*: Created in 1971, this type of floppy consists of a magnetic storage medium enclosed in a cardboard case. It is capable of storing up to 1 MB of data.

- *5¼-inch*: Designed in 1976, this type of floppy has types capable of storing from 100 KB to 1.2 MB of data.

- *3½-inch*: Made in 1987, this type of floppy is enclosed in a rigid plastic envelope. It is also called a micro floppy. Despite its smaller size, it stores a larger amount of data, generally between 720 KB and 1.4 MB.

Compact Discs

A *compact disc (CD)* is a polycarbonate plastic disc with one or more metal layers that is used for storing digital data. It is a standard medium for distributing large quantities of information in a dependable package. The diameter of a standard CD is 120 mm, and the diameter of a mini CD is 80 mm.

Polycarbonate plastic (substrate layer) is impressed with microscopic bumps that are arranged as a single continuous spiral track of data. The polycarbonate plastic is coated with a thin aluminum (reflective) layer that covers the bumps. Then a thin acrylic (protective) layer is sprayed over the aluminum. The label is then printed on the acrylic layer.

The single track of data spirals from the center of the disc to the outside edge. The extended bumps that make up the track are 0.5 microns wide, 0.83 microns long, and 125 nanometers high.

Types of Compact Discs

There are different types of compact discs used for data storage. The following are some of the more common types:

- **CD-ROM** *(compact disc read-only memory)*: This is the most basic type of optical disc used with computers. The most common CD-ROM format holds 700 MB of data. When a user purchases a CD-ROM, it already has the data on it. A user cannot write new data to the disc.

- *CD-R (compact disc–recordable)*: This type of compact disc can be written to once. The user must have a CD recorder to write data to the disc. The CD recorder uses a laser to write data onto a blank data track.

- *CD-RW (compact disc–rewritable)*: This type of disc can be written to many times. As with a CD-R, a user must have a CD recorder to write data to the disc.

Reading a CD

A CD drive is used to read data—whether it is audio data, video data, or application data—from a CD. A drive is made up of the following main parts:

- *Drive motor*: This rotates the disc at speeds between 200 and 500 rpm. The speed is dependent on which part of the CD is being read.

- *Laser and lens system*: This reads the bumps on the disc.

- *Tracking mechanism*: This moves the laser assembly to follow the spiral track.

DVDs

A *DVD*, also called either a ***digital versatile disc*** or a digital video disc, is used for storing digital data and has a much higher storage capacity than a CD. A single-sided, single-layer DVD (DVD-5) can hold up to 4.7 GB of data, and a double-sided, dual-layer DVD (DVD-18) can hold up to 17 GB of data. DVDs are commonly used to store movies, as they have enough space to hold video and multiple audio tracks. A DVD has the same dimensions as a CD. As with a CD, data is encoded in the form of small pits and bumps in the data track of a DVD.

A DVD is composed of many layers made of plastic, all adding up to a thickness of 1.2 mm. Each layer is formed through an injection-molding process using polycarbonate plastic. This forms a disc that contains microscopic bumps arranged in a single continuous spiral track of data. A thin aluminum (reflective) layer is applied to the polycarbonate layer to form the inner layers of the disc. A semi-reflective gold layer, used for the outer layers, allows the laser to focus on either the outer or inner layers. All the layers are coated with lacquer and compressed together under infrared light.

The label of a single-sided disc is printed on the non-readable side. The label of a double-sided disc is printed only on the non-readable area that is near the hole in the middle.

Every writeable layer of a DVD consists of a spiral track of data. On single-layer DVDs, the track always spirals from the center of the disc to the outside edge. The extended bumps that make up the track are 320 nanometers wide, 400 nanometers long, and 120 nanometers high.

Recordable DVDs

There are different types of recordable DVD formats, all with slightly different features:

- *DVD-R (SL or DL)*: This is a recordable, non-rewriteable format for DVDs. The single-layer (SL) version supports single-sided 4.7 GB DVDs (DVD-5s). The dual-layer (DL) version supports 8.5 GB DVDs (DVD-9s). A user can write data to a DVD-R only once.

- *DVD+R (SL or DL)*: This is a recordable, non-rewriteable format for DVDs. The single-layer (SL) version supports single-sided 4.7 GB DVDs (DVD-5s). The dual-layer (DL) version supports 8.5 GB DVDs (DVD-9s). A user can write data to a DVD+R only once. There are some significant technical differences between DVD+R and DVD-R that tend to make DVD+R a more reliable format.

- *DVD-RW (SL or DL)*: This is a rewriteable version of a DVD-R, with the same storage capacity. According to the standard, a DVD-RW can be written to 1000 times.

- *DVD+RW (SL or DL)*: This is a rewriteable version of a DVD+R, with the same storage capacity. According to the standard, a DVD+RW can be written to 1000 times. One advantage of a DVD+RW is that a user can add data to a disc without erasing the whole disc.

- *DVD-RAM*: This type of disc is easy to read from and write to, so it is ideal for use in video cameras. Unlike other DVD formats, DVD-RAM data is stored on the disc in concentric tracks, not one long spiral. These discs can be written to 100,000 times, and they can last up to 30 years. They also have better error-checking and error-correction capabilities. However, there are fewer devices compatible with DVD-RAM, and the discs tend to cost more than DVD-R or DVD+R media.

HD DVDs

HD DVDs were originally called Advanced Optical Discs (AODs) and were developed as a successor to standard DVDs. An *HD DVD* is the same physical size as a standard DVD (120 mm), but it holds more data. Whereas a DVD holds up to 4.7 GB of data per layer, an HD DVD holds up to 15 GB per layer.

It has a bumpy layer that reflects light from a laser to a sensor, which creates a digital signal.

HD DVDs store more data than DVDs for the following reasons:

- HD DVDs use 405-nanometer blue-violet lasers instead of 650-nanometer red lasers.

- Because of the shorter wavelength lasers, the pits used in HD DVDs can be smaller and arranged closer together. Whereas the track pitch of a standard DVD is 0.74 microns, the track pitch of an HD DVD is 0.4 microns.

- HD DVDs use more efficient compression techniques to reduce the sizes of the files they store.

Blu-ray Discs

Blu-ray is the next-generation optical medium patented by Sony. A Blu-ray disc holds a large amount of data and is generally used to store high-definition video and audio. The laser used to read the data is focused on smaller areas, so more data can be stored on a disc that is the same size as a CD or DVD. Blu-ray discs are not readable on standard CD and DVD players and readers.

The following are the specifications for Blu-ray:

- *Recording capacity*: 27 GB

- *Laser wavelength*: 405 nm (blue-violet laser)

- *Lens numerical aperture (NA)*: 0.85

- *Data transfer rate*: 36 Mbps

- *Disc diameter*: 120 mm

- *Disc thickness*: 1.2 mm

- *Protection layer thickness*: 0.1 mm

- *Minimum pit length*: 0.15 microns

- *Track pitch*: 0.32 microns

- *Recording format*: Phase change recording

- *Tracking format*: Groove recording

- *Video recording format*: MPEG2 video

- *Audio recording format*: AC3, MPEG1, and Layer 2

- *Video and audio multiplexing format*: MPEG2 transport stream

A single-layer Blu-ray disc holds 27 GB of data, and a dual-layer Blu-ray disc holds 50 GB of data. The format also offers interactive features that allow users to connect to the Internet and directly download subtitles and other movie features.

The following are the advantages of Blu-ray:

- A user can record high-definition television (HDTV) without any quality loss.

- A user can instantly skip to any spot on a disc.

- A user can record one program on a disc, even if he or she is watching another one.

- It generates playlists.

- It edits or reorders the programs that are recorded on a disc.

- It automatically searches for an unfilled space on a disc to avoid recording over a program.

- A user can access the Web to download subtitles and other additional features.

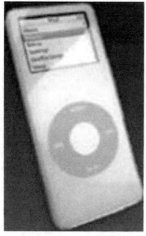

Figure 2-1 An iPod
nano uses flash memory
for data storage.

iPod

The *iPod* is a class of portable digital audio players that are designed and marketed by Apple Computer. The user interface is designed around a central scroll wheel.

The standard iPod stores media on a built-in hard drive, but the smaller iPod shuffle and iPod nano (Figure 2-1) use flash memory. Apple iPods operate as external data storage devices when connected to a computer.

iPods support various audio file formats. For formats that aren't supported, such as Ogg Vorbis, FLAC, and Windows Media Audio (WMA), the file has to be converted to a compatible format before it is placed on an iPod. A user can use *iTunes,* the digital media player application most commonly used to interact with an iPod, to perform this conversion.

The following are the file formats iPods support:

- MP3
- M4A/AAC
- Protected AAC
- AIFF
- WAV
- Audible audiobook
- Apple Lossless

The following are the features of iPods:

- They are used to play music files and videos.
- They are used to store pictures.
- They are used to store backup data files.
- They are used to store addresses and contacts.
- They are used to play games.
- They have up to 20 hours of battery life.
- Their storage capacities range from 1 GB to 120 GB, and this increases with each new iteration.
- They act as mass storage devices. The iPod uses the Apple HFS+ file system when the device is run with a Mac, and the FAT32 file system when it is used with a Windows PC.

Figure 2-2 The Zune has a large screen and can take digital photos.

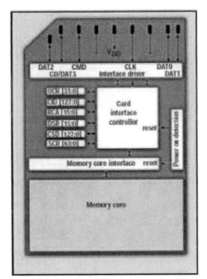

Figure 2-3 This is the inside of an SD card.

Zune

The *Zune* is a portable digital music player that was developed by the Microsoft Corporation. It can hold 30 GB of data. Figure 2-2 shows a Zune.

The following are the features of Zune:

- It takes digital photos.
- It contains a three-inch LCD video screen that works in portrait mode to view pictures and videos.
- It contains a built-in FM tuner that works with American, Japanese, and European frequencies.
- A user can share full-length tracks, home recordings, playlists, and pictures wirelessly from one Zune player to another.

Flash Memory Cards

Flash memory cards are solid-state electronic flash memory data storage devices. They are used in digital cameras, cell phones, handheld devices, laptop computers, digital music players, video game consoles, and other electronic devices. Each sector of flash memory can be erased and written to only a limited number of times. There are various types of flash memory cards, all with different storage capacities and features.

Secure Digital (SD)

An SD card is small and thin. A standard SD card is 32 mm long, 24 mm wide, and 2.1 mm thick. A mini SD card is 21.5 mm long, 20 mm wide, and 1.4 mm thick. This type of card has storage capacities ranging from 8 MB to 4 GB. It also supports digital rights management (DRM) technology. SD cards usually come preformatted with the FAT32 file system. SDHC cards support capacities greater than 4 GB. These cards are not compatible with older devices that accept SD cards. However, SDHC readers accept older SD cards. The SD interface has also been used for SDIO devices, which are small devices such as GPS receivers, Bluetooth adapters, Ethernet adapters, and FM tuners that are compatible with the SD standard. Figure 2-3 shows the inside of an SD card.

Figure 2-4 This CF card holds
4 GB of data.

Figure 2-5 This Memory Stick
holds 128 MB of data.

Figure 2-6 This MMC
holds 1 GB of data.

CompactFlash (CF)

There are two types of CF cards: Type I cards are 3.3 mm thick, and Type II cards are 5 mm thick. CF is one of the older flash memory types. The cards are larger than most of the newer types, but people still use this type of card because of its large capacity and low cost. CF cards have storage capacities ranging from 2 MB to 100 GB. CF cards have a controller chip that attempts to prevent the premature wearing out of a particular sector by spreading the data out over the device when writing. Microdrives, which are miniature hard disks, were designed to fit into Type II slots, and CF cards can easily fit into a PC Card slot with an adapter. Figure 2-4 shows a CF card.

Memory Stick (MS)

There are various types of Memory Sticks, with capacities ranging from 4 MB to 32 GB. These cards are typically used with digital cameras, PDAs, and the Playstation Portable (PSP). Memory Sticks support high-speed data transfers, with a maximum speed of 160 Mbps. Figure 2-5 shows a Memory Stick.

MultiMediaCard (MMC)

An MMC is 32 mm long, 24 mm wide, and 1.4 mm thick, so it is almost the same size as an SD card. The SD format is actually a successor to MMC, and MMCs can fit into most devices that support SD cards. MMC supports storage capacities up to 8 GB. Figure 2-6 shows an MMC.

xD-Picture Card (xD)

An xD-Picture Card is 20 mm long, 25 mm wide, and 1.78 mm thick. The xD-Picture Card format supports storage capacities up to 8 GB. As the name implies, these cards are used primarily in digital cameras, particularly those made by Olympus and Fujifilm, developers of the format. Some cameras that use xD cards use the cards to provide certain photographic features, such as a panoramic function. xD cards support fast data transfer rates, and they are smaller than many older card types. Figure 2-7 shows an xD-Picture Card.

SmartMedia (SM)

SM cards are 45 mm long, 37 mm wide, and 0.76 mm thick. The storage capacities of SM cards range from 2 MB to 128 MB. These cards can be used with PC Card slots, CF Type II slots, and 3½-inch floppy drives using adapters. Its larger size makes it impractical for use in most modern devices. Figure 2-8 shows an SM card.

USB Flash Drives

USB flash drives are NAND-type flash memory data storage devices integrated with a USB 1.1 or 2.0 interface. They are small in size, lightweight, easily detachable, and rewritable. The storage capacities of USB drives typically range from 8 MB to 64 GB. They are usually used for relatively quick portable storage and have replaced

Figure 2-7   This xD-Picture Card holds 512 MB of data.

Figure 2-8   This SmartMedia card holds 64 MB of data.

the floppy disk for this purpose. They use the USB mass storage standard, which is supported by the latest versions of operating systems such as Linux, Mac OS, and Windows.

They are also known as pen drives, thumb drives, jump drives, USB keys, USB sticks, key drives, and vault drives.

A USB flash drive consists of a small printed circuit board enclosed in a robust plastic or metal casing. The USB connector is usually protected by a detachable cap. A USB drive does not require batteries and instead gets its power from the device it is connected to. To access the data that is stored on a flash drive, a user must connect the drive to a USB port or USB hub attached to a computer or some other device.

The following are the components of a USB flash drive:

- Male type-A USB connector
- USB mass storage controller
- Jumpers and test pins
- NAND flash memory chip
- Crystal oscillator
- LED
- Write-protect switches

The following are the common uses of USB flash drives:

- To transfer data from one computer to another
- To perform system administration tasks
- To transfer applications
- To hold music
- To boot operating systems

Chapter Summary

■ This chapter has discussed digital media devices such as magnetic tapes, floppy disks, CDs, DVDs, iPods, flash memory cards, and USB flash drives.

■ A magnetic tape is a nonvolatile storage medium consisting of a thin plastic strip with a magnetic coating.

■ A CD is an optical disc used to store digital data.

■ A Blu-ray disc offers significantly more storage space than an HD DVD—50 GB on a dual-layer disc compared to HD DVD's 30 GB.

- A flash memory card is a solid-state electronic flash memory data storage device.
- USB flash drives are NAND-type flash memory data storage devices integrated with a USB interface.

Review Questions

1. For what purpose are magnetic tapes most often used, and what feature makes them ideal for this purpose?

2. Describe the three sizes of floppy disks and their storage capacities.

3. Describe the physical structure of a Blu-ray disc.

4. How does an iPod differ from a Zune?

5. Compare and contrast the different kinds of compact discs.

6. Describe the physical structure of a DVD.

7. List the parts of a CD drive and describe each part.

8. Discuss the uses of flash memory cards.

9. Describe the physical structure of a USB flash drive.

10. What file formats does the iPod support?

Hands-On Projects

1. Follow these steps:

   ▪ Navigate to Chapter 2 of the Student Resource Center.

   ▪ Read the document titled "Flash Memory Guide.pdf."

   ▪ Read the document titled "DIGITAL MEDIA STORAGE—FACILITIES AND PROCEDURES.pdf."

Chapter 3

Windows, Linux, and Macintosh Boot Processes

Objectives

After completing this chapter, you should be able to:

- Understand boot loaders
- Understand boot sectors
- Describe the basic system boot process
- Explain the MS-DOS boot process
- Explain the Windows XP boot process
- Explain the Linux boot process
- Explain the Mac OS X boot process

Key Terms

BIOS (Basic Input/Output System)   the program a personal computer's microprocessor uses to get the computer system started after a user turns it on; it also manages data flow between the computer's operating system and attached devices such as the hard disk, video adapter, keyboard, mouse, and printer.

Booting   the process of loading an operating system into a computer's main memory, or random access memory (RAM); once the operating system is loaded, the computer is ready for users to run applications.

Boot sequence   the steps that a computer system takes after a system has been powered on

Bootstrapping   see *booting*

CMOS (complementary metal-oxide semiconductor)   the semiconductor technology used in the transistors that are manufactured for most of today's computer microchips; computers contain a small amount of battery-powered CMOS memory to hold the date, time, and system setup parameters.

Cold boot (hard boot)   the startup of a computer from a powered-down, or off, state

Firmware   the software programs or instructions stored in the read-only memory (ROM) of a hardware device that provide the necessary instructions during the boot process for the computer to find the installed operating system and continue to boot up; it is considered a hybrid because it is made up of both software and hardware

Kernel the principal part of an operating system that loads first and is stored in physical memory (RAM); it is generally designed to be as small as possible and only contain essential instructions to maintain critical functions such as memory, process, and disk management.

NVRAM (nonvolatile random access memory) memory that retains its information even when the computer is turned off, by connecting it to a battery source

Warm boot (soft boot) the process of restarting a computer that is already turned on, via the operating system; restarting returns the computer to its initial state. A warm boot is necessary when a program encounters an error, and it is impossible to recover from it.

Introduction to Windows, Linux, and Macintosh Boot Processes

This chapter focuses on the boot processes for the major operating systems available today. *Booting*, also called *bootstrapping*, is the process of loading an operating system into a computer's main memory. This step takes place during the *boot sequence*, which is the set of steps a computer system takes after it has been powered on. The chapter begins by covering some basic information about the boot process. It then discusses the boot process for the legacy operating system MS-DOS before moving on to discussing the boot processes for Windows, Linux, and Mac OS.

Boot Loader

A boot loader or boot manager is a program that loads the operating system into a computer's memory when the system is booted. Multiple-stage boot loaders—where a number of small programs call each other, and the last program loads the operating system—are common.

Boot Sector

A boot sector is a memory sector of a hard disk, floppy disk, or similar data storage device that contains code for bootstrapping systems. The boot sector on a disk is always the first sector on the first track. Each valid boot sector has two bytes (0x55AA), called a boot sector signature, at the end of the sector. Figure 3-1 shows an example of a boot sector.

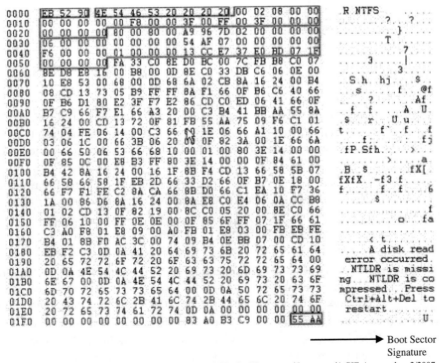

Boot Sector Signature

Source: http://www.windowsserver.it/Portals/0/articoli/bootrecord/bootrecord1.GIF. Accessed on 2/2007.

Figure 3-1 This shows a boot sector, including the boot sector signature.

```
OFFSET 0 1 2 3  4 5 6 7  8 9 A B  C D E F  *0123456789ABCDEF*
000000 fa33c08e d0bc007c 8bf45007 501ffbfc *.3.....|..P.P...*
000010 bf0006b9 0001f2a5 ea1d0600 00bebe07 *................*
000020 b304803c 80740e80 3c00751c 83c610fe *.....t....u.....*
000030 cb75efcd 188b148b 4c028bee 83c610fe *.u......L.......*
000040 cb741a80 3c0074f4 be8b06ac 3c00740b *.t....t.......t.*
000050 56bb0700 b40ecd10 5eebf0eb febf0500 *V........^......*
000060 bb007cb8 010257cd 135f730c 33c0cd13 *..|...W.._s.3...*
000070 4f75edbe a306ebd3 bec206bf fe7d813d *Ou...........}.=*
000080 55aa75c7 8bf5ea00 7c000049 6e76616c *U.u.....|..Inval*
000090 69642070 61727469 74696f6e 20746162 *id partition tab*
0000a0 6c650045 72726f72 206c6f61 64696e67 *le.Error loading*
0000b0 206f7065 72617469 6e672073 79737465 * operating syste*
0000c0 6d004d69 7373696e 67206f70 65726174 *m.Missing operat*
0000d0 696e6720 73797374 656d0000 00000000 *ing system......*
0000e0 00000000 00000000 00000000 00000000 *................*
0000f0 TO 0001af SAME AS ABOVE
0001b0 00000000 00000000 00000000 00008001 *................*
0001c0 0100060d fef83e00 00000678 0d000000 *..........X....*
0001d0 00000000 00000000 00000000 00000000 *................*
0001e0 00000000 00000000 00000000 00000000 *................*
0001f0 00000000 00000000 00000000 000055aa *..............U.*
```

Figure 3-2   This shows the code for a master boot record.

There are two major kinds of boot sectors:

- *Volume boot record*: It is the first sector of a data storage device that has not been partitioned, or the first sector of an individual partition on a data storage device that has been partitioned. It contains code to load and invoke the operating system or other stand-alone program installed on that device or within that partition.

- *Master boot record*: It is the first sector of a data storage device that has been partitioned. It contains code to locate the active partition and to invoke its volume boot record. A master boot record contains the following structures:

  - *Master partition table*: It is a small bit of code that contains a complete description of the partitions that are contained on the storage device.

  - *Master boot code*: The master boot code is a small bit of computer code loaded and executed by the BIOS to start the boot process. The **BIOS** is the program a personal computer's microprocessor uses to get the computer system started after a user turns it on.

Figure 3-2 shows a master boot record, and Figure 3-3 shows the structure of a master boot record.

Basic System Boot Process

After a computer's power is turned on, it goes through a number of steps:

1. The system clock generates a series of clock ticks, which initializes the CPU.

2. The CPU looks to the system's startup program in the ROM BIOS for its first instruction.

3. The first instruction is to run the power-on self-test (POST), in a predetermined memory address.

4. POST checks the BIOS chip and then tests CMOS RAM. **CMOS (complementary metal-oxide semiconductor)** memory holds the system date, time, and setup parameters.

5. If there is no battery failure, POST checks the inventoried hardware devices such as the video card; secondary storage devices, such as hard drives and floppy drives; ports; and other hardware devices, such as the keyboard and mouse, to check whether they are functioning properly.

6. CPU initialization is completed if everything is fine.

7. The BIOS looks into the CMOS chip to find the drive where the OS is installed.

8. The BIOS then checks the boot record of the drive to find the beginning of the OS and the subsequent program file that initializes the OS.

9. The BIOS copies its files into memory after OS initialization.

Master boot record

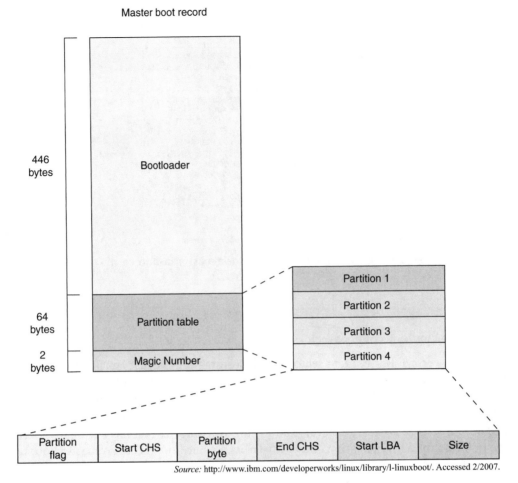

Source: http://www.ibm.com/developerworks/linux/library/l-linuxboot/. Accessed 2/2007.

Figure 3-3 This shows the structure of a master boot record.

10. The OS takes over control of the boot process.

11. The OS performs another inventory of the system's memory and memory availability, and loads the device drivers that it needs to control the peripheral devices, such as a printer, scanner, optical drive, mouse, and keyboard.

MS-DOS Boot Process

After a computer running MS-DOS is turned on, it goes through the following steps:

1. The BIOS initiates power-on self-test (POST). POST performs the following actions:

   a. Initializes the keyboard and other system hardware, such as the video card

   b. Tests the computer's RAM

   c. Checks the disk drives

   d. Attempts to find a valid operating system

   If all goes well in POST, the computer continues with these steps:

2. The BIOS searches for the file IO.SYS in the root directory and loads it into RAM.

3. IO.SYS provides services for peripherals such as printers, modems, and disk drives.

4. IO.SYS loads a file called MSDOS.SYS, which is an extension of ROM or the BIOS.

5. MSDOS.SYS acts as a gateway for communication between DOS and the BIOS.

6. MSDOS.SYS loads the CONFIG.SYS file.

7. CONFIG.SYS stores system configurations.

8. CONFIG.SYS is processed and executed.

9. MSDOS.SYS loads the COMMAND.COM program file into memory.

10. COMMAND.COM is a command interpreter that contains all the internal DOS instructions, such as DIR, CD, and CLS.

11. COMMAND.COM loads an optional file called AUTOEXEC.BAT and executes it.

Windows XP Boot Process

After the power supply is switched on, a computer running Windows XP goes through the following steps:

1. The power supply performs a self-test and sends the power-good signal to the processor.

2. The timer chip stops sending reset signals to the processor, allowing the CPU to begin operations.

3. The CPU loads the ROM BIOS starting at ROM memory address FFFF:0000.

4. The ROM BIOS contains a JMP (jump) instruction that points to the actual address of the ROM BIOS code.

5. The ROM BIOS performs a basic test of central hardware to verify basic functionality.

6. The BIOS searches for adapters that may need to load their own ROM BIOS routines.

7. Startup BIOS routines scan memory addresses C000:0000 through C780:0000 to find video ROM.

8. The ROM BIOS checks to see if this is a *cold boot* (the startup of a system from a powered-down state) or a *warm boot* (the restart of a system that is already on).

9. If this is a cold boot, the ROM BIOS executes a full POST (power-on self-test). If this is a warm boot, the memory test portion of the POST is switched off.

10. POST can be broken down into two components:

    • A video test initializes the video adapter.

    • A video adapter tests the video card and video memory, and displays configuration information or any errors.

11. The BIOS locates and reads the configuration information stored in CMOS.

12. The BIOS examines the disk for a master boot record (MBR).

13. With a valid MBR loaded into memory, the BIOS transfers control of the boot process to the partition loader code.

14. The partition loader, or boot loader, examines the partition table for a partition marked as active.

15. The partition loader then searches the very first sector of that partition for a boot record.

16. The active partition's boot record is checked for a valid boot signature and, if found, the boot sector code is executed as a program.

17. NTLDR, a hidden system file in the root directory of the system partition, controls loading of Windows XP in four stages:

    • *Initial boot-loader phase*: NTLDR switches the processor from real mode to protected mode, which places the processor in 32-bit memory mode and turns memory paging on. It then loads the appropriate file system drivers to allow NTLDR to load files from a partition formatted with any of the file systems supported by XP. If the file BOOT.INI is located in the root directory, NTLDR will read its contents into memory.

    • *Operating system selection*: If BOOT.INI contains entries for more than one operating system, NTLDR will stop the boot sequence at this point, display a menu of choices, and wait for a specified period of time for the user to make a selection. A user can press F8 at this stage of the boot sequence to display various boot options (Figure 3-4), including "Safe Mode" and "Last Known Good Configuration."

    • *Hardware detection*: If the selected operating system is XP, NTLDR locates and loads the DOS-based NTDETECT.COM program to perform hardware detection. If this computer has more than one defined hardware profile, NTLDR will stop at this point and display the Hardware Profiles/Configuration Recovery menu. After the user selects a hardware configuration, NTLDR begins loading the XP kernel (NTOSKRNL.EXE).

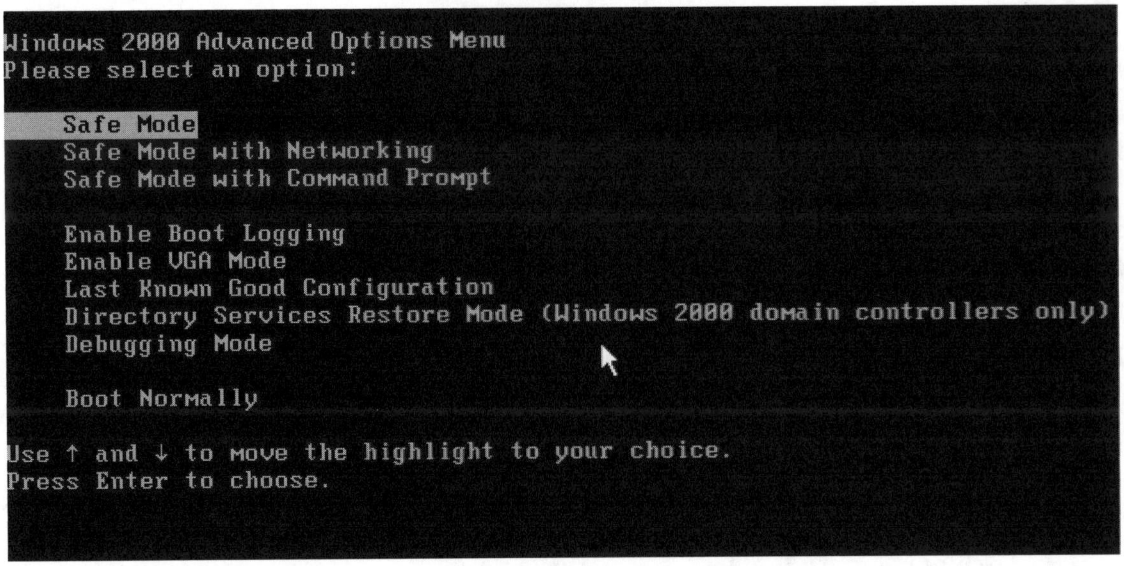

```
Windows 2000 Advanced Options Menu
Please select an option:

    Safe Mode
    Safe Mode with Networking
    Safe Mode with Command Prompt

    Enable Boot Logging
    Enable VGA Mode
    Last Known Good Configuration
    Directory Services Restore Mode (Windows 2000 domain controllers only)
    Debugging Mode

    Boot Normally

Use ↑ and ↓ to move the highlight to your choice.
Press Enter to choose.
```

Figure 3-4 A user can select from various boot options by pressing F8 during the boot process. While this example shows Windows 2000, the options are the same for XP.

- *Configuration selection*: NTLDR now loads device drivers that are marked as boot devices. After loading these drivers, NTLDR relinquishes control of the computer to the device drivers.

18. NTOSKRNL goes through two phases in its boot process:
   - *Phase 0*: XP disables interrupts during phase 0 and enables them before phase 1. The hardware abstraction layer (HAL) is called to prepare the interrupt controller.
   - *Phase 1*: All executive subsystems are reinitialized in the following order:
     1. Object Manager
     2. Executive
     3. Microkernel
     4. Security Reference Monitor
     5. Virtual Memory Manager
     6. Cache Manager
     7. Local Procedure Calls (LPCs)
     8. I/O Manager
     9. Process Manager

19. I/O Manager starts loading all the system driver files:
   - It first loads the boot devices.
   - It assembles a prioritized list of drivers and attempts to load each in turn.
   - It launches the Session Manager Subsystem (SMSS).
   - SMSS loads the win32k.sys device driver, which implements the Win32 graphics subsystem.

20. Win32k.sys switches the screen into graphics mode.

21. The services subsystem starts all services marked as Auto Start.

22. Once all devices and services are started, the boot is deemed successful, and this configuration is saved as the last known good configuration.

23. The WINLOGON.EXE file starts the logon process. It is a login manager file that is responsible for all login and logout procedures.

24. The Local Security Authority (LSASS.EXE) process displays the logon dialog box (Figure 3-5).

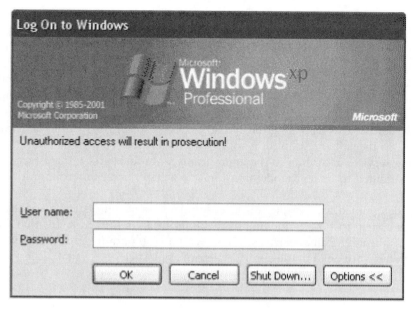

Figure 3-5   This is the logon dialog box for Windows XP Professional.

Linux Boot Process

The Linux boot process comprises five major steps:

- *Step 1, boot manager*: It is responsible for starting the booting process.
- *Step 2, init*: This process initializes booting.
- *Step 2.1, /etc/inittab*: This file contains lines with four fields: id, run level, action, and process.
- *Step 3, services*: This initiates the services that run at startup.
- *Step 4, more inittab*: This step starts all processes configured as "respawn" processes.

Step 1: Boot Manager

When a Linux computer is booted, the processor first checks system memory for the BIOS (Basic Input/Output System) and runs it. The BIOS program is written into permanent ROM and is always available for use. This BIOS program provides the lowest-level interface to all available peripheral devices, and controls the first step of the boot process.

The BIOS tests the system, looks for and checks peripherals, and then looks for a bootable device to boot the system. Usually, it checks the floppy drive or CD-ROM drive for bootable media, if available, and then it looks to the hard drive. The order of the drives used for booting is usually controlled by a particular BIOS setting on the system. The BIOS looks for a master boot record (MBR) starting at the first sector on the first hard drive, loads its contents into memory, and then passes control to it.

The MBR contains instructions on how to load the LILO (Linux Loader) or GRUB boot loader, using a preselected operating system. The MBR then loads the boot loader, which takes over the process (if the boot loader is installed in the MBR). In the default Red Hat Linux configuration, LILO uses the settings in the MBR to display boot options in a menu. Once LILO has received the correct instructions for the operating system to start, either from its command line or configuration file, it finds the necessary boot file and hands off control of the machine to that operating system.

Step 2: init

The kernel, once it is loaded, finds init in sbin and executes it. The **kernel** is the principal part of an operating system that loads first and is stored in physical memory (RAM). When init starts, it becomes the parent of all of the processes that start up automatically on Linux. The first thing init does is read its initialization file, /etc/inittab. This instructs init to read an initial configuration script for the environment, which sets the path, starts swapping, checks the file systems, and so on. Basically, this step takes care of everything that a system needs to have done at initialization, such as setting the clock, initializing serial ports, and so forth.

Then init continues to read the /etc/inittab file, which describes how the system should be set up in each run level, and sets the default run level. A run level is a configuration of processes. All UNIX-like systems can be run in different process configurations, such as single-user mode, which is referred to as run level 1 or run level S (or s). In this mode, only the system administrator can connect to the system. It is used to perform maintenance tasks without risk of damaging the system or user data. At this run level, the system doesn't provide any user services, so they all are disabled. Another run level is the reboot run level, or run level 6, which shuts down all running services according to the appropriate procedures and then restarts the system. Commonly, run level 3 is configured to be text mode on a Linux machine, and run level 5 initializes the graphical login and environment.

After having determined the default run level for the system, init starts all of the background processes necessary for the system to run, by looking in the appropriate rc directory for that run level. Init runs each of the kill scripts (their file names start with a *K*) with a stop parameter. It then runs all of the start scripts (their file names start with an *S*) in the appropriate run level directory so that all services and applications are started correctly.

Step 2.1: /etc/inittab

The /etc/inittab file plays an important role in the Linux booting process. Each entry in the inittab file has four fields separated by a colon and has the following format: "id:runlevel:action:process." Here, "id" is a two-character unique identifier, "runlevel" indicates the run level that has been set, "action" indicates how the process is to be run, and "process" is the command to be executed.

- *Identifier*: This is a two-character string that uniquely identifies an object.
- *Run level*: Run levels effectively correspond to a configuration of processes in the system. Each process started by the init command is assigned one or more run levels in which it can exist. The numbers zero through six represent run levels. For example, if the system is in run level one, only those entries with a one in the run level field are started. The run level field can define multiple run levels for a process by selecting more than one run level in any combination from zero through six. If no run level is specified, the process is assumed to be valid at all run levels.
- *Action*: This tells the init command how to treat the process specified in the process field. The following actions are recognized by the init command:
  - *boot*: Execute the process when the system is booting.
  - *bootwait*: Execute the process when the system is booting, and wait for it to finish executing.
  - *ctrlaltdel*: Execute the process when init receives the interrupt signal (SIGINT).
  - *initdefault*: Enter the specified run level after the system boots.
  - *kbrequest*: Execute the process when a special key combination is pressed on the console keyboard.
  - *off*: If the process associated with this entry is currently running, send the warning signal (SIGTERM) and wait 20 seconds before terminating the process with the kill signal (SIGKILL). If the process is not running, ignore this entry.
  - *once*: When the init command enters a run level that matches the entry's run level, start the process, and do not wait for its termination. When it ends, do not restart the process. When the system enters a new run level, and the process is still running from a previous run level change, the program will not be restarted. All subsequent reads of the /etc/inittab file while the init command is in the same run level will cause the init command to ignore this entry.
  - *ondemand*: Execute the process whenever the specified run level is entered.
  - *powerfail*: Execute the process associated with this entry only when the init command receives a power fail signal (SIGPWR).
  - *powerokwait*: Execute the process associated with this entry only when the init command receives a power fail signal (SIGPWR) and when the file /etc/powerstatus exists with the word "OK" as its contents.

- *powerwait*: Execute the process associated with this entry only when the init command receives a power fail signal (SIGPWR), and wait until it terminates before continuing to process the /etc/inittab file.

- *respawn*: If the process does not exist, start the process. Do not wait for its termination (continue scanning the /etc/inittab file). Restart the process when it dies. If the process exists, do nothing and continue scanning the /etc/inittab file.

- *syswait*: Execute this process during system boot, before any boot or bootwait processes.

- *wait*: When the init command enters the run level that matches the entry's run level, start the process and wait for its termination. All subsequent reads of the /etc/inittab file, while the init command is in the same run level, will cause the init command to ignore this entry.

- *Command*: A command is a shell process to execute. The following commands are the only supported methods for modifying the records in the /etc/inittab file:

  - *chitab*: changes records in the /etc/inittab file

  - *lsitab*: lists records in the /etc/inittab file

  - *mkitab*: adds records to the /etc/inittab file

  - *rmitab*: removes records from the /etc/inittab file

Run Levels

Linux systems generally use eight run levels. Run levels define what services or processes should be running on the system. The /etc/inittab file has information on which run level to start the system at, and it lists the processes to be run at each run level. The init process can run the system in one of eight run levels. The system can only run one of the eight run levels at a time. The main run levels are numbered from 0 to 6.

They are as follows:

- *Run level 0*: Halt system

- *Run level 1*: Single-user mode

- *Run level 2*: Basic multiuser mode without NFS

- *Run level 3*: Full multiuser mode (text based)

- *Run level 4*: Unused

- *Run level 5*: Multiuser mode with graphical user interface

- *Run level 6*: Reboot system

Run levels 1 and 2 are generally used for debugging purposes, and are not used during normal operations. Most desktop Linux distributions boot into run level 5, which starts the graphical login prompt. This allows the user to use the system with the X-Windows server enabled. Most servers boot into run level 3, which starts the text-based login prompt.

Linux run levels can be changed using the telinit command. If a user wants to switch from text-based operations to the graphical interface, he or she needs to type **telinit 5** at the root prompt. This puts the system into run level 5.

Each run level is maintained in its own directory structure, where the user can define the order in which the services must start. These directories are located in the /etc/rc.d/ directory. Under this directory are subdirectories corresponding to each run level, such as rc1.d, rc2.d, and rc3.d.

It is also possible to change the run level during booting. This can be done either by the LILO or GRUB boot loader. If the system uses LILO as the boot manager, the user can append the run level to the boot command, as in the following examples:

- LILO: linux 3

- LILO: linux 5

This changes the system to run in the specified run level.

Step 3: Services

The Linux services are specified in the directory /etc/init.d or /etc/rc.d/init.d. The directory /etc/rc.d/init.d contains the start and stop scripts. Figure 3-6 shows the Service Configuration utility.

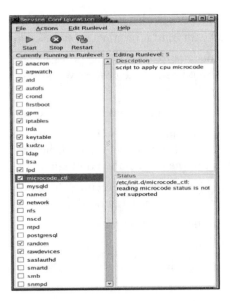

Figure 3-6 Users can change various options for system services using the Service Configuration utility.

Step 4: More inittab

The init program retrieves all lines in /etc/inittab with the action set to "respawn" for the current run level and starts those processes. Respawn commands are restarted when they end, so they will run continuously as long as the system is in run level 5.

Finally, the system is booted and ready to accept login requests.

Mac OS X

Mac OS X is based on the BSD Darwin engine. The Mac OS X startup process is nothing like other UNIX systems. Most significantly, Mac OS X has nothing like the /etc/init.d directory. Instead, it finds its startup items in either /System/Library/StartupItems (for system startup items) or /Library/StartupItems (for locally installed startup items).

In order to set an application to start at system startup, a user needs to perform the following basic steps:

- Create a subdirectory under /Library/StartupItems. For example, if the user is setting up a startup item for MySQL, he or she might create the directory /Library/StartupItems/MySQL.

- Put a startup file in that subdirectory. It should have the same name as its parent folder, as in /Library/StartupItems/MySQL/MySQL. For example, the user can look at the Mac OS X's startup item for Apache, /System/Library/StartupItems/Apache/Apache.

- At a minimum, add a StartupParameters.plist file to that subdirectory. Again, see an existing startup item for a template.

- If the user used a control variable to determine whether the daemon starts at boot (Apache uses WEBSERVER), the user must set that variable to -YES- or -NO- in /etc/hostconfig.

Mac OS X Hidden Files and Key Directories

In UNIX, files can be hidden, or made invisible, by prefixing the file name with a period (.), as in .vol. This makes the invisible in the Finder, as well as when the user issues an ls command with the -a option. Mac OS X uses a file in the root directory (.hidden) to maintain a list of files that should be hidden from the Finder. Mac OS X uses a file system called HFS+, in which the files and directories can have a hidden attribute set using the SetFile command—for example, **SetFile -a V <filename>.** Table 3-1 shows a list of hidden files and important directories in Mac OS X.

._whatever	These files are created on volumes that don't natively support full HFS file characteristics (e.g., UFS volumes and Windows file shares). When a Mac file is copied to such a volume, its data fork is stored under the file's regular name, and the additional HFS information (resource fork, type and creator codes, etc.) is stored in a second file (in AppleDouble format), with a name that starts with "._".
.DS_Store	This file is created by the Finder to keep track of folder view options, icon positions, and other visual information about folders. A separate .DS_Store file is created in each directory to store information about that directory.
~/.Trash	This is used to store files and folders from the boot volume that a particular user has thrown in the trash but that haven't been erased yet.
/.Spotlight-V100	This is used to store metadata indexes and indexing rules for Spotlight (version 1.00). This file is only created under Mac OS X 10.4.
/.hidden	This contains a list of files for the Finder to hide.
/.hotfiles.btree	This is used to track commonly used small files so their positions on disk can be optimized.
/bin	The programs in /bin include the more common and fundamental applications that are used from the UNIX command line as well as several shells (the programs that provide the command line itself).
/dev	This directory contains device special files. It keeps track of the devices (disks, keyboards, monitors, network connections, etc.) attached to the system.
/etc	On a typical UNIX system, the /etc folder contains all the configuration files for a system, including both documents specifying configuration information as well as scripts for actually performing various configuration tasks. On OS X, some of the configuration information stored here is overridden by NetInfo or other directory services, but the /etc files still exist.
/Network	This is the physical location of the Network item that appears at the Computer level in the Finder. It provides a place to attach networkwide resources and server volumes.
/mach /mach.sym /mach_kernel	This is the Mach kernel (which runs at the very core of Mac OS X), along with a couple of shortcuts for getting to it.
/private	This is a directory of drivers for certain peripherals.
/private/Network	This is used to handle nonstatic amounts of network volumes under OS X 10.1.
/sbin	The /sbin directory is similar to /bin, except it contains binaries that are specifically used for system administration.
/tmp	Programs that need temporary space on the hard disk are usually set up to write temporary files to the /tmp directory.
/usr	The /usr directory contains many subdirectories that have binaries and files specifically of use to the normal user.
/usr/bin	This is another place where UNIX binaries are kept.
/usr/lib	This folder contains libraries available for programming on Mac OS X.
/usr/libexec	This folder holds various daemon programs, system maintenance scripts, and other UNIX-style programs that users don't usually run directly.
/usr/sbin	This is another place where UNIX binaries are kept.
/usr/share	This folder contains various data and text files that multiple architectures can share.
/usr/standalone	This folder contains boot loader programs for various computer architectures.
/var	Sometimes, processes controlled by the operating system need a place to store variable files. Processes like printing and programs that store log files use subdirectories in the /var directory to store those files.
/var/backups	This folder is used to store backups of critical system information.
/var/db	This folder holds various databases of system information.
/var/log	System event logs are kept in this directory.
/var/root	This is the root account's home directory.

Table 3-1 **This is a list of the hidden files and important directories in Mac OS X**   *(continues)*

/var/run	This folder stores status information about processes (especially daemons) running on the system.
/var/tmp	This is another place for programs to store temporary data.
/var/vm	This folder is used to store the swap files for Mac OS X's virtual memory.
/var/vm/app_profile	This holds information about various applications' virtual memory usage.
/Volumes	The /Volumes directory is the mount point for all of the drives (other than the boot volume) connected to the system. The Finder hides the /Volumes directory itself, but displays its contents at the Computer level.

Table 3-1 This is a list of the hidden files and important directories in Mac OS X *continued*

Mac OS X Boot Process

The boot process in Mac OS X depends on three important parts: Mac's Open Firmware, the boot loader, and the typical Mac OS X boot sequence. The firmware is not part of Mac OS X, but it plays an important role in the operation of the machine and is useful in debugging. *Firmware* is the software programs or instructions stored in the read-only memory (ROM) of a hardware device that provide the necessary instructions during the boot process for the computer to find the installed operating system and continue to boot up.

Open Firmware

Open Firmware is a nonproprietary, platform-independent boot firmware that is similar to a PC's BIOS. Open Firmware is stored in ROM and is the first stored program executed upon power-up. A user can start Open Firmware by pressing the key combination Command-Option-O-F just as the user powers up the computer. A welcome message is displayed with some other verbiage at the prompt.

The user can continue booting the machine by typing **mac-boot,** or can shut it down by typing **shutdown.** It is more convenient to access a Mac's Open Firmware from another computer over the network by using the following command:

```
0 > dev /packages/telnet
```

```
Upon success, Open Firmware displays the following:
```

```
0 > dev /packages/telnet ok
```

```
If the command is successful, the user can run a telnet server on the system as
follows:
```

```
"enet: telnet,10.0.0.1" io
```

This runs a telnet server on the machine with IP address 10.0.0.1 (the user can choose any appropriate address). Thereafter, the user can connect to Open Firmware on this machine using a telnet client.

The following are examples of commands a user can execute from the Open Firmware prompt:

- The following command prints the device tree:

    0 > **dev / ls**

- And the following is sample output from that command:

ff880d90:	/cpus
ff881068:	/PowerPC,750@0
ff881488:	/l2-cache
ff882148:	/chosen
ff882388:	/memory@0
ff882650:	/openprom
ff882828:	/client-services

- The following command provides information about the installed RAM:

    0 > **dev /memory .properties ok**

- And the following is sample output from that command:

name	memory
device_type	memory
reg	00000000 10000000
	10000000 10000000
slot-names	00000003
	SODIMM0/J25LOWER
	SODIMM1/J25UPPER
dimm-types	DDR SDRAM
dimm-speeds	PC2700U-25330

- The following command lists files in the root directory of the disk (partition) referred to by the alias "hd":

  0 > dir hd:

- And the following is sample output from that command:

Size/ bytes	GMT date	time	File/Dir Name
6148	12/25/ 3	4:25:25	.DS_Store
156	9/12/ 3	20:41:59	.hidden
589824	12/25/ 3	6:45: 6	.hotfiles.btree

- The following command expands the alias "hd" and gives the complete path of the device in the tree (the user can type devalias by itself to see a list of current aliases, along with what they refer to):

  0 > devalias hd

- And the following is sample output from that command:

  /pci@f4000000/ata-6@d/disk@0 ok

Thus, Open Firmware is a powerful tool for controlling, debugging, and exploring a computer running Mac OS X.

Boot Loader

BootX can load kernels from various file systems such as HFS+, HFS, UFS, ext2, and TFTP. In addition to Mach-O, BootX can also load ELF kernels, although Mac OS X does not use this feature.

BootX (/System/Library/CoreServices/BootX) is the default boot loader for Mac OS X.

The sequence of events when BootX starts executing (after being handed control by Open Firmware) is described below:

- BootX first initializes the Open Firmware client interface (that it would use to talk to the firmware) and retrieves the firmware version.

- It then creates a pseudodevice called sl_words (*sl* stands for "secondary loader") in the firmware, and defines various FORTH words in it.

- BootX looks up the options device in the firmware, which contains various variables (that a user can see and set using the printenv and setenv commands in Open Firmware).

  0 > dev /options .properties

name	options
little-endian?	false
real-mode?	false
auto-boot?	true
diag-switch?	false
. . .	
boot-command	mac-boot

- BootX looks up the chosen device, which contains handles for entities such as the boot input/output devices, the memory, the MMU, the PMU, the CPU, and the PIC. For example, the following command at the Open Firmware prompt shows the contents of the chosen device:

  0 > dev /chosen ok

  0 > .properties

name	chosen
stdin	ffbc6e40
stdout	ffbc6600
memory	ffbdd600
mmu	. . .

  . . .

- BootX initializes handles to the MMU and memory using the chosen device.
- BootX initializes handles to the boot display and the keyboard (if present).
- BootX checks if the security mode is "none," or BootX checks if the "verbose" (Cmd-V) or "single user" (Cmd-S) flags were specified, and sets the output level accordingly.
- BootX checks if the system is booting in Safe Mode.
- BootX claims memory for various purposes.
- BootX finds all displays and sets them up. It does this by searching for nodes of type "display" in the device tree. The primary display is referred to by the screen alias.
- While opening the display(s), BootX also sets the screen color to the familiar whitish gray.
- BootX looks up the boot device, boot arguments, and other components, and determines where to get the kernel from (from a network device, from a block device, or from some other location). BootX uses this information to construct the path to the kernel file (mach_kernel). If booting from a block device (which is the usual case), BootX calculates the path to the kernel extension cache and the extensions directory (usually /System/Library/Extensions).
- At this point, BootX draws the Apple logo splash screen and starts the spinning cursor. If booting from a network device, BootX draws a spinning globe instead.
- Depending on various conditions, BootX tries to retrieve and load the kernel cache file.
- The next step is to "decode" the kernel. If the kernel header indicates a compressed kernel, BootX tries to decompress it (typically, LZSS compression is used, as this kind of data is compressed once but expanded many times). Since the kernel binary can potentially be a "fat" binary (code for multiple architectures residing in the same binary), BootX checks if it indeed is fat and, if so, "thins" it (figures out the PowerPC code).
- BootX attempts to decode the file as a Mach-O binary. If this fails, BootX also tries to decode it as ELF.
- If the previous fails, BootX gives up, draws the failed boot picture, and goes into an infinite loop.
- If BootX is successful so far, it saves file system cache hits, misses, and evicts; sets up various boot arguments and values (such as whether this is a graphical or verbose boot, whether there are some flags to be passed to the kernel, and the size of installed RAM); and also calls a recursive function to flatten the device tree.
- Finally, BootX calls the kernel, immediately before which it "acquiesces" Open Firmware, an operation as a result of which any asynchronous tasks in the firmware, timers, or DMA stop.

Mac OS X Boot Options

Following is a list of Mac OS X boot options:

- *C*: Forces most Macs to boot from the CD-ROM drive instead of the internal hard drive; only works with Apple ROM drives and with bootable CD discs
- *D*: Forces the first internal hard drive to be the startup disk

- *N*: Netboot (New World ROM machines only); looks for the BOOTP or TFTP server on the network to boot from

- *R*: Forces PowerBooks to reset their screen to default size (helpful if the machine has been hooked up to an external monitor or projector)

- *T*: Target Disk Mode (Firewire); puts machines with built-in Firewire into Target Disk Mode so a device attached with a Firewire cable will show up as a hard drive on the system

- *Mouse button held down*: Ejects any mounted removable media

- *Shift*: Disables all extensions (Mac OS 7–9) or disables login items (Mac OS X 10.1.3 or later)

- *Option*: When using an Open Firmware New World ROM–capable system, the System Picker will appear and query all mounted devices for bootable systems, returning a list of drives and what OS they have on them. On Old World systems, the machine will simply boot into the default OS without any Finder windows open.

- *Space bar*: Brings up Apple's Extension Manager at startup to allow the user to modify his or her extension set

- *Command-V*: Boots Mac OS X into verbose mode, reporting every console message generated during startup

- *Command-S*: Boots Mac OS X into single-user mode

- *Command-Option*: Rebuilds the desktop

- *Command-Option-P-R*: Erases PRAM if held down immediately after startup tone; the machine will chime when it has erased the PRAM

- *Command-Option-N-V*: Erases **NVRAM (nonvolatile RAM),** memory that retains its information even when the computer is turned off, by connecting it to a battery source

- *Command-Option-O-F*: Boots the machine into Open Firmware (New World ROM systems only)

- *Command-Option-Shift-Delete*: Forces the Mac to start up from its internal CD-ROM drive or an external hard drive

- *Command-Option-Shift-Delete-# (where # = a SCSI device ID)*: Boot from a specific SCSI device

Below is a list of Mac OS X boot options that work on older computers only:

- *Command-Option-I*: Forces the Mac to read the disc as an ISO-9000 formatted disc

- *Command*: Boots with virtual memory turned off

- *Command-Option-T-V*: Forces Quadra AV machines to use a TV as a monitor

- *Command-Option-X-O*: Forces a Mac Classic to boot from ROM

- *Command-Option-A-V*: Forces the system to recognize an AV monitor correctly

Mac OS X Boot Sequence

1. As stated previously, Open Firmware is a program, or set of instructions, that is stored in ROM and is the first operation to execute when a computer powers on. Open Firmware looks for hardware installed on the computer to initialize the boot drive. Open Firmware then loads a file of type tbxi (BootX) from the boot partition of the hard drive and executes it. This file contains information about booting. Open Firmware can directly load ELF, XCOFF, and bootinfo. BootX reads the root partition out of NVRAM. Control then passes to /System/Library/CoreServices/BootX, the boot loader. BootX copies Mac OS X device drivers from the boot partition into memory and disables all address translations. It loads the kernel. At this time, Open Firmware is no longer accessible.

2. The init routine of the kernel executes.

3. The kernel determines the root device of the booting system.

4. The kernel initializes Mach/BSD data structures.

5. The kernel initializes I/O Kit.

6. The kernel starts /sbin/mach_init. This process maintains mappings between service names and the Mach ports that provide access to those services.

7. After the kernel processes have started, the following user-level steps take place:

   - The mach_init process starts /sbin/init, the traditional BSD init process. The init process determines the run level and runs /etc/rc.boot, which sets up the machine enough to run in single-user mode. The rc.boot process determines the type of boot, which could be multiuser, safe, CD-ROM, network, etc. For example, if it sets the sysctl variable kern.netboot, then it is a network boot. The process /etc/rc.netboot handles various aspects of network booting; for instance, it performs network and (if any) local mounts. The process cr.boot checks to see if any file systems require a consistency check.

   - Single-user and CD-ROM boots do not run fsck. Safe mode always runs fsck. The rc.boot process handles the return status of fsck.

   - The /etc/rc process finally launches /sbin/SystemStarter, which handles the startup items. These items are located in /System/Library/StartupItems and /Library/StartupItems.

8. Finally, the Mac OS X desktop is loaded with login windows by default, and the login window application loginwindow.app under /System/Library/CoreServices is executed for the console device. The user can put the system into nongraphical login mode using /etc/ttys.

Installing Mac OS X on Windows XP

Encountering and investigating Mac operating systems or files that need to be examined can be problematic for a computer forensic investigator generally more familiar and more comfortable with Windows operating systems, especially if he or she has only that system on the computer being used to examine the files. The following proceedure will help to resolve this dilemma and facilitate both the examination of the Mac boot process and the files themselves.

1. Use the Darwin installation CD to partition the hard disk.

2. Set prom_driver_graphic to "path/to/video.x".

3. Set prom_env_bootargs to "" for Mac OS X 10.2.

4. Start PearPC, wait, and follow the instructions given by the installer.

5. Click the **Customize** button, and uncheck **Additional Print Drivers, Additional Asian Fonts,** and **Localized Files.**

6. Click on the **Install** button and wait until installed.

7. Download BootCD onto a Mac running Mac OS X 10.2.

8. Use BootCD to create a .dmg file containing a stripped-down OS X system with any required applications. This process takes approximately half an hour on a dual 1-GHz G4.

9. Convert the .dmg that is created with BootCD into a .iso that PearPC can use by typing the following command: **hdiutil convert /path/to/bootableosx.dmg -format UDTO -o /path/to/output.iso**

10. Copy the output .iso to the machine on which PearPC has to run.

11. Edit PearPC's configuration file so that it uses the .iso file as an emulated CD-ROM drive.

12. Start PearPC with the configuration file.

A Mac running OS X directly from a CD is slow, and emulating OS X is even slower.

Tool: PearPC

PearPC is an architecture-independent PowerPC emulator that can run most PowerPC operating systems. The following are some of the features of PearPC:

- PearPC is based on C++, C, and (on x86 platforms) assembler code, and it's supported host platforms are POSIX-X11 and Win32.

- The following operating systems run in PearPC:
  - Mandrake Linux 9.1 for PPC installer
  - Mandrake Linux 9.1 for PPC after installation

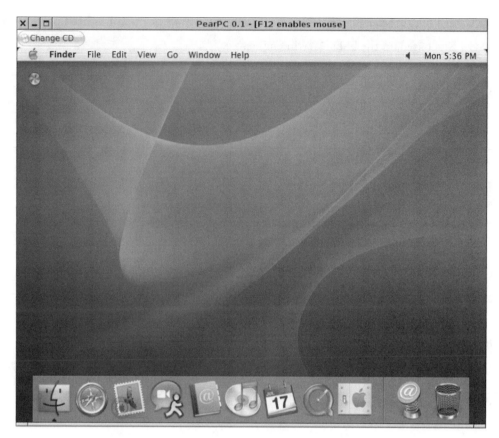

Figure 3-7   Users can run a number of operating systems on PearPC, including Mac OS X, as shown here.

- Darwin for PPC
- Mac OS X 10.3
- NetBSD for PPC

The following are some of the limitations of PearPC:

- CPU emulation is slow; however, this only minimally affects the speed of emulated hardware.
- PearPC will most probably run only on 32-bit architectures.
- A lot of unimplemented features are fatal and cause PearPC to abort.
- PearPC lacks a save/restore machine-state feature.
- It does not support hard disks with storage capacities greater than 128 GB.

Figure 3-7 shows Mac OS X running on PearPC.

Chapter Summary

- Booting is a process that starts operating systems when the user turns on a computer system.
- A boot loader is a small program that loads an operating system into a computer's memory when the system is booted.
- A boot sector is a sector of a hard disk, floppy disk, or similar data storage device that contains code for bootstrapping systems.

- The master boot record is the first sector of a data storage device that has been partitioned.
- Mac OS X is based on the BSD Darwin engine.

Review Questions

1. What does the term booting mean?

   _____

   _____

2. Describe the purpose of the master boot record.

   _____

   _____

3. Write down the basic system boot process.

   _____

   _____

4. What is a kernel?

   _____

   _____

5. Explain the Mac OS X boot process.

   _____

   _____

6. What is the role of a boot loader in booting?

   _____

   _____

7. Explain the Windows XP boot process.

   _____

   _____

8. Briefly explain the purpose of the BIOS.

   _____

   _____

9. Briefly explain the purpose of CMOS.

   _____

   _____

10. Explain the difference between a cold boot and a warm boot.

    _____

    _____

Hands-On Projects

1. Note the boot process of a computer running Windows XP.

2. Note the boot process of a computer running Macintosh and compare it with one running Linux.

3. Perform the following steps:

   ■ Navigate to Chapter 3 of the Student Resource Center.

   ■ Read the document titled "BootX.pdf."

Chapter 4

Windows Forensics I

Objectives

After completing this chapter, you should be able to:

- Collect volatile and nonvolatile information
- Perform Windows memory analysis
- Perform Windows registry analysis
- Perform Windows file analysis

Key Terms

Cache   a set of duplicate data that is stored in a temporary location to allow rapid access for computers to function more efficiently

Driver   a program that allows the operating system of a computer to communicate with a hardware device attached to the computer

Metadata   data about data, or more simply, embedded electronic data not necessarily seen on the monitor or a printed document

Net file   command that displays the names of all open shared files on a system and the number of file locks, and closes individual shared files and removes file locks

Net sessions   command that shows not only the names of the users accessing the system via a remote login session but also the IP addresses and the types of clients from which they are accessing the system

Nonvolatile information   memory information that does not require power to remain stored, such as the swap file stored on a computer's hard drive

Port   a logical connection that allows data to be sent from one application to another directly; there are 65,536 available ports on a computer, with the first 1,024 being well-known ports (0–1023)

Process   a section or instance of an application or program that is being run sequentially

Promiscuous mode   the state of a network interface card where it will register all network traffic, rather than only that traffic arriving with the card's own MAC address as the destination

Service   a process requiring no user interaction that runs on a computer and facilitates the functioning of the computer operating system and associated applications

Swap file   a space on a hard disk (nonvolatile memory) used as the virtual memory extension of a computer's random access memory

Volatile information   memory information stored in the random access memory of a computer that requires electricity to remain stored there

Introduction to Windows Forensics, Part I

This chapter focuses on Windows forensics. It starts by covering the different types of volatile and nonvolatile information an investigator can collect from a Windows system. It then goes into detail about collecting and analyzing data in memory, the registry, and files.

Volatile Information

Investigators are more interested in volatile information. *Volatile information* is information that is lost the moment a system is powered down or loses power. Volatile information usually exists in physical memory, or RAM, and consists of information about processes, network connections, open files, clipboard contents, and the like. This information describes the state of the system at a particular point in time.

When performing a live response, one of the first things investigators should collect is the contents of RAM. By collecting the contents of RAM first, investigators minimize the impact of their data collection on the contents of RAM.

The following are some of the specific types of volatile information that investigators should collect:

- System time
- Logged-on user(s)
- Open files
- Network information
- Network connections
- Process information
- Process-to-port mapping
- Process memory
- Network status
- Clipboard contents
- Service/driver information
- Command history
- Mapped drives
- Shares

System Time

The first piece of information an investigator should collect when investigating an incident is the system time. The system time gives context to the information collected later in the investigation and enables an investigator to establish an accurate timeline of events that have occurred on the system. Not only is the current system time important for the investigator, but the amount of time that the system has been running, or the uptime, is also important.

An investigator also records the real time, or wall time, when recording the system time. Having both allows the investigator to later determine whether the system clock was inaccurate.

An investigator can find the system time and date using the **date/t** and **time/t** commands, as shown in Figure 4-1.

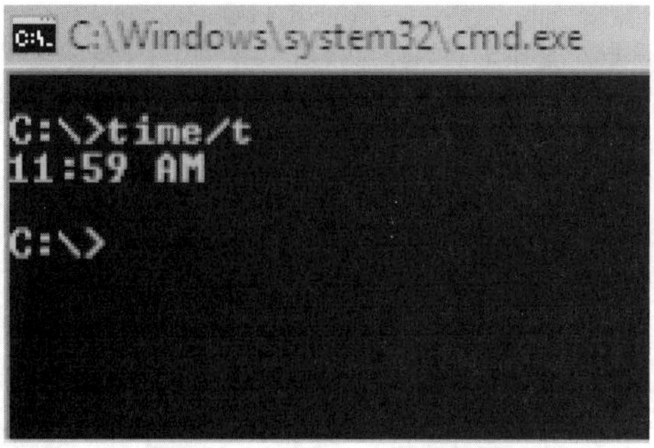

Figure 4-1 An investigator can use the **time/t** command to find the system time.

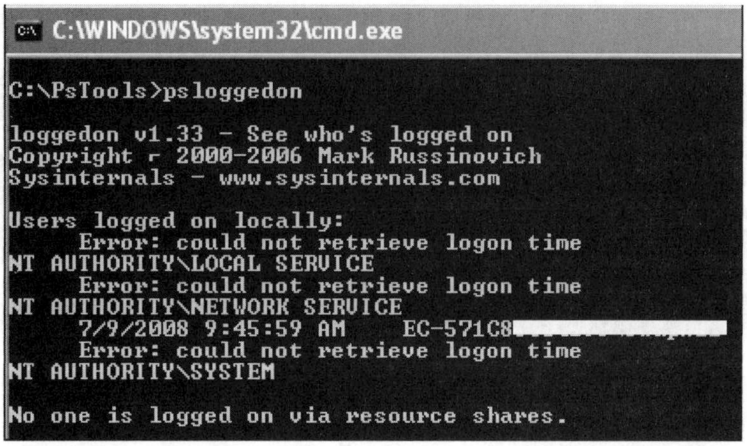

Figure 4-2 PsLoggedOn shows all the users logged into a system.

Logged-On Users

During an investigation, an investigator needs to find out which users are logged on to the system. This includes people who are logged on locally (via the console or keyboard) as well as remotely (such as via the **net use** command or via a mapped share). This information allows an investigator to add context to other information he or she collects from the system, such as the user context of a running process, the owner of a file, or the last access times on files. This information is also useful to correlate against the Security Event Log, particularly if the appropriate auditing has been enabled.

The following are some of the tools and commands an investigator can use to determine logged-on users:

- *PsLoggedOn*: This is the best-known tool for determining logged-on users. This tool shows the investigator the names of the users logged on locally as well as those users who are logged on remotely. Figure 4-2 shows some sample output from PsLoggedOn.

- *Net Sessions*: The **net sessions** command shows not only the names of the users accessing the system via a remote login session but also the IP addresses and the types of clients from which they are accessing the system.

- *LogonSessions*: This command-line tool lists all the active logon sessions on a system. LogonSessions provides more information than the other tools. It lists the authentication package used, type of logon, active processes, and so on. Figure 4-3 shows some sample output from LogonSessions.

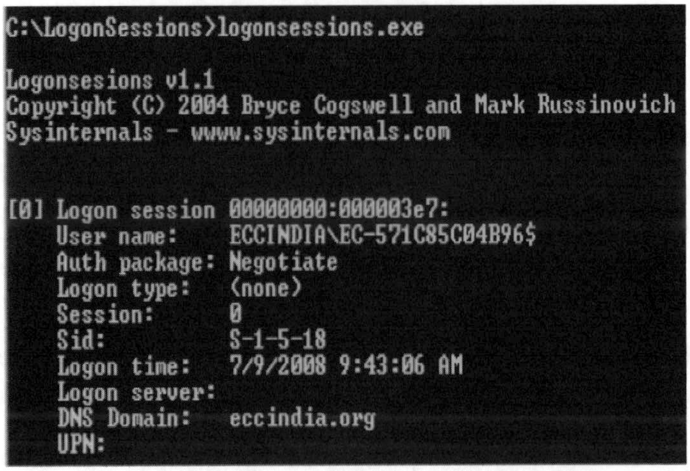

```
C:\LogonSessions>logonsessions.exe

Logonsesions v1.1
Copyright (C) 2004 Bryce Cogswell and Mark Russinovich
Sysinternals - www.sysinternals.com


[0] Logon session 00000000:000003e7:
    User name:    ECCINDIA\EC-571C85C04B96$
    Auth package: Negotiate
    Logon type:   (none)
    Session:      0
    Sid:          S-1-5-18
    Logon time:   7/9/2008 9:43:06 AM
    Logon server:
    DNS Domain:   eccindia.org
    UPN:
```

Figure 4-3   LogonSessions displays a great deal of
information about the active logon sessions on a system.

```
C:\WINDOWS\system32\cmd.exe - OPENFILES                              _ □ ×

C:\>OPENFILES

Files Opened Locally:
--------------------

ID    Process Name          Open File (Path\executable)
====  ====================  =====================================================
12    explorer.exe          C:\Documents and Settings\Admin
72    explorer.exe          C:\..6595b64144ccf1df_6.0.2600.5512_x-ww_35d4ce83
116   explorer.exe          C:\..6595b64144ccf1df_6.0.2600.5512_x-ww_35d4ce83
148   explorer.exe          C:\..6595b64144ccf1df_6.0.2600.5512_x-ww_35d4ce83
156   explorer.exe          C:\..6595b64144ccf1df_6.0.2600.5512_x-ww_35d4ce83
168   explorer.exe          C:\..6595b64144ccf1df_6.0.2600.5512_x-ww_35d4ce83
```

Figure 4-4   Openfiles shows all files open on a system.

Open Files

If there are users logged into a system remotely, investigators should also see what files they have open, if any. A user in a corporate environment could have a share available to allow other users to view images or download songs. Poorly protected Windows systems, such as Windows 2000 systems that are connected to the Internet with no administrator password and no firewall, are vulnerable to remote users.

The following are some of the tools and commands an investigator can use to determine what files are open:

- *Net File*: The **net file** command displays the names of all open shared files on a system and the number of file locks, and closes individual shared files and removes file locks.

- *PsFile*: PsFile is a command-line application that shows a list of files on a system that are open remotely. It also allows a user to close open files either by name or by file identifier.

- *Openfiles*: This command is used to list or disconnect all files and folders that are open on a system. Figure 4-4 shows some sample output from Openfiles.

NetBIOS Name Table Cache

Sometimes when intruders gain remote access to a system, they want to know that other systems are available on the network and can be seen (in the network-centric sense) by the system they have compromised. Intruders can find this information in a variety of ways; sometimes they execute batch files on the system, and other times they launch **net view** commands via SQL injection (by using a browser to send commands to the system through the Web and database servers). When connections are made to other systems using NetBIOS communications, the systems will maintain a list of other systems they have connected to. By viewing the contents of the name table cache, an investigator might be able to determine other systems that have been affected. A *cache* is a set of duplicate data that is stored in a temporary location so that a computer system can rapidly access that data. In this case, it is a set of systems that a computer has connected to.

For example, consider a setup where the network consists of one laptop and several VMware sessions that appear as standalone systems on a virtual network. To demonstrate the caching of NetBIOS names, a user can start a Windows 2000 VMware session and log in to view the IP address that was assigned via DHCP. The user can then return to the host operating system (Windows XP Pro SP2) and at a command prompt type **nbtstat -A 192.168.1.22** to view the "remote" system's name table. Then the user can type **nbtstat -c** to view the cached NetBIOS names on the host operating system.

Network Connections

As soon as possible after an incident is reported, the investigator should collect information regarding network connections to and from the affected system. This information can expire over time, and if too much time passes, that information will be lost. An investigator might approach a system and, after an initial look, determine that the attacker is still logged into the system. Or the investigator could find that a worm or an IRCbot is communicating from the system, searching for other systems to infect, updating itself, or logging into a command-and-control server. This information can provide important clues and add context to other information that the investigator has collected.

Netstat

The netstat command allows a user to collect information regarding network connections on a Windows system. This command-line tool provides a simple view of TCP and UDP connections and their state, network traffic statistics, and so on. Netstat is a native tool, meaning that it is provided as part of the operating system distribution. The most common way to run netstat is with the -ano switches (Figure 4-5), which tell the program to display the TCP and UDP network connections, the listening ports, and the identifiers of the processes (PIDs) using those network connections. Running netstat with the -r switch displays the routing table (Figure 4-6).

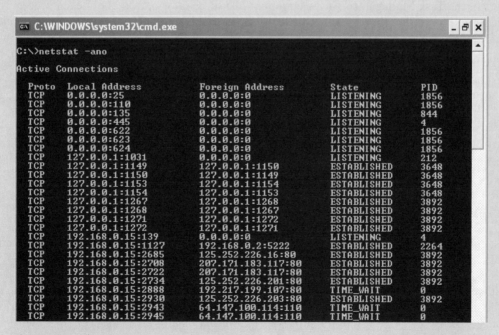

Figure 4-5   The **netstat -ano** command shows all network connections and what processes are using those connections.

(continues)

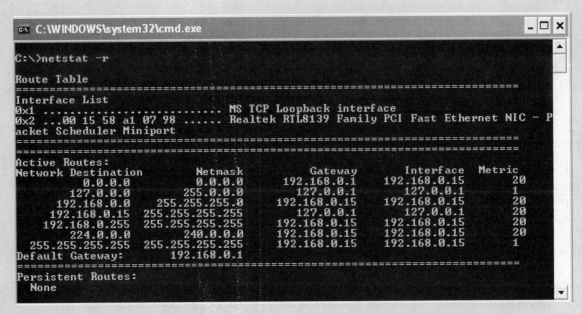

Figure 4-6   The **netstat -r** command shows the routing table.

Process Information

An investigator needs to discover what processes are running on a potentially compromised system. A **process** is a section or instance of an application or program that is being run sequentially. When viewing the running processes in the Task Manager, the investigator can see some information about each process. However, there is much more information that is not visible in Task Manager that the investigator needs to collect.

The following are the types of information an investigator needs to know about running processes:

- The full path to the executable image (.exe file)
- The command line used to launch the process, if any
- The amount of time that the process has been running
- The security/user context that the process is running in
- Which modules the process has loaded
- The memory contents of the process

Figure 4-7 shows a screenshot of Task Manager.

Tool: Tlist

The tlist command, included as part of the MS Debugging Tools, displays information about running processes. For example, the -s switch displays the session identifier, PID, process name, associated services, and command line used to launch the process.

The tlist command also allows an investigator to search for all processes that have a specific module loaded, using the -m switch. For example, wsock32.dll provides networking functionality and is described as the Windows Socket 32-Bit DLL. To list all the processes that have this module loaded, an investigator would type the following command:

tlist -m wsock32.dll

Image Name	PID	User Name	Memory (...	Commit Size	NP Pool	PF Delta	Base Pri	I/O Other
AcroRd32.exe	2140	ECCIND...	22,028 K	31,704 K	9 K	0	Normal	4,322
Alcxmntr.exe	2728	ECCIND...	224 K	7,104 K	3 K	0	Normal	343
avgtray.exe	2712	ECCIND...	2,112 K	5,376 K	6 K	0	Normal	1,723
csrss.exe	512		1,004 K	1,980 K	5 K	0	High	3,485
dwm.exe	2496	ECCIND...	564 K	1,540 K	3 K	0	Normal	357
explorer.exe	2540	ECCIND...	12,684 K	35,256 K	32 K	1	Normal	36,576
MSASCui.exe	2704	ECCIND...	784 K	5,116 K	10 K	0	Normal	506
POWERPNT.EXE	2836	ECCIND...	8,248 K	106,964 K	74 K	0	Normal	5,770
SNAP32.EXE	620	ECCIND...	964 K	1,432 K	2 K	0	Normal	289
taskeng.exe	2396	ECCIND...	1,296 K	9,312 K	8 K	0	Normal	2,859
taskmgr.exe	3856	ECCIND...	2,208 K	2,648 K	4 K	0	High	1,263
thunderbird.exe	3756	ECCIND...	14,496 K	24,688 K	10 K	0	Normal	6,850
winlogon.exe	604		148 K	2,072 K	3 K	0	High	2,096
wsqmcons.exe	1380	ECCIND...	216 K	1,624 K	3 K	0	Below ...	159

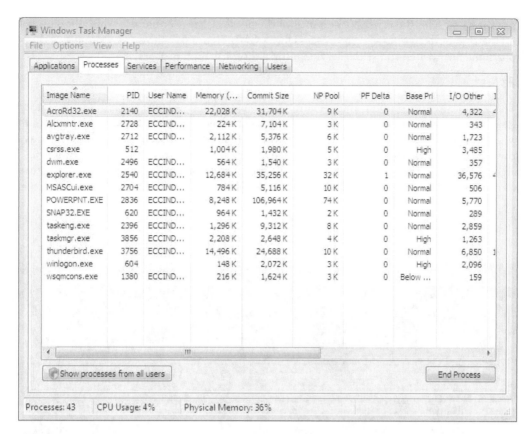

Figure 4-7 The Windows Task Manager shows information about the currently running processes.

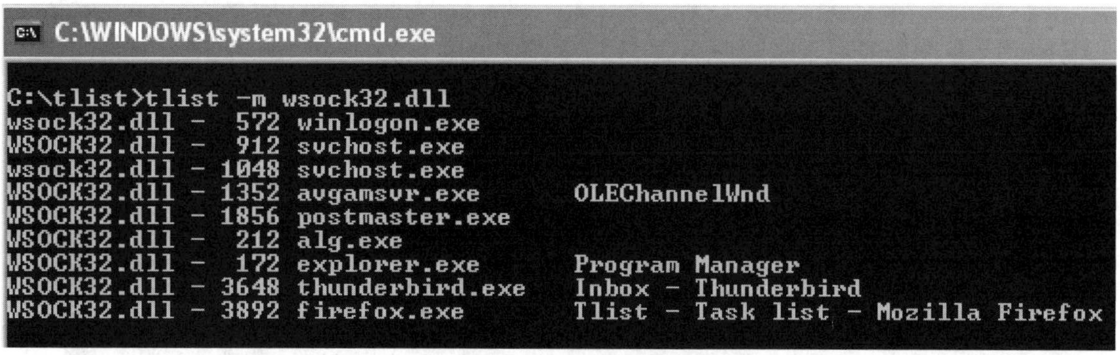

Figure 4-8 This shows the output of the **tlist -m wsock32.dll** command.

This command returns the PID and name for each process that has wsock32.dll loaded, as shown in Figure 4-8.

Tool: Tasklist

The tasklist command, a native utility included with Windows XP Professional and Windows 2003 installations (it is absent from Windows XP Home), is a replacement for tlist. The differences in the two tools are subtle, mostly being the name and the implementation of the switches. The tasklist command does provide options for output formatting, with choices between table, CSV, and list formats. The /v (or verbose) switch provides the most information about the listed processes, including the image name (but not the full path), PID, name and number of the session for the process, the status of the process, the user name of the context in which the process runs, and the title of the window, if the process has a GUI. Figure 4-9 shows an example of this. An investigator can also use the /svc switch to list the service information for each process.

Tool: PsList

PsList displays basic information about running processes on a system, including the amount of time each process has been running (in both kernel and user modes). The -x switch displays details about the threads and memory used by each process. The -t switch displays a task tree in much the same manner as tlist. PsList can also show detailed information about threads or memory used by a process. However, it does not provide the following information about a process: the path to the executable image, the command line used to launch the process, or the user context in which the process runs. Figure 4-10 shows example output from PsList.

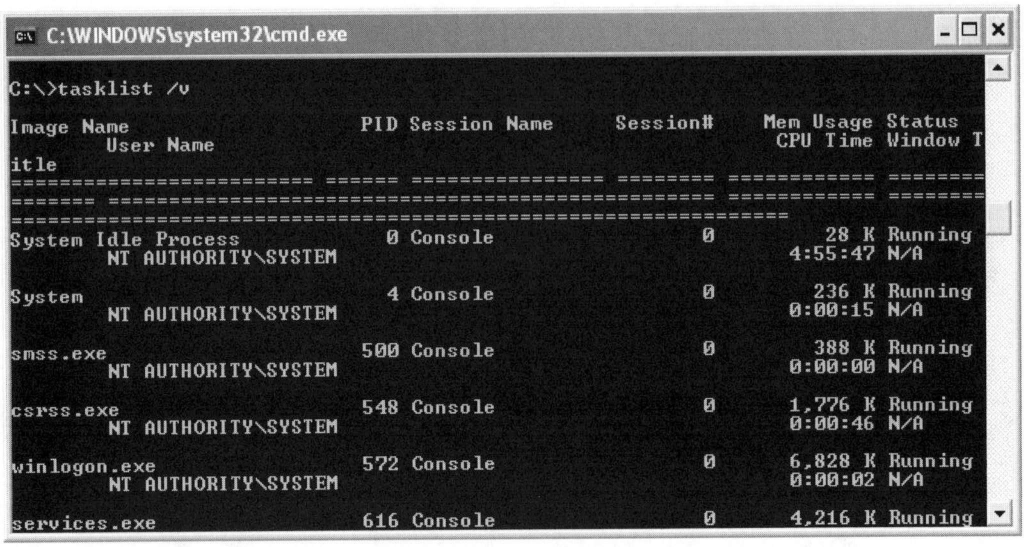

```
C:\WINDOWS\system32\cmd.exe

C:\>tasklist /v

Image Name                     PID Session Name     Session#    Mem Usage Status
        User Name                                                CPU Time Window T
itle
========================= ====== ================ ======== ============ ========
======= =================================================== ============ ========
================================================================
System Idle Process              0 Console                 0         28 K Running
        NT AUTHORITY\SYSTEM                                       4:55:47 N/A

System                           4 Console                 0        236 K Running
        NT AUTHORITY\SYSTEM                                       0:00:15 N/A

smss.exe                       500 Console                 0        388 K Running
        NT AUTHORITY\SYSTEM                                       0:00:00 N/A

csrss.exe                      548 Console                 0      1,776 K Running
        NT AUTHORITY\SYSTEM                                       0:00:46 N/A

winlogon.exe                   572 Console                 0      6,828 K Running
        NT AUTHORITY\SYSTEM                                       0:00:02 N/A

services.exe                   616 Console                 0      4,216 K Running
```

Figure 4-9 Running tasklist with the -v switch shows the most information about the processes running on a system.

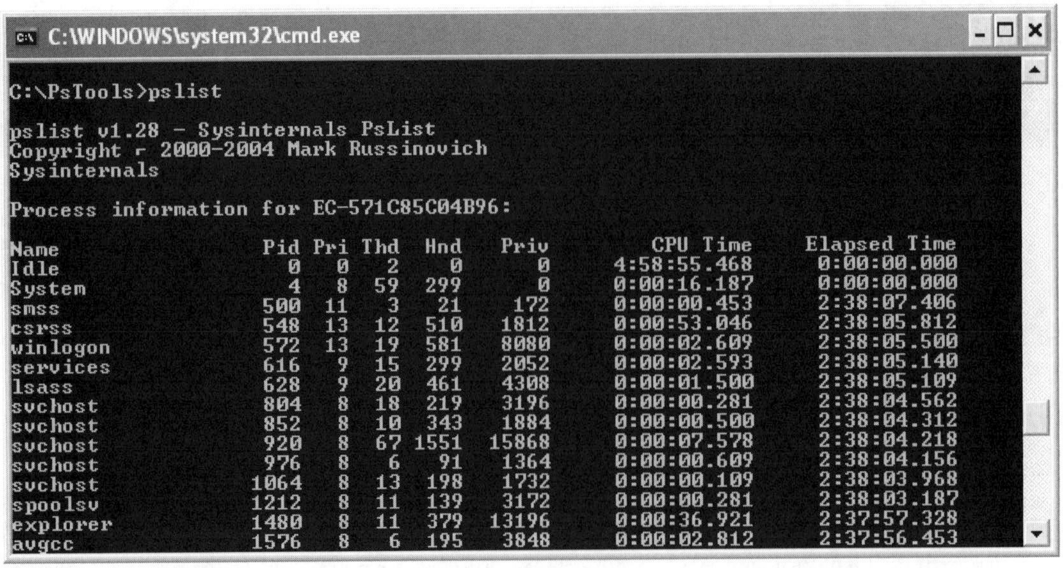

```
C:\WINDOWS\system32\cmd.exe

C:\PsTools>pslist

pslist v1.28 - Sysinternals PsList
Copyright r 2000-2004 Mark Russinovich
Sysinternals

Process information for EC-571C85C04B96:

Name          Pid Pri Thd  Hnd   Priv        CPU Time    Elapsed Time
Idle            0   0   2    0      0     4:58:55.468     0:00:00.000
System          4   8  59  299      0     0:00:16.187     0:00:00.000
smss          500  11   3   21    172     0:00:00.453     2:38:07.406
csrss         548  13  12  510   1812     0:00:53.046     2:38:05.812
winlogon      572  13  19  581   8080     0:00:02.609     2:38:05.500
services      616   9  15  299   2052     0:00:02.593     2:38:05.140
lsass         628   9  20  461   4308     0:00:01.500     2:38:05.109
svchost       804   8  18  219   3196     0:00:00.281     2:38:04.562
svchost       852   8  10  343   1884     0:00:00.500     2:38:04.312
svchost       920   8  67 1551  15868     0:00:07.578     2:38:04.218
svchost       976   8   6   91   1364     0:00:00.609     2:38:04.156
svchost      1064   8  13  198   1732     0:00:00.109     2:38:03.968
spoolsv      1212   8  11  139   3172     0:00:00.281     2:38:03.187
explorer     1480   8  11  379  13196     0:00:36.921     2:37:57.328
avgcc        1576   8   6  195   3848     0:00:02.812     2:37:56.453
```

Figure 4-10 PsList displays basic information about the processes running on a system.

Tool: ListDLLs

ListDLLs shows the modules or DLLs a process is using. ListDLLs shows the full path to the image of the loaded module as well as whether the version of the DLL loaded in memory is different from that of the on-disk image. This information can be extremely important to an investigator because each program loads or imports certain DLLs. These DLLs provide the actual code that is used so application developers do not have to rewrite common functions each time they write a new application. Each DLL makes certain functions available, listing them in their export table, and programs access these functions by listing the DLL and the functions in their import tables.

Spyware, Trojans, and even rootkits use a technique called DLL injection to load themselves into the memory space of a running process. They do not show up in a process listing because they are actually part of another process. This is different from a child process, because the executing malware does not have its own process identifier (PID).

Figure 4-11 shows some example output from ListDLLs.

Tool: Handle

Handle shows the various handles that processes have open on a system. This applies not only to open file handles (for files and directories) but also to ports, registry keys, and threads. This information can be useful for determining which resources a process is accessing while it is running.

Process-to-Port Mapping

When there is a network connection open on a system, some process must be responsible for and must be using that connection. That is, every network connection and open port is associated with a process. A *port* is a logical connection that allows data to be sent from one application to another directly. Several tools are available to an investigator to retrieve this process-to-port mapping. The investigator can use the following tools and commands to retrieve the process-to-port mapping:

- *Netstat command*: On Windows XP and Windows 2003, the netstat command with the -o switch displays the process ID for the process responsible for each network connection, as shown in Figure 4-12. Once information is collected, an investigator will need to correlate it with the output of a tool such as tlist or tasklist to determine the name (and additional information) of the process using the connection. As of SP2, Windows XP's version of netstat has an additional -b option that will display the executable involved in creating each connection or listening port. This switch is also included in netstat in Windows 2003 SP1 and can provide more information about the process using a particular port. In some cases, the output will also show some of the modules (DLLs) used by the process.

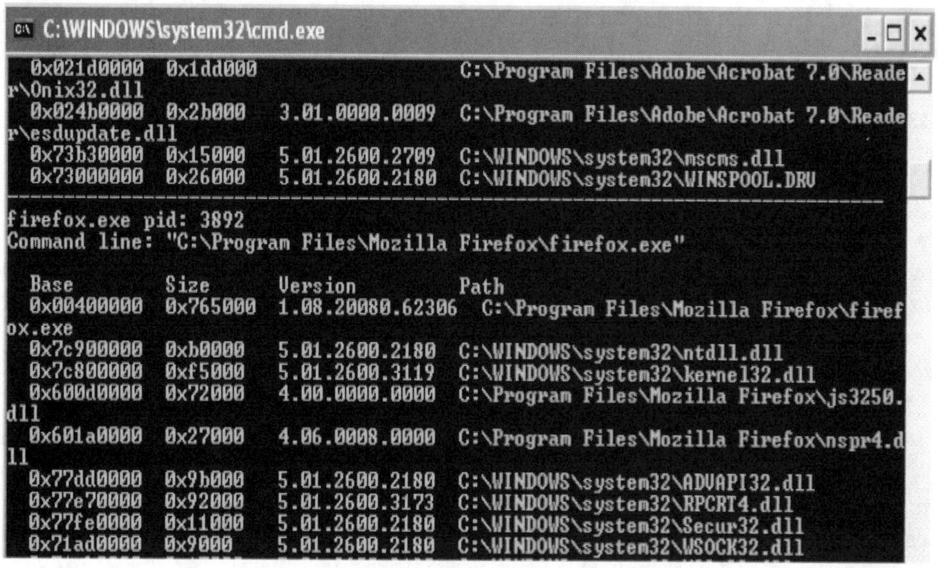

Figure 4-11   ListDLLs displays all the DLLs that a process is using.

Figure 4-12   The **netstat -o** command correlates PIDs and network connections.

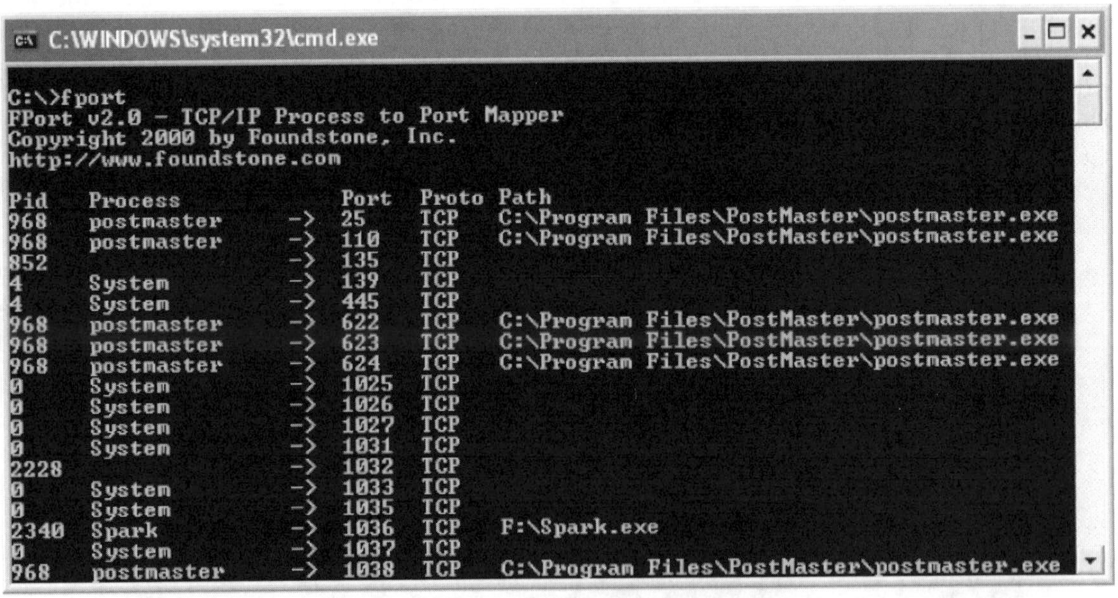

Figure 4-13   The Fport tool shows which processes are using which ports.

- *Fport tool*: Fport has long been one of the tools of choice for obtaining the process-to-port mapping from a Windows system. The output of the tool is easy to understand; however, the tool needs to be executed using an account with administrative privileges. This can be an issue if investigators are responding to a situation in which the logged-in account is a regular user account. Figure 4-13 shows example output from Fport.

- *OpenPorts tool*: This tool allows for multiple output formats (including netstat-style, fport-style, and CSV) and does not require that an account with administrative privileges be used. When run with the -fport switch, OpenPorts provides an fport-style output and displays the PID, the name of the process, the number of the port, the protocol (TCP or UDP), and the path to the executable image for each process. Using the -netstat switch, OpenPorts displays its output similar to that of netstat, so only the PIDs are displayed and not the path to the executable image. Figure 4-14 shows example output from OpenPorts.

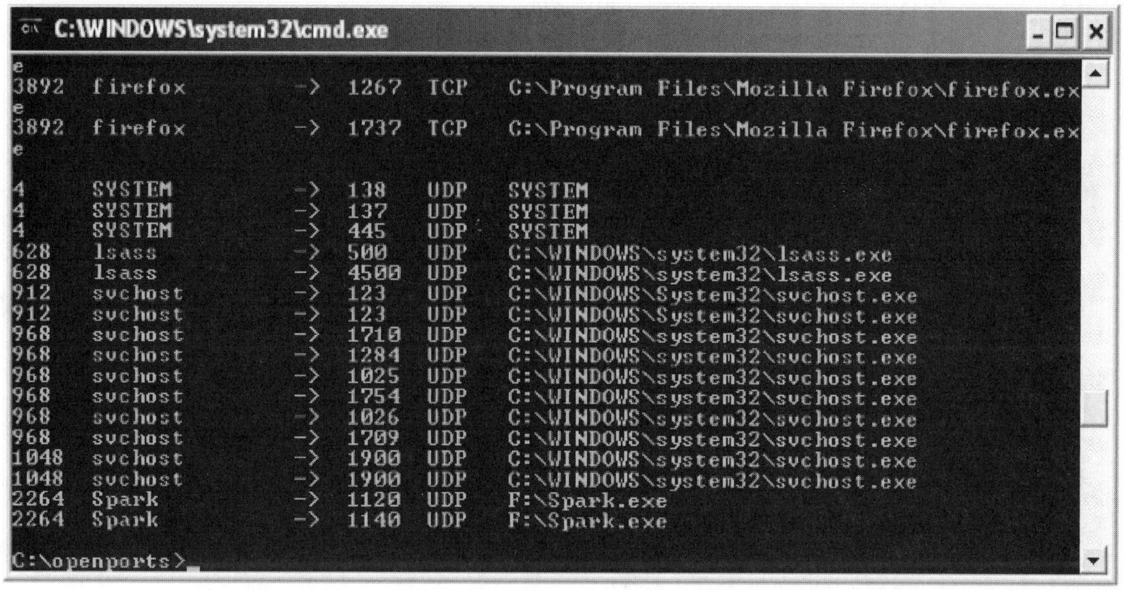

```
C:\WINDOWS\system32\cmd.exe                                          - □ ×
e
3892    firefox          ->  1267    TCP     C:\Program Files\Mozilla Firefox\firefox.ex
e
3892    firefox          ->  1737    TCP     C:\Program Files\Mozilla Firefox\firefox.ex
e
4       SYSTEM           ->  138     UDP     SYSTEM
4       SYSTEM           ->  137     UDP     SYSTEM
4       SYSTEM           ->  445     UDP     SYSTEM
628     lsass            ->  500     UDP     C:\WINDOWS\system32\lsass.exe
628     lsass            ->  4500    UDP     C:\WINDOWS\system32\lsass.exe
912     svchost          ->  123     UDP     C:\WINDOWS\System32\svchost.exe
912     svchost          ->  123     UDP     C:\WINDOWS\System32\svchost.exe
968     svchost          ->  1710    UDP     C:\WINDOWS\system32\svchost.exe
968     svchost          ->  1284    UDP     C:\WINDOWS\system32\svchost.exe
968     svchost          ->  1025    UDP     C:\WINDOWS\system32\svchost.exe
968     svchost          ->  1754    UDP     C:\WINDOWS\system32\svchost.exe
968     svchost          ->  1026    UDP     C:\WINDOWS\system32\svchost.exe
968     svchost          ->  1709    UDP     C:\WINDOWS\system32\svchost.exe
1048    svchost          ->  1900    UDP     C:\WINDOWS\system32\svchost.exe
1048    svchost          ->  1900    UDP     C:\WINDOWS\system32\svchost.exe
2264    Spark            ->  1120    UDP     F:\Spark.exe
2264    Spark            ->  1140    UDP     F:\Spark.exe

C:\openports>
```

Figure 4-14   OpenPorts displays the process-to-port mapping for all the processes running on a system.

Network Status

Getting information about the status of the network interface cards (NICs) connected to a system can be important to an investigation. For instance, today many laptops come with built-in wireless NICs, so it may not be clear by looking at the desktop whether or not the system is connected to a wireless access point and, if so, what IP address it is using. Knowing the status of the NICs prior to the acquisition of a system can provide insight into a follow-on investigation.

The following are tools used for network status detection:

- Ipconfig command
- PromiscDetect tool
- Promqry tool

Tool: Ipconfig

The ipconfig command is a utility native to Windows systems that the investigator can use to display information about the NICs and their status. The most useful switch for investigators is /all, which is used to display the network configuration of all the NICs on the system, as shown in Figure 4-15. This information includes the state of the NIC, whether DHCP is enabled or not, the IP address of the NIC, and more. This information might be useful during an investigation, because there may be need of network traffic logs, and the IP address of the system could have been modified at some point. Also, many Web-based e-mail services record the IP address of the system from which an e-mail was drafted (this information is retrieved by the browser) in the headers of the e-mail.

Tool: PromiscDetect

Sometimes compromised systems will have a network "sniffer" installed to capture network traffic, such as login credentials to other systems, or to develop a picture of what other systems are on the network and what services they are running. Some malware payloads include this capability, or it can be a follow-on download installed by an attacker. For the NIC to capture network traffic in this manner, it has to be placed in "promiscuous" mode. This is not something an administrator or investigator will see, because there is nothing obvious to indicate that the NIC is in promiscuous mode. *Promiscuous mode* refers to the state of a network interface card where it will register all network traffic, rather than only than the traffic arriving with the card's own MAC address as the destination. There is no System Tray icon or Control Panel setting that clearly indicates to the investigator that the system is being used to "sniff" traffic.

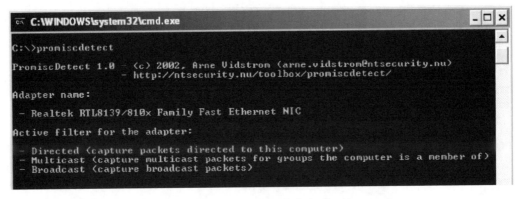

Figure 4-15   The **ipconfig /all** command displays information about all the NICs on a system.

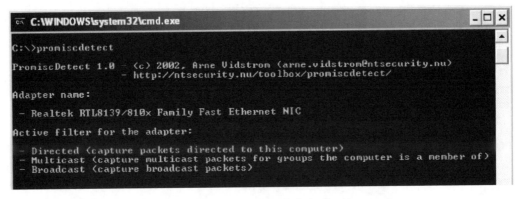

Figure 4-16   PromiscDetect shows the status of NICs installed in a system.

There are tools available that can detect if the NIC is in promiscuous mode. One such tool is PromiscDetect; another is Promqry. The primary difference between the two tools is that Promqry can be run against remote systems, allowing an administrator to scan systems within the domain for systems that might be sniffing the network.

Figure 4-16 PromiscDetect shows example output from PromiscDetect.

Tool: Promqry

Promqry is used for detecting when Windows computers on your network have network interfaces operating in promiscuous mode (sniffing network traffic). It has both a command line interface and a GUI. An investigator or administrator can run the command line version and dump its output to a text file. Promqry cannot detect standalone sniffers or sniffers running on non-Windows operating systems. Figure 4-17 shows example output from Promqry.

Clipboard Contents

The clipboard is simply an area of memory where data can be stored for later use. Most Windows applications provide this functionality through the **Edit** option on the menu bar. Clicking **Edit** reveals a drop-down menu with choices like **Cut, Copy,** and **Paste**. The clipboard is often used to facilitate moving data in some

Figure 4-17 Promqry displays whether a NIC is in promiscuous mode.

fashion—between documents or between application windows on the desktop. The user selects text or other data, chooses **Copy**, and then chooses **Paste** to insert that data somewhere else. The **Cut** functionality removes the data from the document the user is working on, and that data goes into the clipboard. What people don't always realize is that something that they copy to the clipboard on a Monday will still be there on Thursday if they don't replace the clipboard contents with something else and if they don't log out.

Pclip is a command-line utility that an investigator can use to retrieve the contents of the clipboard.

Service/Driver Information

Services and drivers are started automatically when the system starts, based on entries in the registry. A *driver* is a small program that allows a computer system to communicate with a hardware device attached to the system. A *service* is a noninteractive program that helps the operating system and applications perform their tasks. Most users do not even see these services running as processes on the system. Not all services are necessarily installed by the user or even the system administrator. Some malware installs itself as a service or even as a system driver.

Command History

The command history can provide valuable information to an investigator. To see these previously typed commands in a command shell, an investigator can scroll up in the window, but that only goes so far. If the attacker typed the cls command to clear the screen, the investigator would not be able to use the scroll bar to see any of the commands that had been entered. Instead, the investigator can use the **doskey /history** command, which will show the complete history of the commands typed into that prompt.

Mapped Drives

During an investigation, the investigator might want to know what drives or shares the system under investigation has mapped to. These mappings could have been created by the user, and they might be an indication of malicious intent. There might be no persistent information within the file system or registry for these connections to be mapped shares on other systems, though the volatile information regarding drive mappings can be correlated to the network connection information that the investigator has already retrieved.

Shares

Besides resources used by the system, an investigator also needs to acquire information regarding those resources that the system is making available. Information about shares available on a system is maintained in the HKEY_LOCAL_MACHINE\System\CurrentControlSet\Services\lanmanserver\Shares key, but it can also be retrieved from a live system using a command such as share.

Nonvolatile Information

Nonvolatile information is kept on secondary storage devices and persists after a system is powered down. It is nonperishable and can be collected after the volatile information is collected. The following are some of the specific types of nonvolatile information investigators collect:

- Hidden files
- Slack space
- Swap files
- Index.dat files
- Metadata
- Hidden ADS (alternate data streams)
- Windows Search index
- Unallocated clusters
- Unused partitions
- Hidden partitions
- Registry settings
- Connected devices
- Event logs

Examining File Systems

An investigator should run **dir /o:d** in the C:/%systemroot%/system32 directory at a command prompt. This command enables the investigator to examine:

- The time and date of the installation of the operating system
- The service packs, patches, and subdirectories that automatically update themselves often

When examining the files, the investigator should focus on recently dated files.

Registry Settings

Several registry values and settings could impact the follow-on forensic analysis and investigation. There are several tools for collecting information from the registry. An investigator can use reg (a command-line tool that is part of the Windows 2000 Support Tools and is native to Windows XP and 2003) to access and manage the registry.

The following are two registry values that can greatly affect an investigation:

- *ClearPageFileAtShutdown*: This particular registry value tells the operating system to clear the page file when the system is shut down. Because Windows uses virtual memory, some memory used by processes is paged out to the page file. When the system is shut down, the information within the page file remains on the hard drive and can contain information such as decrypted passwords, portions of IM conversations, and other strings and bits of information that might provide important leads in an investigation. However, if this file is cleared during shutdown, this valuable information will be more difficult to obtain.

- *DisableLastAccess*: Windows has the ability to disable updating of the last access times on files. This was meant as a performance enhancement, particularly on high-volume file servers. On normal desktops and laptops, this setting does not provide any noticeable improvement in performance. To activate this capability, a user sets the following value to 1: HKEY_LOCAL_MACHINE\System\CurrentControlSet\Control\FileSystem\DisableLastAccess.

  On Windows XP and 2003 systems, this setting can be queried or enabled via the fsutil command. For example, to query the setting, a user can enter the following command:

  fsutil behavior query disablelastaccess

Another area of the registry that can provide valuable information in an investigation is the Protected Storage area. The information held in Protected Storage is maintained in an encrypted format in the registry. If an investigator acquires an image of the system, tools such as AccessData's Forensic Toolkit can decrypt and recover the information.

Microsoft Security IDs

The Microsoft security IDs are generally available in the Windows registry. An administrator or investigator can find these IDs in the HKEY_LOCAL_MACHINE\SOFTWARE\Microsoft\WindowsNT\CurrentVersion\ProfileList key.

Event Logs

Event logs are stored in files within the file system, and they can change rapidly depending on how they are configured and what events are being audited.

Depending on how the audit policies are configured on the victim system and how investigators are accessing it as the first responder, entries can be generated within the event logs.

Investigators can use tools such as PsLogList and DumpEvt to retrieve the event records, or they can copy the event log files themselves off the system.

Index.dat File

The Internet Explorer Web browser uses index.dat files as a database that is active as long as a user is logged on in Windows. It is a repository of redundant information, such as visited URLs, search queries, recently opened files, and form AutoComplete information. Its role is similar to that of an index file in databases, where a technique called indexing stores the contents of a database in a different order to speed up query responses. Similarly, when the AutoComplete function is enabled in Internet Explorer, every Web address visited is sorted in the index.dat file, allowing Internet Explorer to attempt to find an appropriate match when a user types in an edit field. Separate index.dat files exist for the Internet Explorer history, cache, and cookies. Table 4-1 shows the locations of index.dat files for different versions of Windows.

Connected Devices

An investigator may want to document what devices are connected to a system he or she is investigating. The investigator can use DevCon, available from Microsoft, to document devices that are attached to a Windows system. DevCon, a command-line replacement for the Device Manager, can show available device classes as well as the status of the connected devices. Figure 4-18 shows example output from DevCon.

Slack Space

The space between the end of a file and the end of the disk cluster it is stored in is called the slack space. In computer forensics, investigators examine slack space because it may contain meaningful data.

Slack space can be used to stealthily store data. If a user makes a small file, the rest of the cluster can be used reliably to store hidden data. This data will be invisible to the file system and remain intact as long as the size of the file is not altered.

The procedure to gather information in slack space is as follows:

1. Connect to the target computer and select the media.

2. Create a bit-level copy of the original media.

3. Verify the copy by generating its hash value.

4. Investigate using keyword searches, hash analysis, and file signature analysis using a tool such as EnCase.

Operating System	File Path
Windows 95/98/ME	\Windows\Temporary Internet Files\Content.IE5\ \Windows\Cookies\ \Windows\History\History.IE5\
Windows NT	\Winnt\Profiles\<user name>\Local Settings\Temporary Internet Files\Content.IE5\ \Winnt\Profiles\<user name>\Cookies\ \Winnt\Profiles\<user name>\Local Settings\History\History.IE5
Windows 2000/XP	\Documents and Settings\<user name>\Local Settings\Temporary Internet Files\Content.IE5\ \Documents and Settings\<user name>\Cookies\ \Documents and Settings\<user name>\Local Settings\History\History.IE5\

Table 4-1   These are the locations where an investigator can find the index.dat file

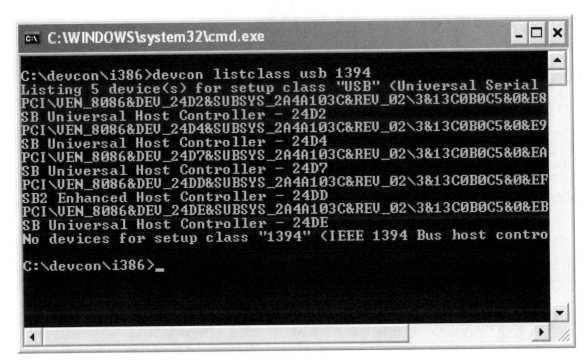

Figure 4-18 This DevCon output shows all USB and Firewire devices in the system.

Tool: DriveSpy

DriveSpy uses familiar DOS commands to navigate a system under investigation. DriveSpy does not use drive letters in the prompt, but rather a drive/partition combination (for example, D0P1:\WINDOWS\SYSTEM) to eliminate confusion in the event the resident operating system has not assigned a drive letter to the drive being processed (such as when examining a FAT32 partition under DOS 6.22).

The following are the types of things DriveSpy processes:

- Large hard drives (greater than 8.4 GB)
- Floppy disks and removable media
- FAT12/16/16x/32/32x partitions
- Hard drives without partitions
- Hidden DOS partitions
- Non-DOS partitions
- Long file names
- File creation (Windows 95/98), modification (DOS), and access dates (Windows 95/98)
- Erased files (with companion long file name if one exists)
- Slack space
- Unallocated space

The following are some of the features DriveSpy includes:

- A built-in sector and cluster hex viewer that can be used to examine DOS and non-DOS partitions
- Configurable logging capabilities to document the investigation (keystroke-by-keystroke if desired)
- The ability to create and restore compressed forensic images of drive partitions
- Full scripting capabilities to automate processing activities

Swap File

A *swap file* is a space on a hard disk used as the virtual memory extension of a computer's real memory (RAM). Having a swap file allows the computer's operating system to pretend that the system has more RAM than it actually does. The least recently used files in RAM can be swapped out to the hard disk until they are needed later so that new files can be swapped in to RAM. In some operating systems, the units that are moved are called pages and the swapping is called paging.

One advantage of a swap file is that it can be organized as a single contiguous space so that fewer I/O operations are required to read or write a complete file. In general, Windows and UNIX-based operating systems provide a swap file of a default size that the user or a system administrator can usually change.

On Windows, the swap file is a hidden file in the root directory called pagefile.sys. The registry path for the swap file is HKEY_LOCAL_MACHINE\SYSTEM\CurrentControlSet\Control\Session Manager\Memory Management.

Figure 4-19 shows the configuration screen for the swap file.

Windows Search Index

The Windows Search index maintains a record of any document or application on a PC, including the contents of these files. Users can then quickly search for files using a variety of search techniques, including keyword and file name searches.

The system index must complete an initial scan of a PC. Following the initial scan, any new files are indexed when the PC is idle, and these files become searchable shortly thereafter. Subsequent scans for new files or e-mail messages require a fraction of the time and PC resources to keep the index up to date.

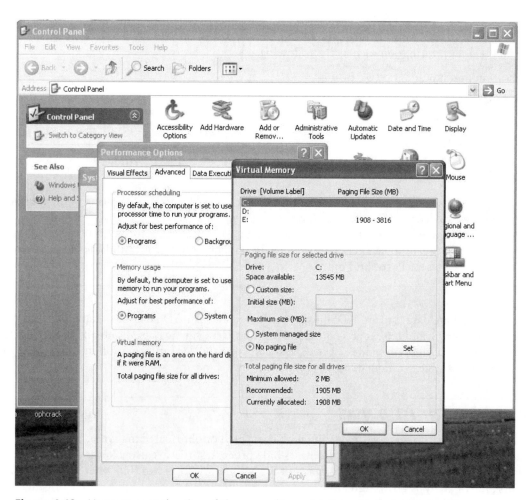

Figure 4-19   Users can set the size of the swap file or let the system determine the best size.

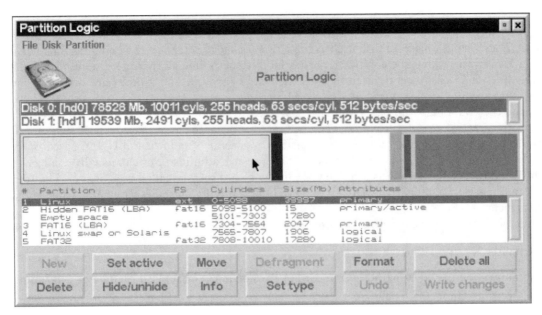

Figure 4-20   Partition Logic allows a user to create partitions or perform operations on existing partitions.

Tool: Search Index Examiner

Passware Search Index Examiner displays all the items indexed by Windows Search. It lists all the files in the index and includes information such as the following:

- Creation and modification dates
- Author
- E-mail recipients
- Content summaries

Hidden Partitions

A hidden partition is a logical section of a disk that is not accessible to the operating system. Hidden partitions may contain files, folders, confidential data, or backups of the system.

An investigator can use a tool such as Partition Logic to collect the information from the hidden partition. Partition Logic can create, delete, erase, format, defragment, resize, copy, and move partitions. Figure 4-20 shows the main screen for Partition Logic.

Hidden ADS

Through an alternate data stream (ADS), users can hide data. An ADS can be created by running a command like **notepad visible.txt:hidden.txt** at a command prompt. Data can be copied into an ADS by using a command like **type atextfile > visible.txt:hidden2.txt**. A user can copy the ADS information in a new file by using a command like **more <visible.txt:hidden2.txt> newfile.txt**.

Windows Memory Analysis

Malware analysts look to memory in dealing with encrypted or obfuscated malware, because when the malware is launched, it is decrypted in memory. Rootkits hide processes, files, registry keys, and even network connections from view, but by analyzing the contents of RAM, investigators can find what has been hidden.

As this area of analysis grows and more investigators pursue RAM as a viable source of valuable information and evidence, it will become easier to extract information from RAM and correlate that to what is found during postmortem forensic analysis.

Importance of a Memory Dump

A memory dump contains the contents of physical memory at the time the dump is created. It is often used to diagnose a bug in a program, as programs create a memory dump when they halt unexpectedly.

The information in memory dumps is in binary, octal, or hexadecimal format. An investigator can check memory dump information using DumpChk.

EProcess Structure

Each process on a Windows system is represented as an executive process, or EProcess, block. This EProcess block is a data structure in which various attributes of the process, as well as pointers to a number of other attributes and data structures (threads and the process environment block) relating to the process, are maintained. Because the data structure is a sequence of bytes, each sequence with a specific meaning and purpose, an investigator can read and analyze these structures. The size and even the values of the structures change not only between operating system versions (for example, Windows 2000 to XP) but also between service packs of the same version of the operating system (Windows XP to XP SP2).

It is relatively easy for an investigator to view the contents of the EProcess structure (or any other structure available on Windows). First, the investigator must download and install the Microsoft Debugging Tools and the correct symbols for the operating system and service pack. Then, he or she must download LiveKD from SysInternals and, for convenience, copy it into the same directory as the debugging tools. Once this is done, the investigator must open a command prompt, change to the directory where the debugging tools are installed, and type the following command:

debug>**livekd –w**

This command will open WinDbg, the GUI interface to the debugger tools. To see what the entire contents of an EProcess block look like (with all the substructures that make up the EProcess structure broken out), the command is **dt -a -b -v _EPROCESS**. The -a switch shows each array element on a new line, with its index, and the -b switch displays blocks recursively. The -v switch creates more verbose output, telling the overall size of each structure.

An important element of a process that is pointed to by an EProcess structure is the process environment block, or PEB. This structure contains a great deal of information, but the elements that are important to forensic investigators are the following:

- A pointer to the loader data (referred to as *PPEB_LDR_DATA*) structure that includes pointers or references to modules (DLLs) used by the process

- A pointer to the image base address, where an investigator can find the beginning of the executable image file

- A pointer to the process parameters structure, which itself maintains the DLL path, the path to the executable image, and the command line used to launch the process

Parsing this information from a dump file can prove to be useful to an investigator.

Process Creation Mechanism

There are a number of steps involved in process creation. These steps can be broken down into six stages:

1. The executable (.exe) file is opened. During this stage, the appropriate subsystem (POSIX, MS-DOS, Win16, etc.) is identified. Also, the Image File Execution Options registry key is checked to see if there is a Debugger value, and if there is, the process starts over.

2. The EProcess object is created. The kernel process block (KProcess), the process environment block, and the initial address space are also set up.

3. The initial thread is created.

4. The Windows subsystem is notified of the creation of the new process and thread, along with the ID of the process's creator and a flag to identify whether the process belongs to a Windows process.

5. Execution of the initial thread starts. At this point, the process environment has been set up and resources have been allocated for the process's thread(s) to use.

6. The initialization of the address space is completed, in the context of the new process and thread.

The process has at least one thread and may begin consuming additional memory resources as the process itself executes.

Parsing Memory Contents

The tools that parse memory contents use a technique of locating and enumerating the active process list, using specific values/offsets (derived from system files) to identify the beginning of the list. Then the tools use the same methodology for walking through the doubly linked list until all the active processes have been identified. The location of the offset for the beginning of the active process list is derived from one of the important system files, ntoskrnl.exe.

Lsproc

Lsproc is a Perl script that locates processes but not threads. It takes a single argument, the path and name to a RAM dump file:

lsproc.pl d:\dumps\drfws1-mem.dmp

The output of Lsproc appears at the console in six columns containing the following: the word *Proc*, the parent process ID (PPID), the process ID (PID), the name of the process, the offset of the process structure within the dump file, and the creation time of the process.

The following is some example output from Lsproc:

Proc	820	324	helix.exe	0x00306020	Sun	Jun	5 14:09:27	2005
Proc	0	0	Idle	0x0046d160				
Proc	600	668	UMGR32.EXE	0x0095f020	Sun	Jun	5 00:55:08	2005
Proc	324	1112	cmd2k.exe	0x00dcc020	Sun	Jun	5 14:14:25	2005
Proc	668	784	dfrws2005.exe(x)	0x00e1fb60	Sun	Jun	5 01:00:53	2005
Proc	156	176	winlogon.exe	0x01045d60	Sun	Jun	5 00:32:44	2005
Proc	156	176	winlogon.exe	0x01048140	Sat	Jun	4 23:36:31	2005
Proc	144	164	winlogon.exe	0x0104ca00	Fri	Jun	3 01:25:54	2005
Proc	156	180	csrss.exe	0x01286480	Sun	Jun	5 00:32:43	2005
Proc	144	168	csrss.exe	0x01297b40	Fri	Jun	3 01:25:53	2005
Proc	8	156	smss.exe	0x012b62c0	Sun	Jun	5 00:32:40	2005
Proc	0	8	System	0x0141dc60				
Proc	668	784	dfrws2005.exe(x)	0x016a9b60	Sun	Jun	5 01:00:53	2005
Proc	1112	1152	dd.exe(x)	0x019d1980	Sun	Jun	5 14:14:38	2005
Proc	228	592	dfrws2005.exe	0x02138640	Sun	Jun	5 01:00:53	2005
Proc	820	1076	cmd.exe	0x02138c40	Sun	Jun	5 00:35:18	2005
Proc	240	788	metasploit.exe(x)	0x02686cc0	Sun	Jun	5 00:38:37	2005
Proc	820	964	Apoint.exe	0x02b84400	Sun	Jun	5 00:33:57	2005
Proc	820	972	HKserv.exe	0x02bf86e0	Sun	Jun	5 00:33:57	2005
Proc	820	988	DragDrop.exe	0x02c46020	Sun	Jun	5 00:33:57	2005
Proc	820	1008	alogserv.exe	0x02e7ea20	Sun	Jun	5 00:33:57	2005
Proc	820	972	HKserv.exe	0x02f806e0	Sun	Jun	5 00:33:57	2005
Proc	820	1012	tgcmd.exe	0x030826a0	Sun	Jun	5 00:33:58	2005
Proc	176	800	userinit.exe(x)	0x03e35020	Sun	Jun	5 00:33:52	2005

In the output, several of the processes have *(x)* after the process name. This indicates that the processes have exited. In these cases, the contents of the physical memory (for example, pages) have been freed for use but have not been overwritten yet.

Lspd

Lspd is a Perl script that allows a user to list the details of a process. Lspd relies on the output of Lsproc to obtain its information. Lspd takes two arguments: the path and name of the dump file and the offset from the Lsproc output of the process that investigators are interested in. Although Lsproc takes some time to parse through the contents of the dump file, Lspd is much quicker.

The following command line is an example of how to use Lspd to get detailed information about the dd.exe process with PID 284:

lspd.pl d:\dumps\dfrws1-mem.dmp 0x0414dd60

The following is the output from this command:

```
Process Name : dd.exe
PID          : 284
Parent PID   : 1112
TFLINK       : 0xff2401c4
TBLINK       : 0xff2401c4
FLINK        : 0x8046b980
BLINK        : 0xff1190c0
SubSystem    : 4.0
Exit Status  : 259
Create Time  : Sun Jun 5 14:53:42 2005
Exit Called  : 0
DTB          : 0x01d9e000
ObjTable     : 0xff158708 (0x00eb6708)
PEB          : 0x7ffdf000 (0x02c2d000)
InheritedAddressSpace: 0
ReadImageFileExecutionOptions: 0
BeingDebugged: 0
CSDVersion   : Service Pack 1
Mutant = 0xffffffff
Img Base Addr = 0x00400000 (0x00fee000)
PEB_LDR_DATA = 0x00131e90 (0x03a1ee90)
Params = 0x00020000 (0x03a11000)
```

Lspd also follows pointers provided by the EProcess structure to collect other data as well. For example, users can see the path to the executable image and the command line used to launch the process. The following is further output for this process:

```
Current Directory Path = E:\Shells\
DllPath =
E:\Acquisition\FAU;.;C:\WINNT\System32;C:\WINNT\system;
C:\WINNT;E:\Acquisition\FAU\;E:\Acquisition\GNU\;E:\Acquisition\CYGWIN\;E:\I
R\bin\;E:\IR\WFT;E:\IR\windbg\;E:\IR\Foundstone\;E:\IR\Cygwin;E:\IR\somarsof
t\;E:\IR\sysinternals\;E:\IR\ntsecurity\;E:\IR\perl\;E:\Static-
Binaries\gnu_utils_win32\;C:\WINNT\system32;C:\WINNT;C:\WINNT\System32\Wbem
ImagePathName = E:\Acquisition\FAU\dd.exe
Command Line = ..\Acquisition\FAU\dd.exe if=\\.\PhysicalMemory
of=F:\intrusion2005\physicalmemory.dd conv=noerror --md5sum --verifymd5 --
md5out=F:\intrusion2005\physicalmemory.dd.md5 --
log=F:\intrusion2005\audit.log
Environment Offset = 0x00000000 (0x00000000)
Window Title = ..\Acquisition\FAU\dd.exe if=\\.\PhysicalMemory
of=F:\intrusion2005\physicalmemory.dd conv=noerror --md5sum --verifymd5 --
md5out=F:\intrusion2005\physicalmemory.dd.md5 --
```

log=F:\intrusion2005\audit.log
Desktop Name = WinSta0\Default

Lspd also retrieves a list of the names of various modules (DLLs) used by the process and whatever available handles (file handles and so on) it can find in memory. For example, Lspd found that dd.exe had the following file handle open:

Type: File
Name = \intrusion2005\audit.log

From the preceding output example the file \intrusion\audit.log is located on the F:\ drive and is the output file for the log of activity generated by dd.exe, which explains why it would be listed as an open file handle in use by the process. Using this information as derived from other processes, an investigator can get an understanding of files he or she should be concerned with during an investigation.

Parsing Process Memory

In the past, investigators have used tools such as Strings or grep searches to parse through the contents of a RAM dump and look for interesting strings (passwords), IP or e-mail addresses, URLs, and the like. However, when investigators are parsing through a file that is about half a megabyte in size, there is not a great deal of context to the information they might find.

Lspm takes the same arguments as Lspd (the name and path of the dump file, and the physical offset within the file of the process structure) and extracts the available pages from the dump file, writing them to a file within the current working directory. To run Lspm against the dd.exe process, an investigator would use the following command line:

lspm.pl d:\dumps\dfrws1-mem.dmp 0x0414dd60

The output of this command looks like this:

Name: dd.exe -> 0x01d9e000
There are 372 pages (1523712 bytes) to process.
Dumping process memory to dd.dmp...
Done.

Extracting the Process Image

When a process is launched, the executable file is read into memory. One of the pieces of information that an investigator can obtain from the process details (via Lspd) is the offset within the dump file to the image base address. Lspd will do a quick check to see whether an executable image can be found at that location. To develop this information further, an investigator can parse the portable executable (PE) file header and see whether it is possible to extract the entire contents of the executable image from the dump file.

Lspi is a Perl script that takes the same arguments as Lspd and Lspm and locates the beginning of the executable image for that process. If the image base address offset does indeed lead to an executable image file, Lspi will parse the values contained in the PE header to locate the pages that make up the rest of the executable image file.

The following command line shows Lspi being run against the dd.exe process:

lspi.pl d:\dumps\dfrws1-mem.dmp 0x0414dd60

The following is the output of this command:

Process Name : dd.exe
PID : 284
DTB : 0x01d9e000
PEB : 0x7ffdf000 (0x02c2d000)
ImgBaseAddr : 0x00400000 (0x00fee000)
e_lfanew = 0xe8
NT Header = 0x4550
Reading the Image File Header
Sections = 4
Opt Header Size = 0x000000e0 (224 bytes)

```
Characteristics:
IMAGE_FILE_EXECUTABLE_IMAGE
IMAGE_FILE_LOCAL_SYMS_STRIPPED
IMAGE_FILE_RELOCS_STRIPPED
IMAGE_FILE_LINE_NUMS_STRIPPED
IMAGE_FILE_32BIT_MACHINE
Machine = IMAGE_FILE_MACHINE_I860
Reading the Image Optional Header
Opt Header Magic = 0x10b
Subsystem : IMAGE_SUBSYSTEM_WINDOWS_CUI
Entry Pt Addr : 0x00006bda
Image Base : 0x00400000
File Align : 0x00001000
Reading the Image Data Directory information
Data Directory RVA Size
-------------- --- ----
ResourceTable 0x0000d000 0x00000430
DebugTable 0x00000000 0x00000000
BaseRelocTable 0x00000000 0x00000000
DelayImportDesc 0x0000af7c 0x000000a0
TLSTable 0x00000000 0x00000000
GlobalPtrReg 0x00000000 0x00000000
ArchSpecific 0x00000000 0x00000000
CLIHeader 0x00000000 0x00000000
LoadConfigTable 0x00000000 0x00000000
ExceptionTable 0x00000000 0x00000000
ImportTable 0x0000b25c 0x000000a0
unused 0x00000000 0x00000000
BoundImportTable 0x00000000 0x00000000
ExportTable 0x00000000 0x00000000
CertificateTable 0x00000000 0x00000000
IAT 0x00007000 0x00000210
Reading Image Section Header Information
Name Virt Sz Virt Addr rData Ofs rData Sz Char
---- ------- --------- --------- -------- ----
.text 0x00005ee0 0x00001000 0x00001000 0x00006000 0x60000020
.data 0x000002fc 0x0000c000 0x0000c000 0x00001000 0xc0000040
.rsrc 0x00000430 0x0000d000 0x0000d000 0x00001000 0x40000040
.rdata 0x00004cfa 0x00007000 0x00007000 0x00005000 0x40000040
Reassembling image file into dd.exe.img
Bytes written = 57344
New file size = 57344
```

The file extracted from the memory dump will not be exactly the same as the original executable file. This is due to the fact that some of the file's sections are writeable, and those sections will change as the process is executing. As the process executes, various elements of the executable code (addresses, variables, and so on) will change according to the environment and the stage of execution. However, there are a couple of ways that an investigator can determine the nature of a file and get some information about its purpose. One of those ways is to see whether the file has any file version information compiled into it, as is done with most files created by legitimate software companies. In the section headers of the image file, there is a section named .rsrc, which is the name often used for a resource section of a PE file. This section can contain a variety of resources, such as dialogs and version strings, and is organized like a file system of sorts.

Memory Dump Analysis and the Page File

Tools such as Lspm that rely solely on the contents of the RAM dump will provide an incomplete memory dump, since memory pages that have been swapped out to the page file (pagefile.sys on Windows systems) will not be incorporated into the resulting memory dump. To overcome this deficiency, in the spring of 2006 Nicholas

Paul Maclean published his thesis work, *Acquisition and Analysis of Windows Memory*, which explains the inner workings of the Windows memory management system and provides an open-source utility called vtop to reconstruct the virtual address space of a process.

Pool Allocations

When the Windows memory manager allocates memory, it generally allocates memory from the 4 KB (4,096 bytes) pages. However, allocating an entire 4 KB page for a sentence copied to the clipboard would be a waste of memory. So the memory manager allocates several pages ahead of time, keeping an available pool of memory. Many of the commonly used pool headers are listed in the pooltag.txt file provided with the Microsoft Debugging Tools.

The downside to searching for memory pool allocations is that although the pool headers do not seem to change between versions of Windows, the format of the data resident within the memory pool changes, and there is no available documentation regarding the format of these memory pools.

Collecting Process Memory

During an investigation, an investigator might be interested in only particular processes rather than a list of all processes, or the investigator might like more than just the contents of process memory available in a RAM dump file. For example, the investigator might have quickly identified processes of interest that required no additional extensive investigation. There are ways to collect all the memory used by a process—not just what is in physical memory but what is in virtual memory or the page file as well.

Tool: PMDump

PMDump is a tool that allows an investigator to dump the contents of process memory without stopping the process. As discussed earlier, this allows the process to continue and the contents of memory to change while being written to a file, thereby creating a "smear" of process memory. Also, PMDump does not create an output file that can be analyzed with debugging tools.

Tool: Process Dumper

Another method for dumping the contents of process memory is a tool called Process Dumper. It dumps the entire process space along with additional metadata and the process environment to the console so that the output can be redirected to a file or a socket.

Tool: UserDump

UserDump allows an investigator to dump any process on the fly, without attaching a debugger and without terminating the process once the dump has been completed. Also, the Microsoft Debugging Tools can read the dump file that UserDump generates. However, UserDump requires the investigator to install a driver for it to work.

Inside the Windows Registry

Administrators directly interact with the registry through some intermediary application, the most common of which are the GUI registry editors that ship with Windows—regedit and regedt32. Windows XP and 2003 distributions also include reg, a command-line tool that can be used from the command prompt or in scripts. Figure 4-21 shows the Registry Editor.

Each of the hives in the Windows registry plays an important role in the functioning of the system. The HKEY_USERS hive contains all the actively loaded user profiles for that system. HKEY_CURRENT_USER is the active, loaded user profile for the currently logged-on user. The HKEY_LOCAL_MACHINE hive contains a vast array of configuration information for the system, including hardware settings and software settings. The HKEY_CURRENT_CONFIG hive contains the hardware profile the system uses at startup. Finally, the HKEY_CLASSES_ROOT hive contains configuration information relating to which application is used to open various files on the system. This hive is subclassed to both HKEY_CURRENT_USER\Software\Classes (user-specific settings) and HKEY_LOCAL_MACHINE\Software\Classes (systemwide settings). Table 4-2 describes the different data types in the registry.

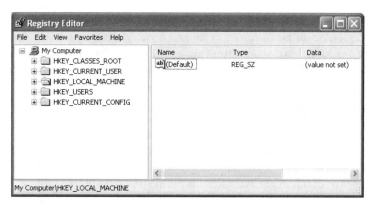

Figure 4-21   There are five main hives in the Windows registry.

Data Type	Description
REG_BINARY	Raw binary data
REG_DWORD	Data represented as a 32-bit (4-byte) integer
REG_SZ	A fixed-length text string
REG_EXPAND_SZ	A variable-length data string
REG_MULTI_SZ	Multiple strings, separated by a space, comma, or other delimiter
REG_NONE	No data type
REG_QWORD	Data represented by a 64-bit (8-byte) integer
REG_LINK	A Unicode string naming a symbolic link
REG_RESOURCE_LIST	A series of nested arrays designed to store a resource list
REG_RESOURCE_ REQUIREMENTS_LIST	A series of nested arrays designed to store a device driver's list of possible hardware resources
REG_FULL_RESOURCE_DESCRIPTOR	A series of nested arrays designed to store a resource list used by a physical hardware device

Table 4-2   This table describes the various data types used in the registry

Registry Structure Within a Hive File

Understanding the basic components of the registry will help an investigator gain extra information through keyword searches of other locations and sources, such as the page file, physical memory, or even unallocated space. By knowing more about the information that is available within the registry, an investigator will know better what is possible and what to look for.

Each type of cell in the registry has a specific structure and contains specific types of information. The following are the types of cells:

- *Key cell*: This type of cell contains registry key information and includes offsets to other cells as well as the LastWrite time for the key (signature: *kn*).

- *Value cell*: This type of cell holds a value and its data (signature: *kv*).

- *Subkey list cell*: This type of cell is made up of a series of indexes (or offsets) pointing to key cells; these are all subkeys to the parent key cell.

- *Value list cell*: This type of cell is made up of a series of indexes (or offsets) pointing to value cells; these are all values of a common key cell.

- *Security descriptor cell*: This cell contains security descriptor information for a key cell (signature: *ks*).

Using these signatures, an investigator can potentially carve registry key and value information out of the unallocated clusters of an acquired image or even out of RAM dumps.

A key cell is 76 bytes long, plus a variable-length name. A value cell is only 18 bytes long with a variable-length name and variable-length data. The data type is stored in a 4-byte (DWORD) value located within the value cell itself.

The Registry as a Log File

The key cells within the registry constitute the keys or folders that are visible on opening the Registry Editor. This is the only one of the structures that contains a time value, called the LastWrite time. The LastWrite time is a 64-bit FILETIME object that is analogous to the last modification time of a file. This information provides a time-frame reference for certain user activities on the system, and it also tells when a specific value was added to a key or modified. In addition to the LastWrite times, the registry also maintains time-stamp information in some of the data associated with specific values.

Monitoring Changes to the Registry

Monitoring registry changes is a tough task. One of the ways to do this is by taking a snapshot of the registry, performing an action, taking a snapshot of the registry again, and comparing the two snapshots. One particular tool that is useful for this task is InControl5. Another way to monitor changes to the registry is to use Regmon from Microsoft to monitor the registry in real time.

Registry Analysis

During a live response, an investigator can retrieve and analyze much of the information from within the registry; all of the registry information is available during a postmortem investigation.

ProDiscover provides a simple interface for accessing the registry during postmortem analysis. When a case is loaded into ProDiscover, the investigator need only right-click the **Windows** directory in the Content View and choose **Add to Registry Viewer**. ProDiscover then locates the necessary files to populate the Registry Viewer. ProScript is ProDiscover's scripting language, which is based on Perl and provides an excellent facility for extracting information from the registry in an automated fashion. The ProScript.pm module facilitates an API for writing Perl scripts that interact almost completely with ProDiscover; just about anything that an investigator can do through the ProDiscover user interface can also be done with a ProScript.

System Information

When working with an acquired image of a Windows system during postmortem analysis, an investigator can find a great deal of basic information about the system in the registry. Some basic information is relatively easy to obtain during live response; for example, the investigator can determine the version of the operating system (such as Windows 2000, XP, 2003, or Vista) by simply looking at the shell.

Other information about the system is stored in the registry in the CurrentControlSet key. The active key is numbered 1. Within the Registry Viewer are two ControlSets: ControlSet001 and ControlSet002.

An investigator can find the computer name in the following key, in the ComputerName value:

SYSTEM\CurrentControlSet\Control\ComputerName\ActiveComputerName

An investigator can find the time that the system was last shut down in the following key:

SYSTEM\ControlSet00x\Control\Windows

The ShutdownTime value beneath this key is a FILETIME object that can be correlated with other times on the system, such as Event Log entries and the like, to assist in developing a timeline of activity and system use. The following key could also be of value during an investigation:

SOFTWARE\Microsoft\Windows NT\CurrentVersion

This key holds several values that provide information about the system. The ProductName, CurrentBuildNumber, and CSDVersion values tell about the operating system and version.

Time Zone Information

An investigator can find information about the time zone settings in the following key:

SYSTEM\CurrentControlSet\Control\TimeZoneInformation

This information can be important for establishing a timeline of activity on the system.

Many tools are available to extract information regarding times and dates in UTC/GMT time. The investigator can use the ActiveTimeBias value from the TimeZoneInformation key to translate or normalize the times to other sources from the system, such as entries in log files.

Shares

Windows 2000, XP, 2003, and Vista systems create hidden administrative shares on a system, by default. If a user creates an additional share, such as via the **net share** command, that share will appear in the following key located in the HKEY_LOCAL_MACHINE hive:

SYSTEM\CurrentControlSet\Services\lanmanserver\Shares

An administrator can disable the creation of hidden administrative shares using the following key:

SYSTEM\CurrentControlSet\Services\lanmanserver\parameters

If the value named as AutoShareServe beneath this key is 0, this indicates that the system has been modified specifically to prevent the creation of hidden administrative shares.

Audit Policy

The system's audit policy is maintained in the Security hive, beneath the Policy\PolAdtEv key. The (Default) value is a REG_NONE data type and contains binary information into which the audit policy is encoded. The audit policy extracted from a sample image using a tool called the Offline Registry Parser shows the following:

\SECURITY\Policy\PolAdtEv
LastWrite time: Fri Sep 9 01:11:43 2005
--> Default;REG_NONE;01 17 f5 77 03 00 00 00 03 00 00 00 00 00 00 00
00 00 00 00 00 00 00 00 03 00 00 00 03 00 00 00 00 00 00 00 00 00 03 00 00 00 09 00 00 00

The first DWORD (4 bytes) of the binary data (actually, the first byte) gives the information about whether auditing has been enabled.

Windows 2000 and XP systems have nine event types that can be audited, and each of those areas is represented by a DWORD value in the sequence of bytes. For each of the lettered pairs, 00 means that there is no auditing, 01 means that success events are audited, 02 means failure events are audited, and 03 means that both success and failure events are audited. This information can be useful during an investigation because it will tell about what types of events investigator should expect to see in the Event Log.

Wireless SSIDs

On live systems, Windows XP will maintain a list of service set identifiers (SSIDs) to which it has connected. This list is maintained in the following registry key:

SOFTWARE\Microsoft\WZCSVC\Parameters\Interfaces\{GUID}

Beneath this key, there is a value called ActiveSettings and then several other values called Static#000x, where x is an integer starting at 0. These values are all binary, and the SSIDs for any wireless access points that have been accessed are included within the binary data. Within the binary data, at offset 0x10 is a DWORD value that contains the length of the SSID. The SSID name immediately follows this DWORD value for the number of bytes/characters listed. This can be useful in situations where unauthorized access is an issue or in a case where it is important to trace the IP address that the individual was using.

Autostart Locations

Autostart locations within the registry are locations that allow applications to be launched without any interaction from the user. These locations were originally provided for the user's convenience. Some applications, such as touch-pad drivers and applications on laptops, as well as antivirus and firewall applications, are most useful when they are started automatically.

Attackers often use malware that automatically starts when the system boots or when a user logs in because a user does not have to run a particular program to cause the malware to run in these situations.

On a live Windows XP system, the msconfig command launches the System Configuration Utility. Users can run this command by clicking the **Start** button, choosing **Run**, typing **msconfig** into the textbox, and then pressing Enter. Figure 4-22 shows the System Configuration Utility.

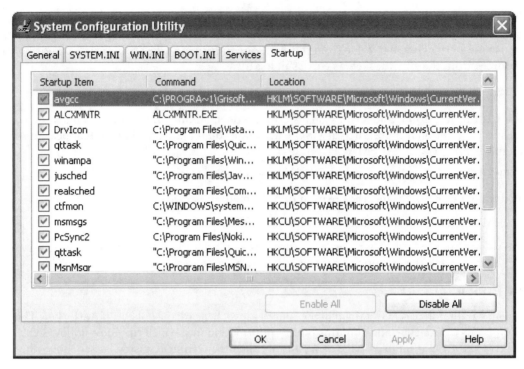

Figure 4-22 The System Configuration Utility allows an administrator to choose which applications and services automatically start.

User Login

When a user logs into a system, the following registry keys are accessed and parsed so that the listed applications can be executed:

1. HKEY_LOCAL_MACHINE\Software\Microsoft\Windows\CurrentVersion\Runonce

2. HKEY_LOCAL_MACHINE\Software\Microsoft\Windows\CurrentVersion\Policies\Explorer\Run

3. HKEY_LOCAL_MACHINE\Software\Microsoft\Windows\CurrentVersion\Run

4. HKEY_CURRENT_USER\Software\Microsoft\Windows NT\CurrentVersion\Windows\Run

5. HKEY_CURRENT_USER\Software\Microsoft\Windows\CurrentVersion\Run

6. HKEY_CURRENT_USER\Software\Microsoft\Windows\CurrentVersion\RunOnce

These keys are ignored if the system is started in Safe Mode.

On Windows XP and 2003 systems, if an administrator prefaces the RunOnce values (keys 1 and 6) with an asterisk (*), the associated programs can be run even if the system is started in Safe Mode.

User Activity

Autostart registry locations that fall under this category are those that are accessed when the user performs an action, such as opening an application like Internet Explorer or Outlook.

The following are two keys that investigators should check for the presence of malware:

- HKEY_LOCAL_MACHINE\Software\Classes\Exefile\Shell\Open\command

- HKEY_CLASSES_ROOT\Exefile\Shell\Open\command

When a user double-clicks a file, Windows scans the registry for that file class and then determines what actions to take, based on the registry settings for the file class.

Any other data in this key should be considered suspicious and investigated immediately.

This functionality does not apply to just the Exefile entry beneath HKEY_CLASSES_ROOT. Some malware will modify other entries of the same type to ensure its persistence on the system.

For example, some backdoors modify values in the following key:

HKEY_CLASSES_ROOT\Word.Document.x\shell\open\command

Windows operating systems provide the ability to alert external functions when certain events occur on the system, such as when a user logs on or off or when the screensaver starts. The following registry key handles these notifications:

HKLM\Software\Microsoft\Windows NT\CurrentVersion\Winlogon\Notify\

Entries beneath this key point to DLLs that receive notifications of certain events. Googling for Winlogon\ Notify will give a long list of links to malware that uses this key's functionality.

It is a good idea for an investigator to sort the subkeys beneath Notify based on their LastWrite times and pay particular attention to any entries that are near the date of the suspected incident. An investigator should also take note of any entries that list DLLs in the DLLName value that have suspicious file version information or no file version information at all. Beneath the WinLogon key (listed previously) is a value named TaskMan that might be of interest to investigators, because it allows the user to choose an application to replace the Task Manager.

Enumerating Autostart Registry Locations

One tool investigators can use to retrieve information from autostart locations in the registry on a live system is AutoRuns.

AutoRuns will retrieve entries from a number of registry keys and display what it finds. It will also retrieve the description and publisher from the executable file pointed to by each registry value. This information provides a quick indicator to the investigator as to whether anything that could be suspicious is running in one of these locations. Figure 4-23 shows a screenshot from Autoruns.

For postmortem investigations, analysts require tools that allow them to enumerate a registry that has been reconstructed from the component files of a system image. ProDiscover's ProScript capability allows an analyst to use Perl scripts similar to those written for live systems to search the registry in an image during postmortem analysis.

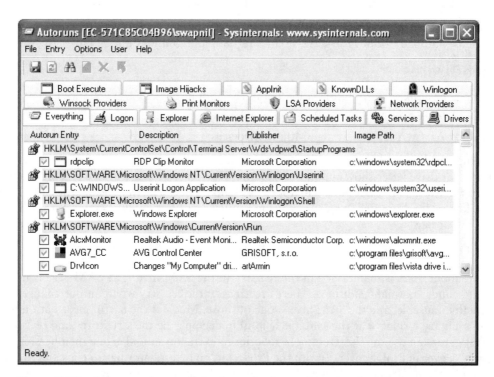

Figure 4-23   Autoruns shows all the items in the registry that have been set to automatically start.

USB Removable Storage Devices

When a USB removable storage device, such as a thumb drive, is connected to a Windows system, footprints or artifacts are left in the registry. When the device is plugged in, the Plug and Play (PnP) Manager receives the event and queries the device descriptor in the firmware for information about the device, such as the manufacturer. The PnP Manager then uses this information to locate the appropriate driver for the device and, if necessary, loads that driver. Once the device has been identified, a registry key is created beneath the following key:

HKEY_LOCAL_MACHINE\System\CurrentControlSet\Enum\USBSTOR

The subkey that is created beneath this key is named with the following form:

Disk&Ven_###&Prod_###&Rev_###

This subkey represents the device class identifier, since it identifies a specific class of device. The fields represented by ### are filled in by the PnP Manager based on information found in the device descriptor. Once the device class ID has been created, a unique instance identifier needs to be created for the specific device. The value iSerialNumber is a unique instance identifier for the device, similar to the MAC address of a network interface card. This value is used as the unique instance ID for the device so that multiple devices of the same class can be uniquely identified on the system.

For devices that do not have a serial number, the PnP Manager will create a unique instance ID for that device, which will look similar to the following:

6&26c97b61&0

If an investigator finds a unique instance ID beneath the USBSTOR key that looks like this, he or she knows that the device that was plugged into the system does not have a serial number in its device descriptor. Investigators should include the use of UVCView in their methodology. This tool allows an investigator to examine the descriptor for any attached USB device. Using this tool, the investigator can associate devices with the system through registry artifacts in the USBSTOR key and in the MountedDevices key. The ParentIdPrefix value can be used to correlate additional information from within the registry.

Using both the unique instance identifier and the ParentIdPrefix, investigators can determine the last time that the USB device was connected to the Windows system. On a live system, the investigator has to look at the following key:

HKEY_LOCAL_MACHINE\SYSTEM\CurrentControlSet\Control\DeviceClasses

A number of subkeys are present beneath this key. Forensic investigators are interested in specific device classes such as {53f56307-b6bf-11d0-94f2-00a0c91efb8b} and {53f5630db6bf-11d0-94f2-00a0c91efb8b}.

MountedDevices

The MountedDevices key stores information about the various devices and volumes mounted on an NTFS file system. The following is the complete path to the key:

HKEY_LOCAL_MACHINE\System\MountedDevices

For example, when a USB removable storage device is connected to a Windows system, it is assigned a drive letter; that drive letter shows up in the MountedDevices key. If the device is assigned the drive letter F:, the value in the MountedDevices key will appear as \DosDevices\F:. An investigator can map the entry in the USBSTOR key to the MountedDevices key using the ParentIdPrefix value found within the unique instance ID key for the device.

Finding Users

Information about users is maintained in the registry in the SAM hive. The SAM hive is not accessible to the administrator under normal conditions. There are areas of the registry where minor changes can leave the system potentially unusable, and the SAM hive is one of those. Much of the useful information in the SAM hive is encoded in a binary format. The file sam.h is helpful in deciphering the structures and revealing information.

An investigator can use the UserDump.pl ProScript to extract user and group membership information from the Registry Viewer in ProDiscover. To run the ProScript, an investigator has to click the **Run ProScript** button on the menu bar and select the location of the ProScript from the **Run ProScript** dialog box. The investigator then selects the UserDump.pl ProScript, and once it has completed, the information parsed from the SAM hive will be visible in the results window, where it can be selected, copied, and pasted into a file or report. The user information is maintained in the F value located at the following path:

SAM\SAM\Domains\Account\Users\{RID}

The F value within the key is a binary data type and must be parsed appropriately to extract all the information. There are some important dates available in the contents of the binary data for the F value, including the following:

- Bytes 8–15 represent the last login date for the account.
- Bytes 24–31 represent the date that the password was last reset.
- Bytes 32–39 represent the account expiration date.
- Bytes 40–47 represent the date of the last failed login attempt.

The sam_parse.pl Perl script not only displays the time stamps available from the user information in the SAM file, it also parses the user flags and the number of times the user has logged into the system. Information about group membership is maintained in the SAM\SAM\Domains\Builtin\Aliases key.

Tracking User Activity

An investigator can use a number of registry keys to track user activity. These registry keys can be found in the NTUSER.DAT file for the user and are updated (i.e., entries added) when a user performs specific actions. When this happens, the key's LastWrite time is updated.

The majority of a user's activity is recorded in the registry in the HKEY_CURRENT_USER hive.

The UserAssist Keys

An investigator can find user information stored in the user's NTUSER.DAT file beneath the following registry key:

Software\Microsoft\Windows\CurrentVersion\Explorer\UserAssist\{GUID}\Count

The GUID is a globally unique identifier; there are two such keys beneath the UserAssist key: {5E6AB780-7743-11CF-A12B-00AA004AE837} and {75048700-EF1F-11D0-9888-006097DEACF9}. Within the HKEY_CLASSES_ROOT hive, the GUID 5E6AB780-7743-11CF-A12B-00AA004AE837 points to the Internet Toolbar, and the GUID 75048700-EF1F-11D0-9888-006097DEACF9 points to the ActiveDesktop.

Beneath each of the Count keys are several values; the value names beneath both keys are ROT13 encrypted and can be easily decrypted.

When the value names are decrypted, they begin with "UEME_" and then one of the following:

- *RUNPATH*: Refers to an absolute path within the file system
- *RUNCPL*: Refers to launching a Control Panel applet
- *RUNPIDL*: Refers to a PIDL, or pointer to an ID list; part of the internal Explorer namespace

MRU Lists

Many applications maintain an MRU list, which is a list of files that have been most recently used. Within the running application, these file names generally appear at the bottom of the drop-down menu when **File** on the menu bar is selected.

The MRU list registry key is the following key:

\Software\Microsoft\Windows\CurrentVersion\Explorer\RecentDocs

This key can contain a number of values, all of which are binary data types. The values investigators are interested in are the ones that have names that are numbers and the one named MRUListEx. The numbered value names contain the names of the files accessed (in Unicode), and the MRUListEx value maintains the order in which they were accessed (as DWORDs).

The RecentDocs key also has a number of subkeys, each one being the extension of a file that was opened (.doc, .txt, .html, etc.). The values within these subkeys are maintained in the same way as in the Recent-Docs key: the value names are numbered, and their data contains the name of the file accessed as a binary data type.

Investigators can find another MRU list in the following key:

\Software\Microsoft\Windows\CurrentVersion\Explorer\RunMRU

The RunMRU MRU list is maintained in clear text and is more easily readable than the RecentDocs key. Entries are added to this key when a user clicks the **Start** button, chooses **Run,** and types a command or the name of a file.

Another key similar to the RunMRU key is the following key:

\Software\Microsoft\Internet Explorer\TypedURLs

This key maintains a MRU list of URLs that a user types into the address bar.

Another key that holds MRU lists is the following:

\Software\Microsoft\Windows\CurrentVersion\Explorer\ComDlg32\OpenSaveMRU

This key maintains MRU lists of files opened via **Open** and **Save As** dialogs within the Windows shell. Similar to the RecentDocs key, the OpenSaveMRU key also maintains subkeys of specific file extensions that have been opened or saved.

Search Assistant MRU Lists   When a user clicks the **Start** button in Windows XP, chooses **Search,** and then chooses **For Files and Folders,** the search terms entered into the dialog box are stored in the following registry key:

Software\Microsoft\Search Assistant\ACMru

The ACMru key generally has some combination of four subkeys:

- *5001*: Contains the MRU list for the Internet Search Assistant
- *5603*: Contains the MRU list for the Windows XP files and folders search
- *5604*: Contains the MRU list that corresponds to searching for a word or phrase in a file
- *5647*: Maintains the MRU list for the computers entered when searching for computers or people

MRU Lists When Connecting to Other Systems   When a user uses the Map Network Drive Wizard to connect to a remote system, an MRU list is created beneath the following key:

Software\Microsoft\Windows\CurrentVersion\Explorer\Map Network Drive MRU

Each entry is given a letter as the value name, and the MRUList value illustrates the order in which the user connected to each drive or share.

Whether the user uses the Map Network Drive Wizard or the **net use** command, the volumes the user added to the system will appear in the following key:

Software\Microsoft\Windows\CurrentVersion\Explorer\MountPoints2

The IP addresses also appear in the following registry key:

Software\Microsoft\Windows\CurrentVersion\Explorer\ComputerDescriptions

Analyzing Restore Point Registry Settings

Restore points were introduced with Windows XP and ME. The purpose of restore points in general is to take a snapshot of a system so that a user can restore the system to a previous restore point if things go wrong.

The settings for restore points are stored in the Registry. They are stored at:

HKEY_LOCAL_MACHINE\Software\Microsoft\WindowsNT\CurrentVersion\SystemRestore

The interval for restore point creation is stored in the RPGlobalInterval value, and the default DWORD data is 86,400. The system restore points can be reset and disabled. The setting for disabling restore points is a value named DisableSR, and it defaults to 0. If the setting has been changed to 1, it means that restore point creation has been disabled.

An investigator can find restore points in numbered folders in the following location:

\System Volume Information\ -restore {GUID}\RP##

A user cannot access folders and files below the System Volume Information folder using the Explorer interface. This is true even if the user has administrative privileges and hidden/system files are set to be visible. This condition makes it difficult for the average user to access, manipulate, or delete these files.

The System Restore utility is in the System Tools folder in the Start menu.

Restore Points

Automatically created restore points have names assigned to them that are stored in the file rp.log located in the root of the folder RP##.

The following are some of the characteristics of restore points and their names:

- When restore points are created on schedule (default = 24 hours), they are named system checkpoints. This name appears in the user interface.

- The restore point name is stored starting at byte offset 16 in the rp.log file.

- If software or unsigned drivers are installed, the system usually creates a restore point. The name of the software or the unsigned driver is used as the name of the restore point.

- A user can manually create restore points, and the user-provided name is stored in this same location.

- The last 8 bytes of the rp.log file are a Windows 64-bit time stamp indicating when the restore point was created.

- Restore points are also created prior to the installation of any Windows automatic updates.

A restore point makes copies of important system and program files that were added since the last restore point. These files, except for registry hive files, are stored in the root of the RP## folder.

Determining the Startup Locations

A user can manually start any service or application on a computer, or services and applications can start automatically. The common startup locations in the registry are listed in Table 4-3.

Registry Key	Notes
HKEY_LOCAL_MACHINE\Software\Microsoft\Windows\CurrentVersion\Run\	All values in this key execute at system startup.
HKEY_LOCAL_MACHINE\Software\Microsoft\Windows\CurrentVersion\RunOnce\	All values in this key execute at system startup and then are deleted.
HKEY_LOCAL_MACHINE\Software\Microsoft\Windows\CurrentVersion\RunServices\	All values in this key are run as services at system startup.
HKEY LOCAL MACHINE\Software\Microsoft\Windows\CurrentVersion\RunServicesOnce\	All values in this key are run as services at system startup and then are deleted.
HKEY_LOCAL_MACHINE\Software\Microsoft\WindowsNT\CurrentVersion\Winlogon\	The value Shell will be executed when any user logs on. This value is normally set to explorer.exe, but it could be changed to a different Explorer in a different path.
HKEY_LOCAL_MACHINE\Software\Microsoft\Active Setup\Installed Components\	Each subkey (GUID name) represents an installed component. All subkeys are monitored, and the StubPath value in subkeys, when present, is a way of running code.
HKEY_LOCAL_MACHINE\Software\Microsoft\Windows NT\CurrentVersion\Winlogon\	The value Userinit runs when any user logs on. It can be appended to have additional programs start here.
HKEY_LOCAL_MACHINE\Software\Microsoft\Windows\CurrentVersion\ShellServiceObjectDelay\	The value Load, if present, runs using explorer.exe after it starts.
HKEY_LOCAL_MACHINE\Software\Microsoft\Windows\CurrentVersion\Policies\Explorer\run\	If Explorer and run are present, the values under run are executed after Explorer starts.
HKEY_LOCAL_MACHINE\SOFTWARE\Microsoft\Windows\CurrentVersion\RunOnceEx\0001\	Per Microsoft KB232509, the syntax to run a program from here is RunMyApp 5 "llnotepad.exe."
HKEY_LOCAL_MACHINE\System\CurrentControlSet\Services\VxD\	When present, subkeys are monitored, and the StaticVxD value in each subkey is a method of executing code.

Table 4-3 This table describes the different startup locations in the registry   *(continues)*

Registry Key	Notes
HKEY_LOCAL_MACHINE\System\CurrentControlSet\ Control\Session Manager\	The value BootExecute contains files that are native applications executed before Windows runs.
HKEY_LOCAL_MACHINE\System\CurrentControlSet\ Services\	This contains a list of services that run at system startup. If the value Start is 2, startup is automatic. If the value Start is 3, startup is manual. If the value Start is 4, the service is disabled. The number of services listed in this key is quite large.
HKEY_LOCAL_MACHINE\System\CurrentControlSet\ Services\Winsock2\Parameters\Protocol_Catalog\Catalog_ Entries\	The subkeys are for layered service providers, and the values are executed before any user login.
HKEY_LOCAL_MACHINE\System\Control\WOW\	Whenever a legacy 16-bit application is run, the program listed in the value cmdline is run.
HKEY_CURRENT_USER\Software\Microsoft\Windows\ CurrentVersion\Run\	All values in this subkey run when this specific user logs on.
HKEY_CURRENT_USER\Software\Microsoft\Windows\ CurrentVersion\RunOnce\	All values in this subkey run when this specific user logs on, and then the values are deleted.
HKEY_CURRENT_USER\Software\Microsoft\Windows\ CurrentVersion\RunOnce\Setup\	For this specific user, this key is used only by setup, and a progress dialog box tracks progress as the values in this key are run one at a time.
HKEY_CURRENT_USER\Control Panel\Desktop\	For this specific user, if a screensaver is enabled, a value named scrnsave.exe is present. Whatever is in the path found in the string data for this value will execute when the screensaver runs.
HKEY_CURRENT_USER\Software\Microsoft\Windows NT\ CurrentVersion\Windows\	For this specific user, the string specified in the value run executes when this user logs on.
HKEY_CURRENT_USER\Software\Microsoft\Windows NT\ CurrentVersion\Windows\	For this specific user, the string specified in the value load runs when this user logs on.
HKEY_CURRENT_USER\Software\Microsoft\Windows\ CurrentVersion\Policies\Explorer\	For this specific user, the string specified in the value run runs when this user logs on.

Table 4-3   This table describes the different startup locations in the registry

Registry Key	Default or Normal Settings
HKEY_CURRENT_USER\Software\Microsoft\Windows\ CurrentVersion\Explorer\Shell Folders\	The value Startup will be C:\Documents and Settings\%UserName%\Start Menu\Programs\Startup, where %UserName% will not be the environment variable but will actually specify the user's name.
HKEY_CURRENT_USER\Software\Microsoft\ Windows\ CurrentVersion\ Explorer\User Shell Folders\	The value Startup will be %USERPROFILE%\Start Menu\ Programs\Startup.
HKEY_LOCAL_MACHINE\Software\Microsoft\ Windows\ CurrentVersion\ Explorer\Shell Folders\	The value Common Startup will be C:\Documents and Settings\ All Users\Start Menu\Programs\Startup.
HKEY_LOCAL_MACHINE\Software\Microsoft\ Windows\ CurrentVersion\ Explorer\User Shell Folders\	The value Common Startup will be %ALLUSERSPROFILE%\Start Menu\Programs\Startup.

Table 4-4   This table describes the different startup folder locations found in the registry

There are also two startup locations within the user profile area:

- C:\Documents and Settings\All Users\Start Menu\Programs\Startup
- C:\Documents and Settings\%UserName%\Start Menu\Programs\Startup

Any executable service or application located in the former will run for all users upon logon, while any in the latter will run only for that specific user when he or she logs on.

User startup folder registry settings are described in Table 4-4.

Cache, Cookie, and History Analysis in Internet Explorer

A cache is a place to store something temporarily. The files a user requests by looking at a Web page are stored on the hard disk in a cache subdirectory under the browser directory. When the user returns to a page he or she recently looked at, the browser can get it from the cache rather than the original server, saving time and decreasing network traffic.

A cookie is information that a Web site puts on a user's hard disk so that the user's system can remember something about the site at a later time. Typically, a cookie records user preferences when using a particular site.

Using the Web's Hypertext Transfer Protocol (HTTP), each request for a Web page is independent of all other requests. For this reason, the Web server has no memory of what pages it has sent to a user previously or anything about a user's previous visits. The following are the directories where cache, cookie, and history information is stored for Internet Explorer:

- *C:\Documents and Settings\<user name>\Local Settings\Temporary Internet Files\Content.IE5*: Stores all IE activities of a user, included cached pages and images

- *C:\Documents and Settings\<user name>\Local Settings\History\History.IE5*: Stores browser history

- *C:\Documents and Settings\<user name>\Cookies*: Stores cookies

Cache, Cookie, and History Analysis in Mozilla, Firefox, and Netscape

Cache, cookie, and history information is stored in the following ways in Mozilla, Firefox, and Netscape:

- Mozilla, Firefox, and Netscape save Web activity in an ASCII file named history.dat.

- Firefox files are located in the following directory:
  \Documents and Settings\<user name>\Application Data\Mozilla\Firefox\Profiles\<random text>.

- Mozilla and Netscape files are located in the following directory:
  \Documents and Settings\<user name>\Application Data\Mozilla\Profiles\<profile name>\<random text>.

Tool: Pasco

Pasco is a command-line tool that investigators can use to examine Internet Explorer data stored in an index.dat file. Pasco parses the file and outputs the results to a field-delimited file. An investigator can then load this file into a spreadsheet program to view the data. The investigator could also use analysis tools on the output file.

Tool: IECacheView

IECacheView reads the cache folder of Internet Explorer and displays the contents in an easily readable GUI. For each file in the cache, the following information is displayed:

- File name
- Content type
- URL
- Last accessed time
- Last modified time
- Expiration time
- Number of hits
- File size
- Folder name
- Full path of the cache file name

An investigator can save this information to a text, HTML, or XML file.

Tool: CacheMonitor II

When an investigator first launches the program, CacheMonitor II scans the cache and displays all of its contents in a list, including information about the cached files. When the cache changes, the investigator can tell CacheMonitor II to rescan the cache. The listing will update to show any changes, and the Status column will update to show that a particular file has changed. Figure 4-24 shows a portion of a screenshot from CacheMonitor II.

Tool: IEHistoryView

IEHistoryView allows an investigator to look at the browsing history of any user on a computer system. The history is displayed in a GUI and includes information for each page, such as the URL, the page title, and how many times the page was visited. The investigator can save the history list to a text, HTML, or XML file. Figure 4-25 shows a screenshot from IEHistoryView.

Tool: IE Cookie Analysis

IE Cookie Analysis reads the index.dat file containing information about cookies. For each cookie, IE Cookie Analysis extracts the following information from index.dat:

- Cookie file name
- Record type (always URL for a cookie)
- Offset in hex to the location of the record in the index.dat
- Record size in bytes

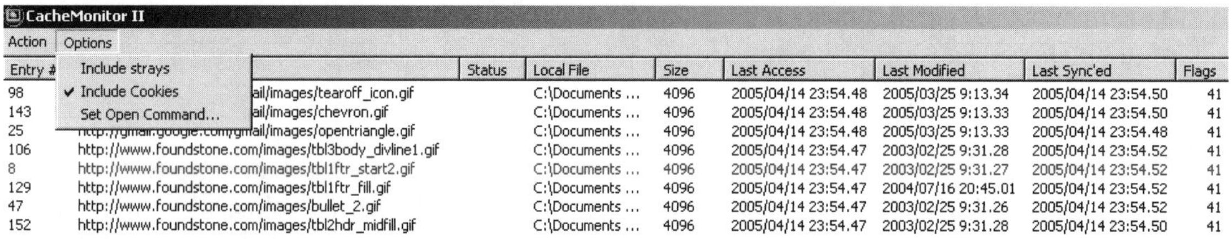

Figure 4-24 A user can scan for changes in the cache using CacheMonitor II.

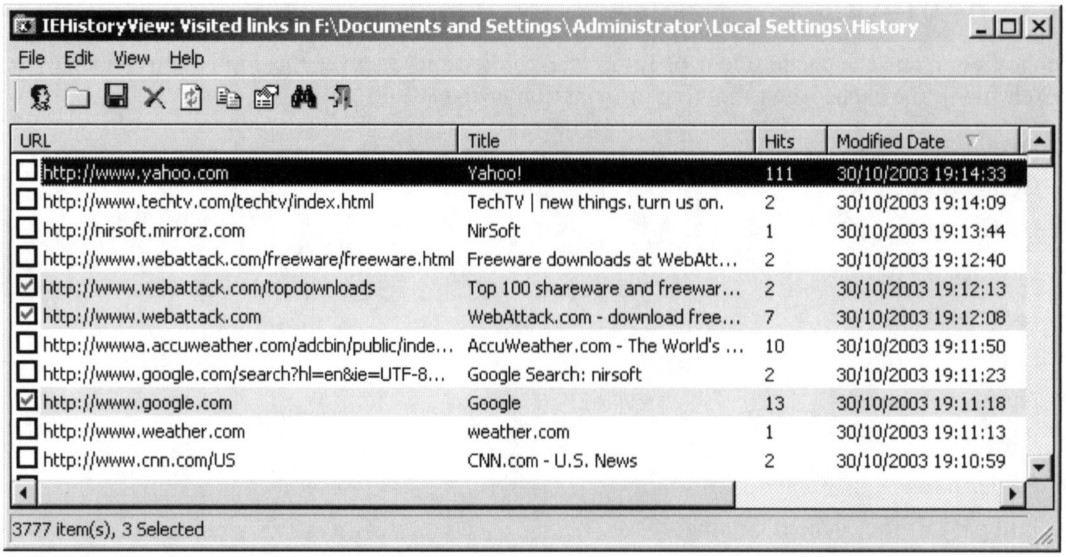

Figure 4-25 IEHistoryView displays the browsing history of any user.

- Number of hits
- Site that created the cookie
- Last modified date
- Last accessed date
- User profile name
- MD5 of the cookie file

An investigator can choose any cookie in the display window of IE Cookie Analysis and open the page that created the cookie in Internet Explorer. He or she can also open the cookie file itself in a text editor such as Notepad or Wordpad.

Tool: IECookiesView

IECookiesView is a utility that displays details about all the cookies stored by Internet Explorer. Using this tool, an investigator can look at the cookies of any user on the computer. The investigator can sort the cookies by any column of information and search for cookies based on the Web site that created them. The investigator can also copy cookie information to the clipboard or save the cookie information to a text file. Figure 4-26 shows a screenshot from IECookiesView.

Tool: IE Sniffer

IE Sniffer offers a suite of tools that allows a user to view and manipulate Internet Explorer cache, history, and cookie files. Of primary interest to the forensic investigator are the Quick Viewer and Hex Viewer. The Quick Viewer allows an investigator to look at the contents of any index.dat file and open any of the URLs in a browser. The Hex Viewer provides a more detailed look at the index.dat files. Figure 4-27 shows a screenshot from IE Sniffer.

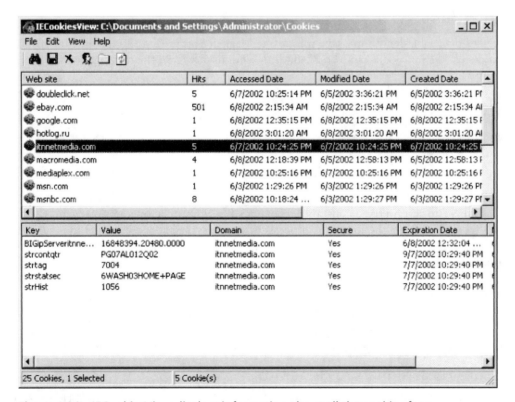

Figure 4-26 IECookiesView displays information about all the cookies for a particular user.

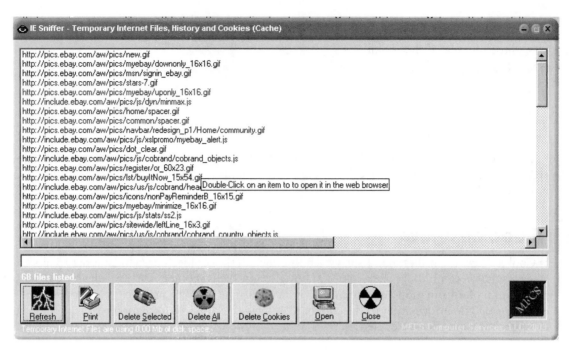

Figure 4-27   IE Sniffer allows a user to view the cache, history, and cookie files for Internet Explorer.

MD5 Calculation

Message-Digest algorithm 5 (MD5) was designed by Ron Rivest in 1991. It is a cryptographic hash function with a 128-bit hash value and is used in security applications and to check the integrity of files.

MD5 Algorithm

MD5 processes a variable-length message into a fixed-length output of 128 bits. The input message is broken up into chunks of 512-bit blocks (sixteen 32-bit little-endian integers); the message is padded so that its length is divisible by 512.

The padding is done as follows:

- First, a single bit, 1, is appended to the end of the message.
- It is followed by as many zeros as are required to bring the length of the message up to 64 bits fewer than a multiple of 512.
- The remaining bits are filled up with a 64-bit integer representing the length of the original message, in bits.

The main MD5 algorithm operates on a 128-bit state, divided into four 32-bit words, denoted A, B, C, and D. These are initialized to certain fixed constants. The main algorithm then operates on each 512-bit message block in turn, each block modifying the state. The processing of a message block consists of four similar stages, termed rounds; each round is composed of 16 similar operations based on a nonlinear function F, modular addition, and left rotation.

Tool: ChaosMD5

ChaosMD5 is a free MD5 generator for Windows. With this program, an investigator can generate an MD5 checksum for any file. It also generates a unique signature for each input file. The investigator can then use the MD5 checksum to check file integrity. Figure 4-28 shows the main screen of ChaosMD5.

Tool: Secure Hash Signature Generator

Secure Hash Signature Generator generates hash signatures for the data stored on a disk drive. An investigator can use these signatures to verify data integrity. The tool is compatible with PATA, SATA, and SCSI drives. It generates MD5 (128-bit signature), SHA1 (160-bit signature), and CRC32 (32-bit signature) hashes.

Figure 4-28   Users can enter text or a file name in ChaosMD5, and it will computer the MD5 checksum.

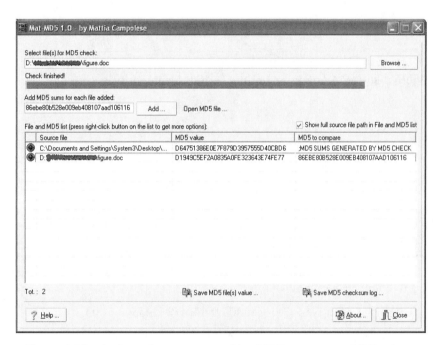

Figure 4-29   An investigator can use Mat-MD5 to compare MD5 values.

Tool: Mat-MD5

Mat-MD5 allows an investigator to check the MD5 hash for a file and compare that hash with other MD5 strings. It processes one or more files and adds the resulting MD5 value to a list. The investigator can then compare that value to any other value in the list. Figure 4-29 shows a screenshot from Mat-MD5.

Tool: MD5 Checksum Verifier

MD5 Checksum Verifier uses MD5 to check the integrity of files. With it, an investigator can create MD5 checksums to verify the files' integrity at a later time. Figure 4-30 shows a screenshot MD5 Checksum Verifier.

Recycle Bin

Forensic investigators are aware of the old adage that when a file is deleted, it is not really gone. This is especially true with the advent of the Recycle Bin on the Windows desktop. The Recycle Bin allows user to retrieve and restore files that have been deleted. A user can open the Recycle Bin, select files that have been thrown away, and restore them to their previous locations.

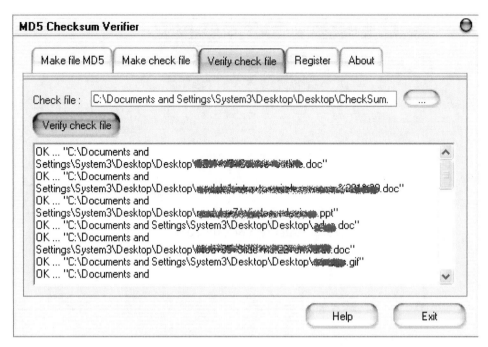

Figure 4-30   MD5 Checksum Verifier verifies file integrity.

When a user selects a file on the desktop or through Windows Explorer and deletes it—it is not really gone. The file is simply moved to the Recycle Bin, which appears by default in the file structure as the Recycler directory at the root of each drive. In many cases, this directory can provide a significant amount of information relevant to an investigation.

As a user on a system begins to delete files through the shell, a subdirectory is created for that user within the Recycler directory; that subdirectory is named with the user's security identifier, or SID. For example, the subdirectory will look something like this:

C:\RECYCLER\S-1-5-21-1454471165-630328440-725345543-1003

When an investigator opens the Recycle Bin from the desktop, the current user's subdirectory is automatically opened for view. Files sent to the Recycle Bin are maintained according to a specific naming convention. When a file is moved to the Recycle Bin, it is renamed using the following convention:

D<original drive letter of file><#>.<original extension>

Prefetch Files

For boot prefetching, the Cache Manager monitors hard page faults and soft page faults that occur during the boot process. It monitors through the first 2 minutes of the boot process, the first minute after all Windows services have started, or the first 30 seconds following the start of the user's shell, whichever comes first. The fault data is processed along with references to files and directories that are accessed, which ultimately allows all this data to be accessed from a single directory rather than requiring that data be retrieved from different files and directories scattered across the hard drive. This, in turn, decreases the amount of time required to boot the system.

During application prefetching, the Cache Manager monitors the first 10 seconds after a process is started. Prefetching is controlled by the following registry key:

HKEY_LOCAL_MACHINE\SYSTEM\ControlSet00x\Control\Session Manager\Memory Management\ PrefetchParameters

Shortcut Files

Shortcuts are files with the extension .lnk that are created and are accessed by users. Users can create shortcuts to applications, documents, folders, removable storage devices, and network shares. Shortcuts can provide information about files (or network shares) that a user has accessed. They also provide information about devices that the user might have attached to the system.

AccessData's Forensic Toolkit (FTK), Windows File Analyzer (WFA), and EnCase provide the ability to parse the contents of shortcut files to reveal information embedded within the files.

Word Documents

Word documents are compound documents, based on Object Linking and Embedding (OLE) technology that defines the file structure. Besides formatting information, Word documents can contain quite a bit of additional information that is not visible to the user, depending on the user's view of the document.

Word documents can maintain not only past revisions but also a list of up to the last 10 authors to edit the file. This has posed an information disclosure risk to individuals and organizations. An investigator can use the Perl scripts wmd.pl and oledmp.pl to list the OLE streams embedded in a Word document.

PDF Documents

Portable document format (PDF) files can also contain metadata such as the name of the author, the date that the file was created, and the application used to create the PDF file. Often, the metadata can show that the PDF file was created on a Mac or that the PDF file was created by converting a Word document to PDF format. As with Word documents, this metadata can pose a risk of information disclosure.

An investigator can use the Perl scripts pdfmeta.pl and pdfdmp.pl to extract metadata from PDF files. The only difference between the two scripts is that they use different Perl modules to interact with the PDF files.

Graphics Files

The metadata present in a JPEG image file depends largely on the application that created or modified it. For example, digital cameras embed exchangeable image file format (Exif) information in images, which can include the model and manufacturer of the camera, and can even store thumbnails or audio information (Exif uses the TIFF image file directory format). Applications such as Adobe's Photoshop have their own set of metadata that they add to JPEG files.

Tools such as Exifer, IrfanView, and the Image::MetaData::JPEG Perl module allow an investigator to view, retrieve, and in some cases modify the metadata embedded in JPEG image files.

File Signature Analysis

An investigator can analyze files with unusual extensions or files with familiar extensions that are in unusual locations with the help of file signature analysis. This technique helps an investigator to determine the nature of these files and to gain some insight into an attacker's technical abilities. File signature analysis involves collecting information from the first 20 bytes of a file and looking for a specific signature or "magic number" that will tell the investigator the type and function of the file. Different file types have different signatures, and these signatures are independent of the file extension.

Forensic analysis tools such as ProDiscover allow an investigator to readily perform file signature analysis and easily view the results. When such tools perform the analysis, they get the file's extension and compare the signature associated with that extension to the information contained in the first 20 bytes of the file.

NTFS Alternate Data Streams

An NTFS alternate data stream (ADS) is a feature of the NTFS file system. ADSs were added to the file system to support the Hierarchal File System (HFS) used by the Macintosh. HFS employs resource forks so that the file system can maintain metadata about the file, such as icons, menus, or dialog boxes.

Creating ADSs

The simplest way to create an ADS is to type the following command:

notepad myfile.txt:ads.txt

Add some text to the Notepad window, save the file, and then close Notepad.
Another way to create an ADS is to use the echo command:

echo "This is another ADS test file" > myfile.txt:ads2.txt

Typing **dir** or viewing the contents of the directory in Windows Explorer will show that the file will be zero bytes in size.

Yet another way to create an ADS is to use the type command to copy another file into the ADS:

type c:\windows\system32\sol.exe > myfile.txt:ads3.exe

ADSs can be added to directory listings as well, using the following syntax:

echo "This is an ADS attached to a directory" > :ads.txt

Enumerating ADSs

Vista allows a user to enumerate ADSs with dir using the /r switch. Lads.exe is another tool that a user can use to list ADSs and can be run against any directory.

Removing ADSs

One way to remove an ADS is to simply delete the file to which the ADS is attached. Another option is to copy the file to a non-NTFS media like a partition formatted in FAT, FAT32, or some other file system.

Executable File Analysis

Executable file analysis is a process of gathering information from an executable file. It is classified into two types as follows:

- *Static analysis*: Static analysis is a process that consists of collecting information about and from an executable file without actually running or launching the file in any way.
- *Dynamic analysis*: Dynamic analysis involves launching an executable file in a controlled and monitored environment so that its effects on a system can be observed and documented.

Documentation Before Analysis

The following is some of the documentation that an investigator should prepare before performing executable file analysis:

- Full path and location of the file
- MAC time stamp
- Operating system and version
- File system
- User accounts
- IP address
- Any references to that file within the file system or registry
- Who found the file and when

Static Analysis Process

The procedure for the static analysis process is as follows:

1. Scan the suspicious file with antivirus software like Norton, AVG, or McAfee.
2. Search for strings.

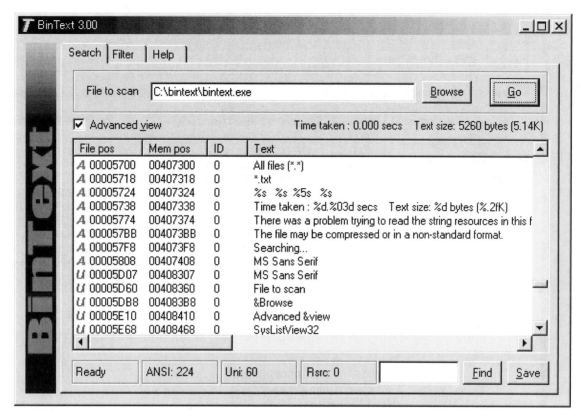

Figure 4-31   BinText displays all the text strings present in a file.

3. Analyze PE header.
4. Analyze import tables.
5. Analyze export table.

Search for Strings

To search for strings, an investigator can run suspicious files through tools such as Strings and BinText to extract all ASCII and Unicode strings of a specific length. This will help the investigator get an idea of the file's nature from the strings within the file. Figure 4-31 shows a screenshot from BinText.

PE Header Analysis

File signatures of a portable executable (PE) file consist of a 64-byte structure called the IMAGE_DOS_HEADER. The last DWORD (e_lfanew) value refers to the address of the new EXE file. This value is defined in the ntimage.h header file. The e_lfanew value points to the location of the PE header. An investigator can use the PEview tool to view the PE header. Figure 4-32 shows a screenshot from PEview.

Import Table Analysis

Information about DLLs and the functions accessed by an executable is maintained in the import table and the import address table of the executable file.

An investigator can use tools such as PEDump and Dependency Walker to access the import table information. He or she can identify the import data directory and parse the structures to determine the DLLs and their functions. The tools also allow the investigator to gather networking code from the import table of the DLLs.

Export Table Analysis

Executable files can import the functions provided by DLLs. DLLs maintain a table of functions available, called an export table. An investigator can collect information about chained or cascading DLL dependencies using PEDump or Dependency Walker. Figure 4-33 shows a screenshot from Dependency Walker.

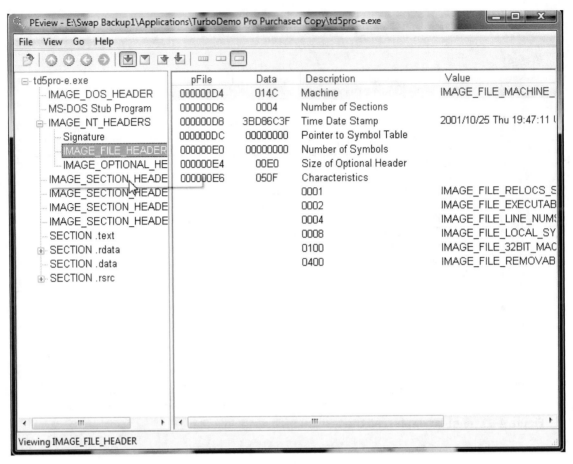

Figure 4-32 An investigator can use PEview to view a file's PE header.

Dynamic Analysis Process

The procedure for the dynamic analysis process is as follows:

- Create a testing environment.
- Use virtualization tools such as Bochs, Parallels, Microsoft's Virtual PC, Virtual Iron, and VMware.
- Start the process of testing the executable.

Creating a Test Environment

The procedure to create a test environment is as follows:

- Run the executables to be tested on a different system than the victim system.
- Do not connect the test system to the victim system through the network.
- Reinstall the operating system after each test.
- Work on a virtual platform.

Collecting Information Using Tools

An investigator can gather network connectivity information using different tools as follows:

- Use network sniffer tools to gather network connectivity information. This will help the investigator know whether the executable is making attempts to communicate to a remote system or to open a port to listen for connections.
- Record TCP and UDP port activity using the Port Reporter tool.
- Use the Process Monitor tool to see files and registry keys that were created or modified, and to view a timeline of activity.

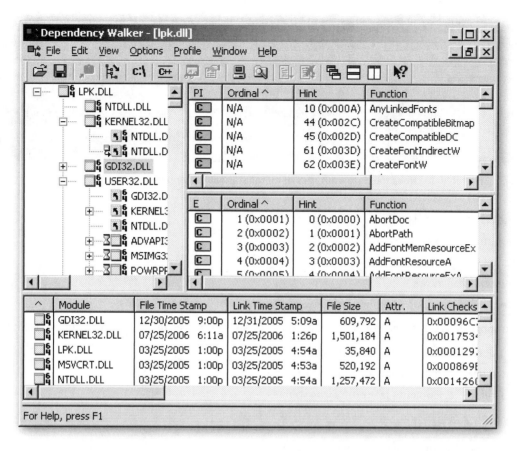

Figure 4-33 An investigator can use Dependency Walker to see what functions are exported in a DLL.

Dynamic Analysis Steps

The steps for actually performing dynamic analysis are as follows:

1. Ensure that all monitoring tools are updated.
2. Ensure that all monitoring tools are configured properly.
3. Create a log storage location.
4. Prepare the executable to be analyzed.
5. Launch baseline phase of snapshot tools.
6. Enable real-time monitoring tools.
7. Launch the executable.
8. Stop real-time monitoring tools and save the data.
9. Launch second phase of snapshot tools and save the data.

Metadata

Metadata is data about data, or more simply, embedded electronic data not necessarily seen on a printed document. It describes various characteristics of data, including when and by whom it was created, accessed, or modified. Because it is not normally seen, users can inadvertently share confidential information when sending or providing files in electronic form.

The following are some examples of metadata:

- Organization name
- Author name
- Computer name
- Network name

Type	Description	Sample Element
Descriptive metadata	Describes and identifies information resources	Unique identifiers, physical attributes, bibliographic attributes
Structural metadata	Provides information about the internal structure of resources	Tags such as title page, table of contents, chapters, parts, errata, index
Administrative metadata	Includes technical data on creation and quality control	Resolution, bit depth, color space, file format, compression, light source, owner, copyright date, copying and distribution limitations

Table 4-5   This table describes the different types of metadata that can appear in a file

- Hidden text or cells
- Document versions
- Template information
- Personalized views
- Nonvisible portions of embedded OLE objects

It is important for investigator to collect metadata, as it provides information about the following:

- Hidden information about the document
- Who tried to hide, delete, or obscure the data
- Correlated documents from different sources

Types of Metadata

Table 4-5 describes the different types of metadata.

Metadata in Different File Systems

The most commonly known metadata about files on Windows systems are the file MAC times; MAC stands for *modified, accessed, and created*. The MAC times are time stamps that refer to the time at which the file was last modified in some way (data was either added to the file or removed from it), last accessed (when the file was last opened), and when the file was originally created.

On the FAT file system, times are stored based on the local time of the computer system, whereas the NTFS file system stores MAC times in Coordinated Universal Time (UTC) format, which is analogous to Greenwich Mean Time (GMT).

Another aspect of file and directory MAC times that an investigator is interested in is the way the time stamps are displayed, based on various move and copy actions.

The following is how time stamps are displayed and changed in the FAT16 file system:

- When a file is copied from one folder to another on the same file system, the file keeps the same modification date, but the creation date is updated to the current date and time.
- When a file is moved from one folder to another on the same file system, the file keeps the same modification and creation dates.
- When a file is copied from a FAT16 partition to an NTFS partition, the file keeps the same modification date, but the creation date is updated to the current date and time.
- When a file is moved from a FAT16 partition to an NTFS partition, the file keeps the same modification and creation dates.

The following is how time stamps are displayed and changed in the NTFS file system:

- When a file is copied from one folder to another on the same file system, the file keeps the same modification date, but the creation date is updated to the current date and time.
- When a file is moved from one folder to another on the same file system, the file keeps the same modification and creation dates.

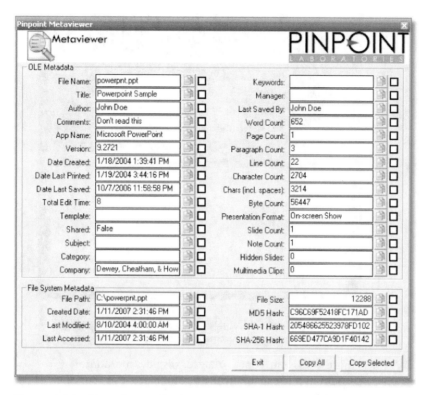

Figure 4-34   Metaviewer displays metadata present in Microsoft Office files.

Viewing Metadata

- An investigator can view some metadata by using the application that created the file. For instance, the investigator can look at the file properties in Microsoft Office or the document properties in Adobe Acrobat.

  In some cases, an investigator has to use other tools to display the metadata. The following are some of the tools investigators can use:

- Metaviewer
- Metadata Analyzer
- iScrub

Tool: Metaviewer

Metaviewer is a utility that integrates into Windows Explorer as a shell extension. It provides access to Microsoft Office metadata and hash values. Figure 4-34 shows a screenshot from Metaviewer.

Tool: Metadata Analyzer

Metadata Analyzer is a tool that analyzes Microsoft Office documents and alerts the user of any private information disclosure. Figure 4-35 shows a screenshot from Metadata Analyzer.

Tool: iScrub

The iScrub tool allows a user to view and manage metadata in documents. The user can capture the metadata and see whether it poses a security risk. The user can then also use the tool to remove any metadata from a file. Figure 4-36 shows a screenshot from iScrub.

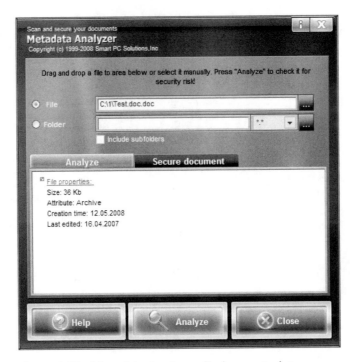

Figure 4-35   Metadata Analyzer displays metadata present in Microsoft Office files and alerts the user of any potential information disclosure.

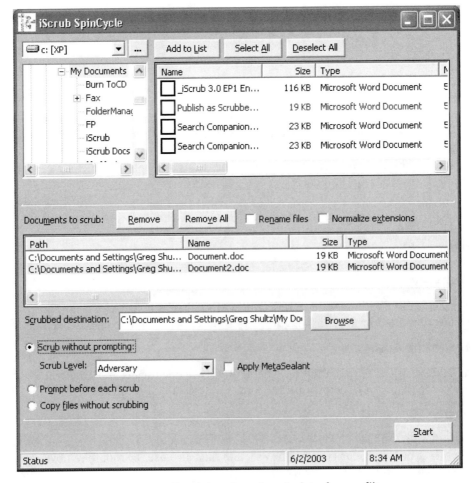

Figure 4-36   A user can use iScrub to wipe all metadata from a file.

Chapter Summary

- During a live response, an investigator should first collect the volatile information or any other information that can change or be lost.
- Several registry values and settings can impact forensic analysis.
- Analyzing the contents of RAM can help an investigator discover what has been hidden.
- Some tools allow an investigator to dump the contents of process memory without stopping the process.
- Registry analysis provides more information to the investigator during a live response.
- The logs generated by the Web server are used for the exploitation of attacks.

Review Questions

1. What kinds of volatile information can an investigator get from a system?

2. What kinds of nonvolatile information can an investigator get from a system?

3. Why is it important for an investigator to capture volatile information first during an investigation?

4. What is the function of a network sniffer?

5. What is the purpose of a browser cache?

6. What are cookies?

7. What is an MRU list?

8. What is metadata and how is it used in Windows files?

9. What is the difference between static analysis and dynamic analysis of an executable file?

10. Describe the MD5 algorithm.

_____

_____

_____

Hands-On Projects

1. Perform the following steps:

   ▪ Navigate to Chapter 4 of the Student Resource Center.

   ▪ Open a command shell.

   ▪ Type **pmdump -list**.

   ▪ Select a process ID.

   ▪ Type **pmdump <pid> myproc.txt**. (Replace <pid> with your selected process ID.)

   ▪ View the myproc.txt file in Wordpad, Notepad, or some other text editor.

2. Perform the following steps:

   ▪ Navigate to Chapter 4 of the Student Resource Center.

   ▪ Install and launch the IE History Viewer program.

   ▪ Display the list of URLs you have visited in the last few days.

3. Perform the following steps:

   ▪ Navigate to Chapter 4 of the Student Resource Center.

   ▪ Install and launch the ChaosMD5 program.

   ▪ Select **File** and click on the browse icon.

   ▪ Choose a file to generate a checksum for and click **Generate MD5**.

   ▪ Select **Text**.

   ▪ Enter some text and click **Generate MD5**.

Chapter 5

Windows Forensics II

Objectives

After completing this chapter, you should be able to:

- Understand event logs
- Understand other audit events
- Understand forensic analysis of event logs
- Understand Windows password issues
- Describe some popular Windows forensic analysis tools

Key Terms

Dynamic Host Configuration Protocol (DHCP)   a service provided by a server in which the server assigns a client machine an IP address upon request

Event   any occurrence that the operating system or a program wants to keep track of or alert the user about

Extensible Markup Language (XML)   a general-purpose specification for markup programming languages that allows the user to define specific elements to aid in sharing structured data among different types of computers with different operating systems and applications

Password cracking   the process of taking a password hash and attempting to determine the associated password that generated that password hash

Introduction to Windows Forensics, Part II

This chapter continues the study of Windows forensics. It starts by covering events and event logs. It then discusses password and authentication issues. The chapter ends with descriptions of various popular Windows forensic tools.

Understanding Events

Whenever an event, such as a user logging on or off, occurs, the operating system logs the event. An *event* can be any occurrence that the operating system or a program wants to keep track of or alert the user about. Some events are recorded by default; others are recorded based on the audit configuration maintained in the PolAdEvt registry key.

Other aspects of event log configuration are maintained in the following registry key:

HKEY_LOCAL_MACHINE\SYSTEM\CurrentControlSet\Services\Eventlog\<Event Log>

Systems that are configured as domain controllers also have File Replication and Directory Service event logs, and systems configured as domain name servers (DNS) also have DNS event logs.

Table 5-1 shows the different types of logon events on a Windows system.

Event Log File Format

The Windows event log (for Windows 2000, XP, and 2003) is stored in a binary format with distinct, recognizable features that can assist an investigator in recognizing and interpreting event log files or simply event records on a system, either in files or located in unallocated space. Each event log consists of a header section and a series of event records. The event log is maintained as a circular buffer, so as new event records are added to the file, older event records are cycled out of the file.

Event Log Header

The event log header is contained in the first 48 bytes of a valid event log file. The event log header consists of 12 distinct DWORD values, nine of which are described in Table 5-2.

The magic number, which appears as "eLfL" in ASCII, is unique to the Windows event log (for Windows 2000, XP, and 2003) and is associated with event records. Microsoft refers to this value as the ELF_LOG_SIGNATURE.

Logon Type	Title	Description
2	Interactive	Indicates that the user logged in at the console
3	Network	Indicates that a user/computer logged into this computer from the network, such as via **net use**, accessing a network share, or a successful **net view** directed at a network share
4	Batch	Reserved for applications that run as batches
5	Service	Service logon
6	Proxy	Not supported
7	Unlock	Indicates that the user unlocked the workstation
8	NetworkClearText	Indicates that a user logged onto a network, and the user's credentials were passed in an unencrypted form
9	NewCredentials	Indicates that a process or thread cloned its current token but specified new credentials for outbound connections
10	RemoteInteractive	Indicates a logon using Terminal Services or a Remote Desktop connection
11	CachedInteractive	Indicates that a user logged onto the computer with credentials that were stored locally on the computer
12	CachedRemoteInteractive	Same as RemoteInteractive; used internally for auditing purposes
13	CachedUnlock	Indicates the logon attempt is to unlock a workstation

Table 5-1   The event logging system keeps track of different types of logon events

Event Record Structure

The basic header for an event record is 56 bytes, slightly larger than the event log header. Although the record size provided in the event record is larger than 56 bytes, the first 56 bytes of the event record constitute an event record header. The event log magic number appears in the second DWORD value of the event record, just as it does for the header.

Details of the content of the first 56 bytes of an event record are shown in Table 5-3.

Having the event record structure definition also makes it possible to reassemble partial event records found in unallocated space. Using the magic number as a guide, an analyst can search through unallocated space. Even if the entire event record is not available, the first 56 bytes provide a road map for reconstructing portions of an event record.

Offset	Size	Description
0	4 bytes	Size of the record, which is always 0x30 (48) bytes
4	4 bytes	Magic number (0x654c664c, or "eLfL" in ASCII)
16	4 bytes	Offset within the event file of the oldest event record
20	4 bytes	Offset within the event file to the next event record to be written
24	4 bytes	ID of the next event record
28	4 bytes	ID of the oldest event record
32	4 bytes	Maximum size of the event file (from the registry)
40	4 bytes	Retention time of event records (from the registry)
44	4 bytes	Size of the record (repeat of DWORD at offset 0)

Table 5-2   The event log header consists of 12 DWORD values, nine of which are listed here

Offset	Size	Description
0	4 bytes	Size of the record in bytes
4	4 bytes	Reserved; magic number
8	4 bytes	Record number
12	4 bytes	Time generated; measured in UNIX time, or the number of seconds elapsed since 00:00:00 1 Jan 1970, in Universal Coordinated Time (UTC)
16	4 bytes	Time written; measured in UNIX time, or the number of seconds elapsed since 00:00:00 1 Jan 1970, in Universal Coordinated Time (UTC)
20	4 bytes	Event ID, which is specific to the event source and uniquely identifies the event; the event ID is used along with the source name to locate the appropriate description string within the message file for the event source
24	2 bytes	Event type (0x01 = Error; 0x10 = Failure; 0x08 = Success; 0x04 = Information; 0x02 = Warning)
26	2 bytes	Number of strings
28	2 bytes	Event category
30	2 bytes	Reserved flags
32	4 bytes	Closing record number
36	4 bytes	String offset; offset to the description strings within this event record
40	4 bytes	Size of the user SID in bytes (if 0, no user SID is provided)
44	4 bytes	Offset to the user SID within this event record
48	4 bytes	Length of the binary data associated with this event record
52	4 bytes	Offset to the data

Table 5-3   The event record header is a 56-byte structure

Vista Event Logs

Vista uses an XML format for storing events, and it supports central collection of event records. *XML* is a general-purpose specification for markup programming languages that allows the user to define specific elements to aid in sharing structured data among different types of computers with different operating systems and applications. Vista has a wide range of categories under which different events can be logged. Tools have been developed for parsing through Vista event logs, and incident responders and forensics analysts use those tools.

On a live Vista system, the wevtutil command retrieves information about the Windows event log that is not readily apparent via the Event Viewer. For example, the following command (Figure 5-1) displays a list of the available event logs on the system:

wevtutil el

An investigator can use the following command (Figure 5-2) to list configuration information about a specific event log, including the file name and path to the file:

wevtutil gl <log name>

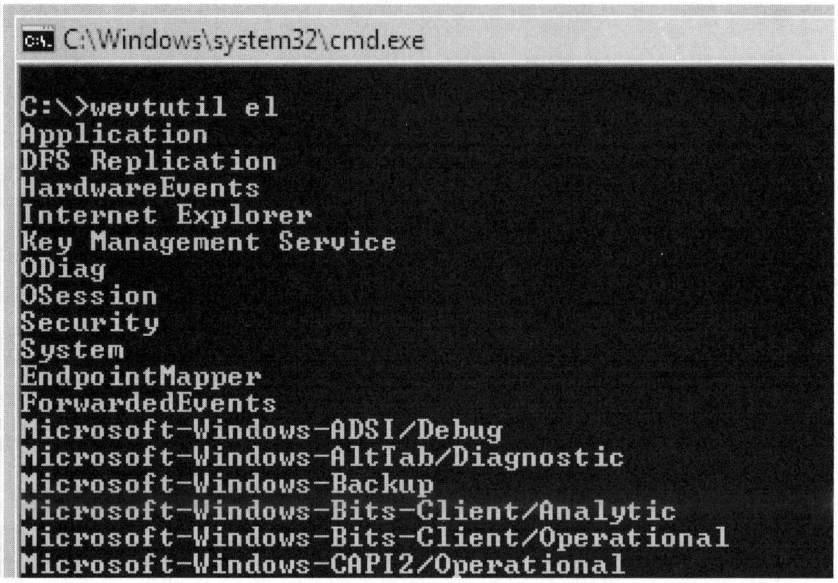

Figure 5-1   An investigator can list all the event logs available using wevtutil.

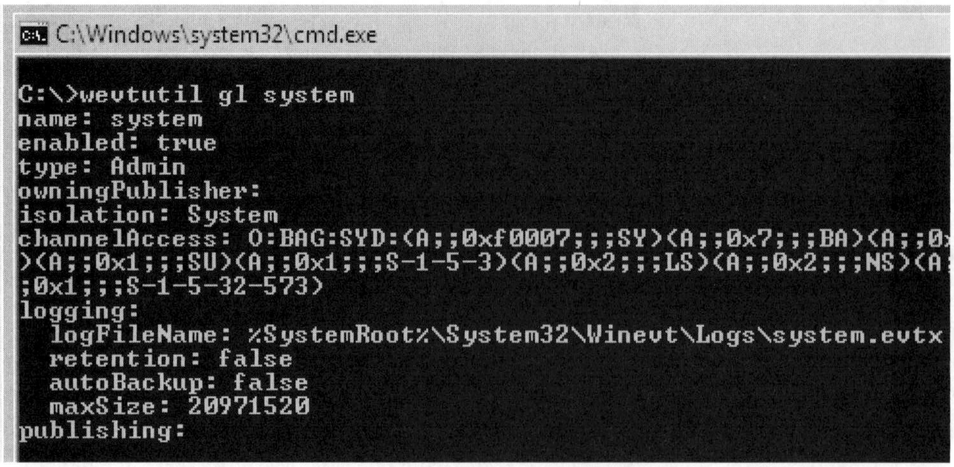

Figure 5-2   An investigator can view configuration information about specific event logs using wevtutil.

Information displayed by this command is also available in the following registry key on a Vista system:

HKEY_LOCAL_MACHINE\System\ControlSet00x\Services\EventLog\log name

IIS Logs

Microsoft's Internet Information Server (IIS) is a popular Web server platform. One of the best ways to uncover attempts to compromise an IIS Web server or to view the details of a successful exploit is to examine the logs generated by the Web server. The IIS Web server logs are most often maintained in the %WinDir%\System32\ LogFiles directory. Each virtual server has its own subdirectory for log files, named for the server itself. The location of the logs is configurable by the administrator and can be modified to point to any location, even a shared drive. By default, the log files are in ASCII format, meaning that they are easily openable and searchable.

IIS Web server logs saved in ASCII format have a simple format, so it is a fairly simple task to use a scripting language to open the file, read each log entry in, one line at a time, and perform processing. IIS logs will generally have column headers located at the top of the file, or that information might be somewhere else in the file if the Web server was restarted. Using the column headers as a key, an investigator can parse each entry for relevant information, such as the request verb (GET, HEAD, or POST), the page requested, and the status or response code that was returned.

Parsing IIS Logs

Managing and configuring IIS through the IIS Management Console is possible only on a system that has IIS installed and running. At the Run window (**Start ->Run**), an investigator can type in either **iis.msc** or **inetmgr** to see the IIS console. Alternatively, the IIS console can be accessed through choosing **Start -> Control Panel -> Administrative Tools -> Internet Services Manager**.

There is a tab for the logging feature in the IIS Management Console. By default, logging is enabled and is configured to use the W3C Extended Log File Format setting. The logs can be optionally written in Microsoft IIS Log File Format or in a database format (ODBC Logging) and therefore managed in a database. In the **General Properties** tab, there is an option to set the time period for each log file. The default is one file per day.

The logs are stored in the format exyymmdd.log. The W3C Extended Log File Format setting will always create a log file that begins with a header that describes the version of IIS that created it, along with the date and time the log started (GMT) and the fields included in the log. Each field name is prefixed with letters that have the following meanings:

- c = client actions
- s = server actions
- cs = client-to-server actions
- sc = server-to-client actions

Table 5-4 describes the IIS log fields used in W3C Extended Log File Format.

Field Name	Description	Logged by Default
date	Date on which the activity occurred	Yes
time	Time at which the activity occurred, expressed in UTC (GMT)	Yes
c-ip	IP address of client making the request	Yes
cs-username	User name of the authenticated user who accessed the server; anonymous users are annotated by a hyphen	Yes
s-sitename	Internet service name and instance number that was serving the request	No
s-computername	Name of the server generating the log entry	No
s-ip	IP address of the server on which the log file was generated	Yes
s-port	Server port number that was used for the connection	Yes
cs-method	Action requested by the client; most often the GET method	Yes

Table 5-4   These are the fields in an IIS log

(continues)

Field Name	Description	Logged by Default
cs-uri-stem	Target of the client's action (default.htm, index.htm, etc.)	Yes
cs-uri-query	Query, if any, the client was requesting (used when sending data to a server-side script)	Yes
sc-status	HTTP status code sent by the server to the client	Yes
sc-win32-status	Windows status code returned by the server	No
sc-bytes	Number of bytes the server sent to the client	No
cs-bytes	Number of bytes the server received from the client	No
time-taken	Length of time the requested action took, expressed in milliseconds	No
cs-version	Protocol version (HTTP or FTP) the client used	No
cs-host	Host header name, if any	No
cs(User-Agent)	Browser type used by client	Yes
cs(Cookie)	Content of cookie (sent or received), if any	No
cs(Referrer)	Site last visited by user; this site provided a link to this current server	No
sc-substatus	Substatus error code	Yes

Table 5-4   **These are the fields in an IIS log** *continued*

Parsing IIS FTP Logs

An FTP (File Transfer Protocol) server sends and receives files using FTP. FTP servers keep detailed logs. FTP logs record the same fields that IIS Web logs do, except for the following:

- cs-uri-query
- cs-host
- cs(User-Agent)
- cs(Cookie)
- cs(Referrer)
- sc-substatus

Table 5-5 shows some of the FTP sc-status codes.

FTP server logging properties are available under the **Properties** button at the bottom of the default FTP Site properties dialog. FTP logs are stored in the following location:

%WinDir%\System32\LogFiles\MSFTPSVC1\exyymmdd.log

Parsing DHCP Server Logs

Dynamic Host Configuration Protocol (DHCP) is a service provided by a server in which the server assigns a client machine an IP address upon request. Microsoft server products (NT Server, Windows 2000 Server, and Windows Server 2003) all provide DHCP service if it is enabled and configured. The server provides the DHCP-assigned IP address for a period called a lease. When the lease expires, depending on the configuration, it can be terminated or renewed.

DHCP Service Activity Logs are created by the DHCP service and stored in the following location by default: %SystemRoot%\System32\DHCP. Logs are stored on a daily basis in the following format:

DhcpSrvLog-XXX.log

In this format, *XXX* is a series of three letters that represents the day of the week on which the log was created.

Table 5-6 describes the DHCP log format.

Error Code	Description
1xx	**Positive Preliminary Replies**
120	Service ready in *nnn* minutes
125	Data connection already open; transfer starting
150	File status okay; about to open data connection
2xx	**Positive Completion Replies**
202	Command not implemented-superfluous at this site
211	System status or system help reply
212	Directory status
213	File status
214	Help message
215	NAME system type, where NAME is an official system name from the list in the Assigned Numbers document
220	Service ready for new user
221	Service closing control connection; logged out if appropriate
225	Data connection open; no transfer in progress
226	Closing data connection; requested file action successful (example, file transfer and so on)
227	Entering passive mode
230	User logged in; proceed
250	Requested file action okay; completed
257	"PATHNAME" created
3xx	**Positive Intermediate Replies**
331	User name okay; need password
332	Need account for login
350	Requested file action pending further information
4xx	**Transient Negative Completion Replies**
421	Service not available; closing control connection
425	Cannot open data connection
426	Connection closed; transfer aborted
450	Requested file action not taken; file unavailable
451	Requested action aborted; local error in processing
452	Requested action not taken; insufficient storage space in system
5xx	**Permanent Negative Completion Replies**

Table 5-5 This describes some of the FTP sc-status codes

Field	Description
ID	DHCP server event ID code
Date	Date on which this record entry was logged by the DHCP service
Time	Time at which this record entry was logged by the DHCP service (stored in local system time zone)
Description	Description of this particular DHCP server event
IP Address	IP address leased to client
Host Name	Host name of the DHCP client to which the IP address is leased
MAC Address	Media access control address (MAC) used by the network interface card (NIC) of the client to which the IP address is leased

Table 5-6 This describes the information in a DHCP log

Parsing Windows Firewall Logs

When logging is enabled, Windows Firewall logs are stored in %SystemRoot%\pfirewall.log. It stores data in the file objects.data, which is located in %SystemRoot%\System32\wbem\Repository\FS\.

When investigators open the Windows Firewall log in a text editor, they will see a header at the top that describes the software and version, the time format, and the fields. Each field is separated from the preceding field with an ASCII space character, represented by the hexadecimal value 0x20; the first eight fields are of forensic significance.

Using the Microsoft Log Parser

Microsoft Log Parser is a powerful and versatile log-parsing tool that uses SQL-like queries. The following command gets all of the information from the System event log:

LogParser.exe -o:DATAGRID "select * from system"

Log Parser accepts three arguments. The first is the input type, specified by the -i switch. The second is the output type, specified by the -o switch. The third is the query, which is in quotation marks.

Figure 5-3 shows the output from the following command:

LogParser.exe -i:EVT -o:DATAGRID "select TimeGenerated, EventID, Message from system"

Evaluating Account Management Events

The account management category of events is used to record changes to accounts and group membership. This includes creation, deletion, and disabling of accounts; modifying which accounts belong to which groups; and account lockouts and reactivations. Various event IDs are associated with changes to accounts. An account can be a domain account or a local account, and can represent a user, computer, or service. Domain account events are recorded on domain controllers, and events related to local accounts are recorded on the local computer that holds the account. When an account is created, event ID 624 is recorded. This event shows the name of the newly created account, along with the name of the account that was used to create it. Another event ID, 642, gives information about changes to an account.

The description for an account creation or deletion event includes the following information:

- The first line of the description summarizes the type of action.
- The account that performed the action is listed in the Caller User Name field.

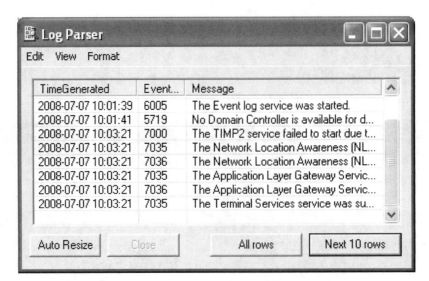

Figure 5-3   An investigator can feed SQL-like queries to Log Parser to get specific information about an event log.

Event ID	Action Indicated
632	Member added to global security group
633	Member removed from global security group
636	Member added to local security group
637	Member removed from local security group
650	Member added to local distribution group
651	Member removed from local distribution group
655	Member added to global distribution group
656	Member removed from global distribution group
660	Member added to universal security group
661	Member removed from universal security group
665	Member added to universal distribution group
666	Member removed from universal distribution group

Table 5-7   This table describes the different group membership event IDs

- The account added or removed is shown in the Member ID field.
- The group affected is listed as the Target Account Name.

Table 5-7 details group membership event IDs.

Interpreting File and Other Object-Access Events

The object-access audit category allows administrators to configure the event logs to record access to various objects on the system. Once auditing is configured, access attempts are recorded in the event logs using three different event IDs: 560, 567, and 562.

When a process needs access to some object, it first opens a handle to that object. A handle is simply a shorthand way of referring to an object, much like the handles used by CB radio operators. In the case of Windows objects, handles are simply numeric identifiers assigned to objects and used by a process to refer to those objects. If a user requests access to a file, some process will open a handle to that file. The file will receive a handle ID, and the process will refer to that file by its handle ID.

Examining Audit-Policy Change Events

When a system is compromised, attackers will frequently attempt to disable auditing. Modifications to the audit policy are recorded as event ID 612 entries. In the audit policy, the + symbols indicate which events are being audited, and the – symbols show which events are not being audited. An investigator can deduce what changes were made by looking at event ID 612 entries and comparing the old policy to the new policy.

The audit policy of the domain controller takes precedence over changes made to the local audit policy on an individual computer; because of this, attackers may not be able to completely disable auditing. If an attacker disables auditing on a computer that is a member of a domain, the domain's Group Policy audit settings may override that change during the next policy update.

Examining System Log Entries

The System event log records events relating to system behavior, including changes to the operating system, changes to the hardware configuration, device driver installation, the starting and stopping of services, and a host of other items of potential investigative interest.

Whenever a service is stopped, the Service Control Manager sends a stop signal to the service and simultaneously sends a message (event ID 7035) to the System event log, advising that the stop signal was sent to a particular service. When the service actually stops, the Service Control Manager sends a message (event ID 7036) to the System event log, advising that the service actually stopped.

Similarly, when a service is started, the Service Control Manager sends a start control signal to the service and simultaneously sends a message (event ID 7035) to the System event log, advising that the start control signal was sent. When the service starts, the Service Control Manager sends a message (event ID 7036) to the System event log, advising that the service actually started.

Examining Application Log Entries

The Application event log contains messages from both the operating system and various programs. All programs can send messages to the Application event log. The user can actually use a program from Microsoft called logevent.exe to send custom messages, typically when batch files are run. This program sends messages to event ID 1 of the Application log, by default, unless another event ID is specified.

Many utilities send messages to the Application log, especially antivirus and other system-protection programs. These security programs send messages relating to their scanning activities, the discovery of malware, and so on. Similar to the Windows Remote Desktop feature, Virtual Network Computing (VNC) allows remote connections. The VNC application records connections to the VNC server, with the IP and port from which the connection originated, in the Application log.

Using EnCase to Examine Windows Event Log Files

An investigator can use EnCase, a forensic tool suite from Guidance Software, to parse Windows event log files by means of an EnScript. The EnScript is provided in the Sweep Case series. There are several reasons why an investigator may opt to use EnCase for this task. First of all, an investigator may wish to keep the processed information within the forensic environment so it may be easily included within the forensic report generated by EnCase. Another more common reason is that EnCase does not rely on the Windows API to process the event logs, and therefore EnCase can process event logs that are reported as "corrupt" by those viewers that rely on the Windows API.

An investigator can use EnCase to locate event log files with its Conditions feature, which is, in essence, a filtering system. With the case mounted in EnCase, the investigator can go to the **Filter** pane (lower-right pane) and select the **Conditions** tab. In the Conditions tree, under **Files** -> **File Details**, the investigator then has to double-click **Search File Extension**.

In the resulting menu, the investigator then types **evt** in the top menu block where <expression> appears. After the investigator clicks **OK**, only files with the extension .evt will be displayed. In the **Table** pane, only the event log files will be visible, as is shown in Figure 5-4.

EnCase Windows Event Log Parser

The Windows Event Log Parser appears as an available module in the right pane of the **Sweep Case Options** dialog. To select it, an investigator places a checkmark in its check box. To see the options available in the Windows Event Log Parser, an investigator can double-click it in the right pane. The Windows Event Log parser can group the events together by any one of six options: Event, Created, Source, Computer, User, or Type. The default is by Event, which is suitable for most uses. Figure 5-5 shows a screenshot from the Windows Event Log Parser.

When the parser has completed its task, it will show bookmarks for each event, arranged in a hierarchical folder structure based on grouping selection, and will have the same results in a spreadsheet. Each event log file (Application, System, and Security) has its own folder. When the grouping is by Event (the default), a folder is created for each event ID, and all like events are grouped under the folder bearing its event ID.

Windows Event Log File Internals

The Windows event log files are, essentially, databases with the records related to the system, security, and applications stored in separate files named SysEvent.evt, SecEvent.evt, and AppEvent.evt, respectively. They are stored in the %SystemRoot%\system32\config folder.

Each of the event log file databases is similarly constructed. Each file has a header, a floating footer of sorts, and records. Database slack exists in the logical portion of the file but is located outside the database proper. To keep the files from becoming fragmented, the operating system may allocate large contiguous cluster runs to the event log files.

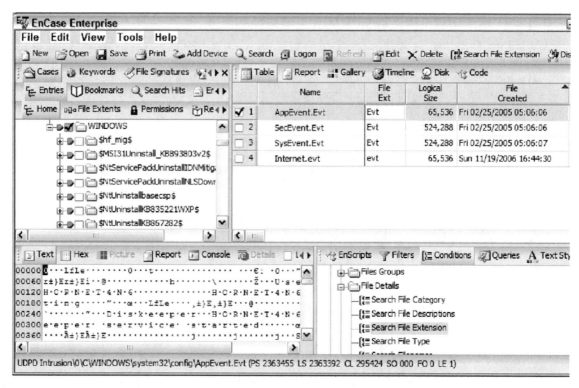

Figure 5-4 EnCase allows an investigator to find the event log files on a system.

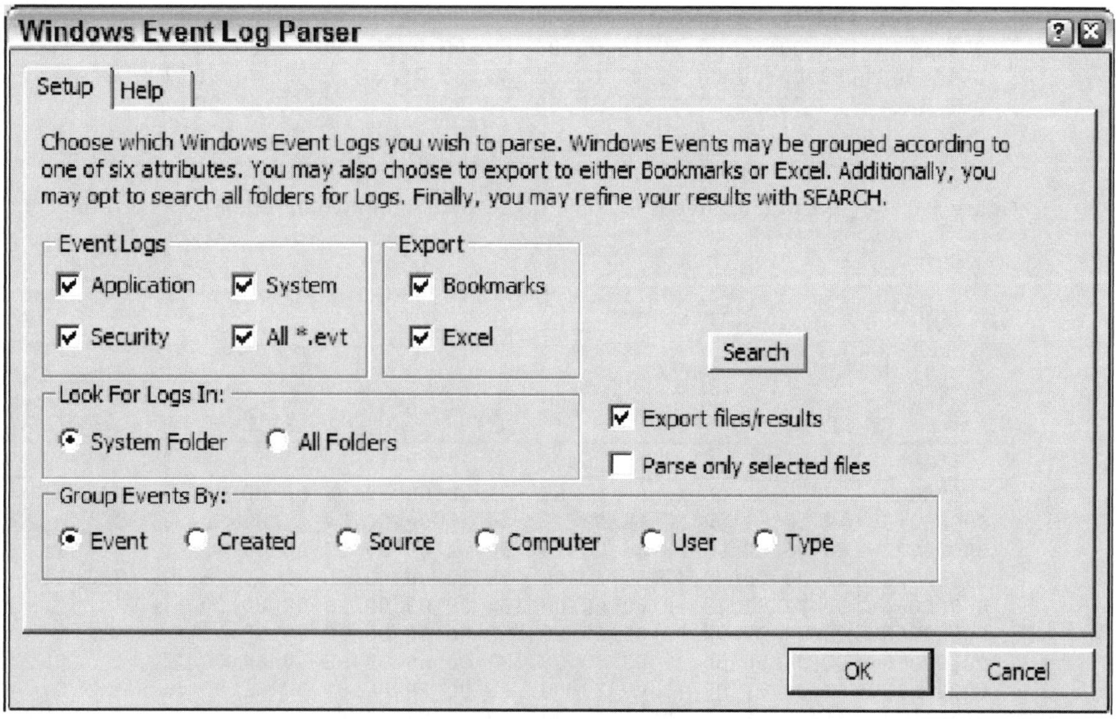

Figure 5-5 An investigator can choose which event logs to parse and how to group those events in Windows Event Log Parser.

Repairing Corrupted Event Log Databases

A Windows event log file will be reported as corrupt when the four critical fields appearing in both the header and the floating footer are out of sync, and when the file status byte is a value other than 0x00 or 0x08.

If a file is reported as corrupt, an investigator can use a hex editor to repair the file status byte. The investigator can look at byte offset 36 and change the value there from its current value to 0x08.

The next step in the repair process is to synchronize the four critical fields in the header with the current values found in the floating footer. To find the floating footer, an investigator can search for the hex string 0x11111111. After locating the floating footer, the investigator needs to locate the byte that immediately follows the string 0x28000000111111112222222233333333444444444. The byte that follows this string is the first byte in the 16-byte string making up the four critical fields (the offset to the oldest event, the offset for the next event, the next event ID number, and the oldest event ID number). The investigator needs to highlight this 16-byte string and copy its hex values (Figure 5-6).

After copying the 16-byte hex string to the clipboard, the investigator needs to paste the 16-byte string into byte offsets 16–31 in the header (Figure 5-7).

After saving the modifications, the investigator can then reopen Windows Event Viewer and open the repaired file without any error (Figure 5-8).

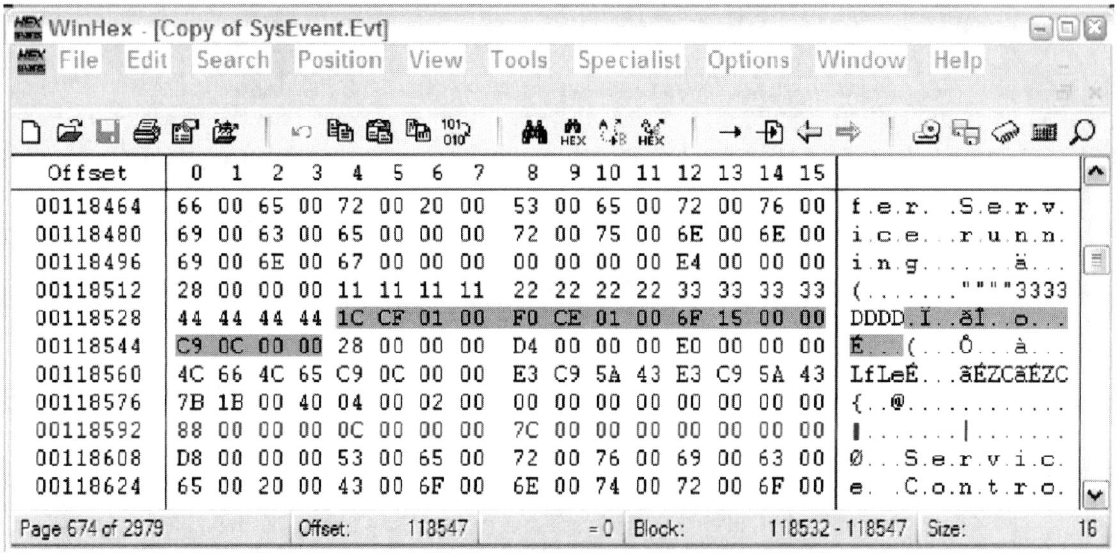

Figure 5-6 An investigator needs to copy this 16-byte string when repairing a corrupt event log.

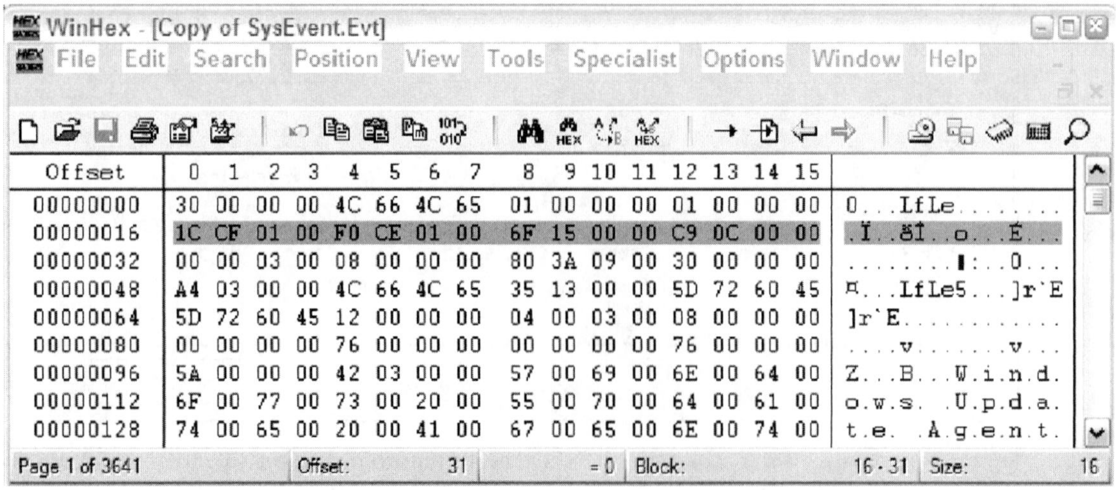

Figure 5-7 The investigator needs to paste the 16-byte string here to repair the event log.

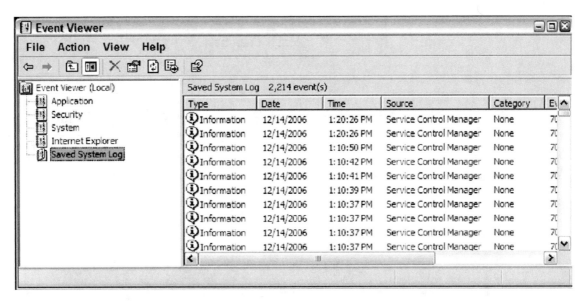

Figure 5-8 The investigator can view the repaired event log in Event Viewer.

Understanding Windows Password Storage

Windows systems store their user and password data in one of two places: the Security Account Manager (SAM) file or Active Directory. Information about local accounts is stored on the local computer's SAM file, which is located in the %SystemRoot%\System32\Config folder; this file exists as a registry hive file. An additional copy of this file may be found in the %SystemRoot%\Repair folder for use by system-recovery utilities in the event the working copy becomes corrupted. The file may also be found in Windows NT Rescue floppy disks that administrators sometimes create for use in repairing damaged systems. Information regarding domain accounts is stored on each domain controller in Active Directory. The Active Directory database information resides on the domain controller in a file called ntds.dit, which is located in the %SystemRoot%\ntds directory.

Hashing Passwords

Windows does not store passwords in plain text. A password is run through a specific algorithm that converts the password into a numeric value. This value, called the hash value or simply the hash of the password, is then stored in lieu of the actual password. Hashing algorithms (also called hash functions) are in a group of algorithms called one-way functions. The algorithm is designed such that whenever a particular password is used as the input to the function, it will always generate the same hash value, and the likelihood of two separate passwords generating the same hash value is low. The hash function is considered one-way because while the same password can be used to consistently generate the same hash value, the resulting hash value cannot be used to determine the original password, as is shown in Figure 5-9. The user first selects a password; the system runs the password through a hash function and calculates the resulting hash value. The system then records the resulting hash value along with the account name in the SAM or ntds.dit file. When a user attempts to authenticate using that account name, the system takes the password that the user provides during the authentication attempt, runs it through the hash function, and compares the resulting hash value to the hash value stored in the password file. If the two are the same, the authentication proceeds. If the two are different, the authentication fails.

Windows Hash Functions

Modern Windows operating systems mainly use two different hash functions and store two different hash values for each password entered. One hash function, called the NT LanMan (NTLM) hash, is a fairly secure hash function and is used in most authentication attempts. The second hash function, called the LanMan (LM) hash, is an older implementation that is less secure. The LanMan hash is still stored for backward-compatibility purposes, so that pre–Windows NT systems can be used to authenticate more current Windows systems.

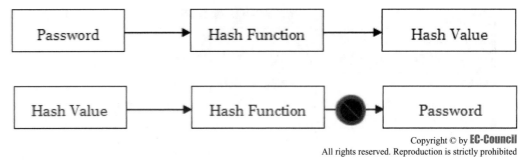

Figure 5-9 In a one-way hash function, the hash value cannot be used to generate the original password.

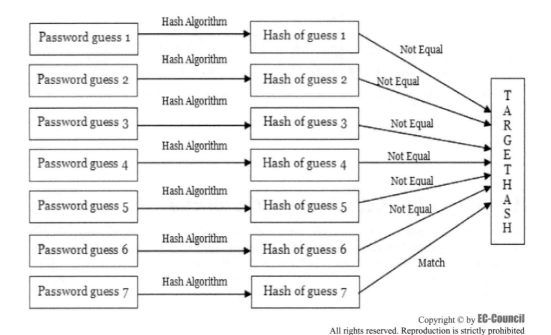

Figure 5-10 An attacker goes through an iterative guessing process until the two hashes match.

Cracking Windows Passwords Stored on Running Systems

The term *password cracking* refers to the process of taking a password hash and attempting to determine the associated password that generated that password hash. The attacker simply guesses what the password may have been. He or she then runs that guess through whatever password-hashing algorithm is used by the target system. The attacker compares the password hash generated by hashing the guess to the password hash that he or she is trying to crack. If the two match, then the guess was correct. If the two do not match, then the guess was incorrect. The more guesses the attacker makes, the greater his or her odds of correctly guessing the password. The process therefore consists of multiple iterations of the following:

1. Guess a possible password.

2. Generate a password hash of the guess using the same hashing algorithm used by the target system.

3. Compare the hash of the guess to the hash of the target account's password.

4. If the two match, the guess was the original password. If the two do not match, start over.

Attackers will utilize a dictionary of possible passwords to facilitate the password-cracking process. The attacker will hash each entry in the dictionary, comparing the resulting hash of each entry to the hash of the password the attacker is trying to crack. Figure 5-10 depicts this process.

Exploring Windows Authentication Mechanisms

When a user logs on to a local computer, the local security subsystem asks the user for a username and password, and the user can enter that information directly into the local computer via the keyboard. When a user is accessing a remote system from across a network connection, the user must have some other mechanism to provide the username and password to the remote computer. The challenge in doing so is to find a way to send that data across the network while minimizing the chance that an attacker who is monitoring the network communication (via a sniffer, for example) would be able to learn the username/password combination. Windows systems use one of three main types of authentication mechanisms to access remote computers: LanMan authentication, NTLM authentication, and Kerberos.

LanMan Authentication

LanMan (LM) authentication is a process that relies on a hash to determine whether a remote user has provided a valid username/password combination. Although a LanMan authentication relies on the LanMan hash, the LanMan hash is never actually sent across the network during an authentication session. The hash itself is considered too sensitive to be sent in clear text over the network. Instead, LanMan authentication uses a fairly simple process to try to protect the LanMan hash value from disclosure to an attacker who may be monitoring the communication, while still making an accurate authentication decision based on the username/password combination provided by the remote user.

Details of the Process

When a user on one computer wishes to authenticate to a remote system (such as when a user tries to map a network drive to another machine, or when he or she tries to access files on a remote share), the user must provide a username and password. The username is sent along with the request to authenticate to the remote machine. In response to this request, the server sends back an 8-byte challenge. The client computer then encrypts the challenge with a key that is based on the LanMan hash of the user's password and sends the encrypted response back to the server (Figure 5-11).

The server machine contains a copy of the user's LanMan hash in its SAM file. The client machine can calculate the appropriate LanMan hash by asking the user to input his or her password and then running the LanMan hash algorithm against that password. The LanMan hash then serves as a shared secret between the two computers, with each knowing the value of the password's LanMan hash. The client encrypts the challenge using the LanMan hash and sends the response. The server then uses its copy of the LanMan hash to independently encrypt the original challenge. If the response sent back from the client matches the encrypted challenge as calculated by the server, then both computers know the LanMan hash for the user's account, and the authentication succeeds.

Attack Methods

A replay attack occurs when an attacker copies the authentication message as it crosses the wire and then resends that message at a later date to impersonate the user. Since the encrypted response is based on an 8-byte challenge, a replay attack is successful only if the challenge issued by the server is the same during the recorded session as it is during the attempted replay.

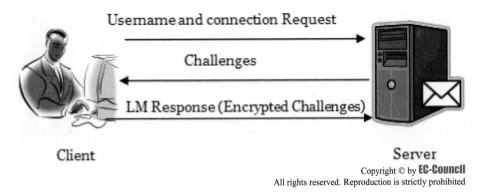

Figure 5-11   The actual LanMan hash is never sent over the network in the LanMan authentication technique.

By providing both the challenge and the encrypted reply to that challenge, the process is vulnerable to a known plain-text attack. In this type of attack, the attacker knows both the encrypted form of a communication (the encrypted LM authentication response) and the original message that was encrypted (the 8-byte challenge issued by the server). This provides the attacker with three parts of a four-part equation.

If an attacker is monitoring the network and captures the authentication message as it passes on the wire, the attacker knows the original message (the challenge), the resulting encrypted message (the response), and the algorithm used to perform the encryption, but still does not know the key that was used to perform the encryption. The LanMan authentication mechanism starts to break down when the complexity (or lack thereof) of its key is examined.

NTLM and Kerberos Authentication

Considering the flaws in the LanMan authentication mechanism, Microsoft developed the New Technology LanMan (NTLM) authentication mechanism. This mechanism is more secure than its predecessor, and attackers do not target it as frequently.

When the NTLM hash is calculated from the original password, it is calculated across the entire case-sensitive password, resulting in a 16-byte hash. The hash is created using the MD4 hash algorithm. This algorithm does not suffer from many of the weaknesses of the LanMan hashing algorithm, since it does not require truncating or padding the password to 14 characters, nor does it split up the password into discreet units. These changes make the NTLM password less susceptible to brute-force cracking. In order to attempt to crack the NTLM authentication exchange, the attacker must guess all possible passwords, trying each password to see if the resulting 21-byte NTLM authentication key can be used to encrypt the server's challenge to produce the client's 24-byte response. Other cryptographic attacks are possible to determine the NTLM hash, but these do not yield any more information about what the original password may have been.

The main problem with the NTLM authentication mechanism is that when a client uses the NTLM authentication, the client also sends the LanMan hash as part of the authentication communication, just in case the server needs it for backward compatibility with other software. Therefore, when NTLM is used for authentication, the LanMan hash is normally also provided, and attackers will choose to focus on the LanMan response, since it is much easier to crack.

Figure 5-12 depicts the NTLM authentication method.

Microsoft also created another version of NTLM authentication, called NTLM version 2 (NTLMv2), with the release of Windows NT Server 4.0 Service Pack 4. It is a more secure algorithm that provides bidirectional authentication and uses a much more complicated authentication mechanism.

Kerberos

The Kerberos authentication mechanism is a secure option available to Windows computers. The Microsoft implementation of Kerberos still uses the NTLM hash as a starting point for identifying that a user knows the correct password, but the Kerberos process is much more robust than LM, NTLM, or NTLMv2. Kerberos relies on a system of security, or access, tickets that are issued by computers designated as ticket-granting authorities. When a user wishes to access a particular remote resource, the user's computer must obtain an appropriate access ticket from the ticket-granting authority (in Windows networks, this is normally a domain controller). Before the ticket-granting authority will issue the ticket, a Kerberos authentication must take place in which the

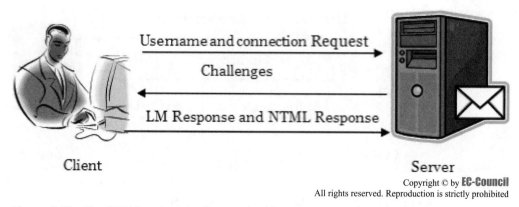

Figure 5-12 The NTLM authentication method is more secure than the LanMan method.

requesting client provides appropriate proof that it knows the correct username/password combination. Once the authentication exchange is complete, an access ticket for the requested resource is issued. This ticket contains information about the computer that made the request, the account that is authorized access, the specific resource that may be accessed, any limitations on the access that should be granted to that resource, and the time duration during which the ticket is valid. Once the ticket is obtained, it can be presented to the desired remote resource, and access will be granted accordingly.

In Kerberos, verification of the user's identity takes place between the domain controller and the client. The file server abdicates any responsibility and makes its authentication decision based solely on the service ticket. Kerberos uses a series of time stamps and cryptographic keys to verify the authenticity of security tickets, resulting in a secure system. The Kerberos system is far more robust and more complex than the LanMan and NTLM systems.

Sniffing and Cracking Windows Authentication Exchanges

Although any authentication mechanism can theoretically be compromised, attackers will generally focus on the weakest link. While Kerberos authentication exchanges are subject to attack, these attacks are much less likely to be successful in a reasonable period of time than attacks against LanMan or even NTLM authentication.

It is important to understand when authentication is carried out between two Windows systems. An authentication takes places whenever a process on one system attempts to access a resource on another system. An example would be when a user attempts to map a network drive to another system, or to access shared files on another system. In the same way, if a program attempts to make such an access without an overt request from a user (such as an automated backup routine attempting to place backups of files onto a remote file server), then the program's process must authenticate to the remote system. This involves providing both an account name and its associated password through one of the authentication mechanisms described in the previous section. When a process needs to access a remote system, it will attempt to authenticate to the remote system by providing the credentials for the account whose security context it is using. No overt action (such as manually typing in a username or password) is necessarily needed.

When the user selects a share existing on another system, his or her computer will automatically attempt to authenticate to the remote system by using the current user's account name and password information to perform a LanMan, NTLM, or Kerberos authentication. This happens immediately and without a prompt to the user.

Sniffing

Although this feature ensures quick and easy access to remote resources, it does have the potential to provide sensitive information to attackers. If a user can be tricked into performing an action that causes his or her computer to attempt to access a remote resource, then the client computer will automatically attempt to authenticate to that remote system. If an attacker controls that remote system, or if the attacker is able to monitor communication between the victim system and the remote system, then the attacker can potentially sniff the authentication attempt and use it to crack the user's password. Armed with the username and password, the attacker can then return to the victim computer at a later date and successfully log on to it using the victim's account. Since a currently logged-on user does not need to manually enter the username and password for subsequent remote authentication attempts, the victim may be totally unaware of the attack.

Cain and Abel

One tool that is useful for an attacker in the scenario described previously is Cain, along with its companion product, Abel. Cain has many different capabilities; among them is a network sniffer that is designed to look for passwords exchanged during various types of authentication exchanges. Cain also has a built-in password cracker that is capable of cracking many different types of passwords and can use rainbow tables to facilitate rapid precomputed hash attacks. Cain's sniffer is even able to use ARP cache-poisoning techniques to defeat the segregation of traffic normally found within a switched network to set up a man-in-the-middle attack and allow sniffing of traffic that the compromised host would not normally receive. Abel acts as a remote sensor for Cain. By installing Abel on a compromised computer, an attacker can use that computer to sniff traffic, sending the results back to a different computer for cracking. This allows the attacker to remotely control the Abel sensor while analyzing the sniffed data from his or her own workstation.

Investigators must thoroughly analyze compromised machines for evidence of what type of malicious software (malware) may have been installed on them and analyze logs to determine what actions may have been taken by that computer to further compromise the security of the network.

Cracking Offline Passwords

Certain tools can extract password data from the SAM files of computers so that an attacker can then feed the data into a password cracker such as RainbowCrack.

A frequent use of such a technique is to defeat the Windows Encrypting File System (EFS). EFS allows data to be stored on a disk in an encrypted format automatically without manual action by the user. Files with the encrypted attribute selected are encrypted before being stored. When the user who created the file attempts to open it, the data is automatically decrypted. If the data is attacked forensically when the system is powered off, the encryption defeats attempts at analysis by rendering the data unintelligible. Early versions of EFS were designed to allow the administrator to override the encryption as a data-recovery agent. On such systems, the user could simply change the administrator's password using any of a number of Linux-based boot disks that allow manual manipulation of the SAM, log in as the administrator, and decrypt the files. Starting with Windows XP, Microsoft has prevented this tactic by making the password a part of the key that encrypts the data. By manually overwriting the password, the user would render all of the encrypted files irretrievable.

One way to recover files encrypted with EFS is to crack the passwords of the users' accounts, make a duplicate working copy of the target hard drive, boot the computer using the working copy of the drive (not the original), log in as the appropriate user, and view the file. Alternatively, if the image is made using EnCase with the Physical Disk Emulator module and VMware, the image itself can simply be booted as a virtual machine. An open-source tool called Live View enables the booting of dd-style images within the free VMware Server product, resulting in a no-cost solution. This whole process can be accomplished with minimal effort.

Tool: Helix

Helix is a customized distribution of the Knoppix Live Linux CD. An investigator can boot into a customized Linux environment that includes customized Linux kernels, hardware detection, and many applications dedicated to incident response and forensics.

Helix is designed not to touch the host computer in any way, and it is forensically sound. It will not automatically mount swap space or any attached devices. It focuses on incident response and forensics tools.

Tools Present on Helix CD for Windows Forensics

The following are the tools present on the Helix CD for Windows forensics:

- Windows Forensics Toolchest (WFT)
- Incident Response Collection Report (IRCR2)
- First Responder's Evidence Disk (FRED)
- First Responder Utility (FRU)
- Security Reports (SecReport)
- MD5 Generator
- Command Shell
- File Recovery
- Rootkit Revealer
- VNC Server
- Putty SSH
- Screen Capture
- Messenger Password
- Mail Password Viewer
- Protected Storage Viewer
- Network Password Viewer
- Registry Viewer
- Asterisk Logger
- IE History Viewer

- IE Cookie Viewer
- Mozilla Cookie Viewer

Figures 5-13, 5-14, and 5-15 show screenshots from Helix.

Figure 5-13   Helix provides a variety of different forensic tools.

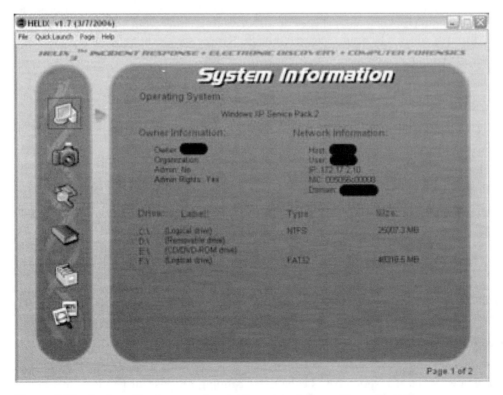

Figure 5-14   An investigator can view basic system information with Helix.

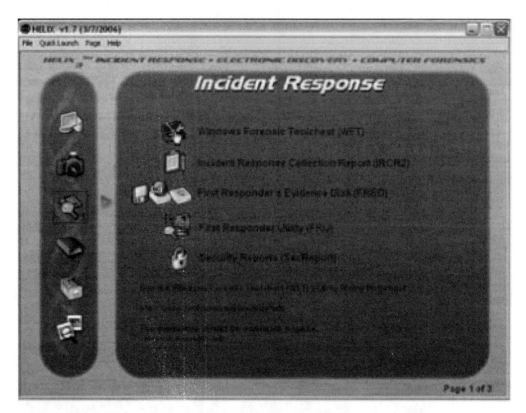

Figure 5-15   Helix provides a forensic investigator with incident response tools.

Helix Tool: SecReport

SecReport comprises two command-line utilities: SecReport collects security information from a Windows-based system, and Delta compares the results of SecReport, either from any two systems or from the same system at two different times. The report generated by SecReport shows the following information:

- Network configuration
- Audit policy
- Event log configuration
- Services
- Applications
- Hotfixes
- Ports open
- Page file settings
- Hardware
- Processors
- Fixed disks

Helix provides the investigator with a graphical front end for the application. Reports should be stored on removable media to prevent contamination of the suspect's system.

Helix Tool: Windows Forensics Toolchest (WFT)

The Windows Forensics Toolchest (WFT) collects security information from a Windows system and provides an automated incident response. It is capable of running other security tools. It produces reports in HTML format.

```
"S:\MyCVSwork\Programs\wft2\code\Release\wft.exe" -noslow -dst c:\wft_out -drive 5 -cfg ..\make...   _ |□| ×|

[WFT]

01:22:37: Reporting 'index.htm'    (md5=3B1B9AE3E60264F04B4D8DD04D07A6B3)
                    'wft_main.htm'  (md5=28CA94C5C43114103A59F84D16855D2E)
                    'wft_info.htm'  (md5=CE40725E9C8165A7F9704AC8C0CAAC14)
                    'wft_log.htm'   (md5=F9CA8ADD0E409EB7C69583640D11A0D6)
                    'wft_cfg.htm'   (md5=7B578805A1443C42592286ED65AC6ED0)

===============================================================
01:22:37: [RUN COMPLETE]
===============================================================
===============================================================
Windows Forensic Toolchest (WFT) v2.0.B5
Copyright (C) 2003-2005 Monty McDougal.  All rights reserved.
http://www.foolmoon.net/security/
===============================================================

Record any checksum(s) below to later verify log integrity

wft_log.txt (md5=D10BA4663695922568501FB086B301D9)
wft_log.htm (md5=5045948747F27DF929E809B8CE1D7F08)

Press any key to continue
```

Figure 5-16   WFT generates MD5 checksums for all of the logs it creates.

WFT is designed to produce output that is useful to the user, but is also appropriate for use in court proceedings. It provides extensive logging of all its actions, along with computing MD5 checksums along the way to ensure that its output is verifiable, as shown in Figure 5-16. It provides a simplified way of scripting incident responses, using a sound methodology for data collection.

It runs from a CD to ensure the forensic integrity of the evidence it collects. In addition to the WFT binary, the CD also must contain any external programs WFT needs. The CD must also include a trusted command shell to ensure that it is used in a forensically sound manner.

Tool: Sigverif

Sigverif is a built-in Windows tool that searches for unsigned drivers on a system. To look for unsigned drivers using Sigverif, an investigator should perform the following steps:

1. Click **Start**, click **Run**, type **sigverif**, and then click **OK**.

2. Click the **Advanced** button.

3. Click **Look for other files that are not digitally signed**.

4. Navigate to the Winnt\System32\Drivers folder, and then click **OK**.

After Sigverif is finished running its check, a list of all unsigned drivers installed on the computer is displayed. The investigator can find the list of all signed and unsigned drivers found by Sigverif in the Sigverif.txt file in the %Windir% folder, typically the Winnt or Windows folder.

Tool: Word Extractor

Word Extractor is a hacking tool that extracts human-understandable words from binary computer files. A hacker could use this tool to try to find hidden text or passwords in a file.

The following are some of the features of Word Extractor:

• Replaces nonhuman words with spaces or dots for better visibility

• Supports drag and drop and text wrapping

• Saves results as text or RTF files

Figure 5-17 shows a screenshot from Word Extractor.

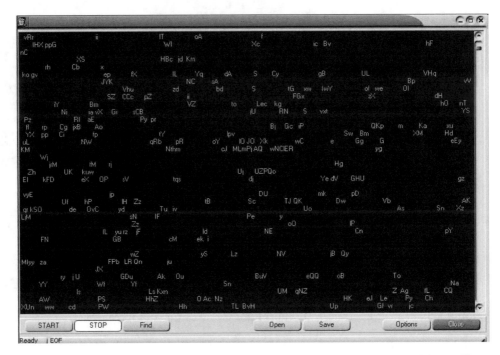

Figure 5-17   Word Extractor shows the human-readable text present in a binary file.

Registry ...	Name	Type	Data	Key Modified Ti...	Data Length
HKLM\HARD...	00000000	REG_BINARY	44 53 44 54 9F ...	8/17/2006 10:5...	17,311
HKLM\HARD...	00000000	REG_BINARY	46 41 43 53 40 ...	8/17/2006 10:5...	64
HKLM\HARD...	00000000	REG_BINARY	46 41 43 50 84 ...	8/17/2006 10:5...	132
HKLM\HARD...	00000000	REG_BINARY	52 53 44 54 34 ...	8/17/2006 10:5...	52
HKLM\HARD...	Component Inf...	REG_BINARY	00 00 00 00 00 ...	8/17/2006 10:5...	16
HKLM\HARD...	Identifier	REG_SZ	AT/AT COMPAT...	8/17/2006 10:5...	17
HKLM\HARD...	Configuration D...	REG_FULL_RES...		8/17/2006 10:5...	84
HKLM\HARD...	SystemBiosDate	REG_SZ	01/27/06	8/17/2006 10:5...	9
HKLM\HARD...	SystemBiosVers...	REG_MULTI_SZ	HP-CPC - 1000...	8/17/2006 10:5...	90
HKLM\HARD...	BootArchitecture	REG_DWORD	0x00000003 (3)	8/17/2006 10:5...	4
HKLM\HARD...	PreferredProfile	REG_DWORD	0x00000000 (0)	8/17/2006 10:5...	4
HKLM\HARD...	Capabilities	REG_DWORD	0x000001a5 (4...	8/17/2006 10:5...	4
HKLM\HARD...	VideoBiosDate	REG_SZ	05/09/08	8/17/2006 10:5...	9
HKLM\HARD...	Component Inf...	REG_BINARY	00 00 00 00 00 ...	8/17/2006 10:5...	16
HKLM\HARD...	Identifier	REG_SZ	x86 Family 15 ...	8/17/2006 10:5...	33
HKLM\HARD...	Configuration D...	REG_FULL_RES...		8/17/2006 10:5...	16
HKLM\HARD...	ProcessorName...	REG_SZ	Intel(R...	8/17/2006 10:5...	48
HKLM\HARD...	VendorIdentifier	REG_SZ	GenuineIntel	8/17/2006 10:5...	13
HKLM\HARD...	FeatureSet	REG_DWORD	0xa0073fff (26...	8/17/2006 10:5...	4
HKLM\HARD...	~MHz	REG_DWORD	0x00000b74 (2...	8/17/2006 10:5...	4
HKLM\HARD...	Update Signature	REG_BINARY	00 00 00 00 03	8/17/2006 10:5	8

10000 item(s), 1 Selected

Figure 5-18   RegScanner shows all of its search results in one list.

Tool: RegScanner

RegScanner scans the registry to find values that match a given set of criteria. It can find registry values by keyword, data length, value type, and modified date. RegScanner then displays all the values in a list and allows the user to double-click on these values to jump to the value in RegEdit. The user can also export the registry values to a file that RegEdit can read. Figure 5-18 shows a screenshot from RegScanner.

Tool: PMDump

PMDump is a tool that dumps the memory contents of a process to a file without stopping the process. PMDump stands for Post-Mortem Dump. An investigator can save the dump information to a secondary storage medium like magnetic tape or disk.

Tool: System Scanner

System Scanner extracts information about processes, including the IDs of all the threads and handles to DLLs, and provides the ability to suspend specific threads of a specific process and to view a process's virtual memory.

When a user starts System Scanner, he or she is shown all the processes currently running on the system, the number of threads per process, and the executable path of each process. The list is updated every five seconds by default, but this is configurable.

Right-clicking on any of the processes allows an investigator to get further information about the process (Figure 5-19). The investigator can also dump the process's virtual memory or view a visual map of it.

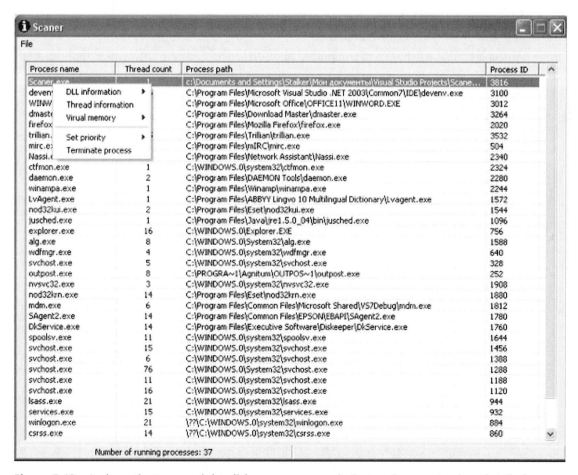

Figure 5-19   An investigator can right-click on any process in System Scanner to view detailed information about the resources the process is using.

Tool: X-Ways Forensics

X-Ways Forensics is a software tool that provides a forensic work environment. The following are some of the features of X-Ways Forensics:

- Disk cloning and imaging, including under DOS
- Examining the complete directory structure inside raw image files, even spanned over several segments
- Native support for FAT, NTFS, ext2, ext3, CDFS, and UDF
- Built-in interpretation of RAID 0 and RAID 5 systems and dynamic disks
- Viewing and dumping physical RAM and the virtual memory of running processes
- Various data recovery techniques and file carving
- Hard disk cleansing to produce forensically sterile media
- Gathering slack space, free space, interpartition space, and generic text from drives and images
- File and directory catalog creation for all computer media
- Easy detection of and access to NTFS alternate data streams (ADS)
- Mass hash calculation for files
- Powerful physical and logical search capabilities for many search terms at the same time
- Support for the file systems HFS, HFS+, ReiserFS, Reiser4, UFS, and UFS2
- Automated file signature check
- Write protection to ensure data authenticity
- Complete case management
- Automated activity logging (audit logs)
- Automated reports that can be imported and further processed by any other application that understands HTML
- Ability to associate comments about files for inclusion in the report or for filtering
- Ability to tag files and add them to customized report tables of notable items
- Dynamic filters based on true file type, hash set category, time stamps, file size, comments, report tables
- Recursive view of all existing and deleted files in all subdirectories
- Ability to copy files off an image or a drive
- Automatic identification of encrypted MS Office and PDF documents
- Ability to automatically find pictures embedded in documents
- Internal viewer for Windows registry files
- Internal viewer for Windows event log files
- Lists the contents of archives directly in the directory browser
- Indexing and searching in an index
- Skin color detection (e.g., a gallery view sorted by skin color percentage greatly accelerates a search for traces of child pornography)
- Detection of host-protected areas (HPAs)
- Supports user creation of hash sets
- Ability to read and write evidence files (.e01 images)
- Ability to create report tables of relevant files
- Ability to copy relevant files to evidence file containers, to pass on selected files to other investigators while retaining all metadata

Figure 5-20 shows a screenshot from X-Ways Forensics.

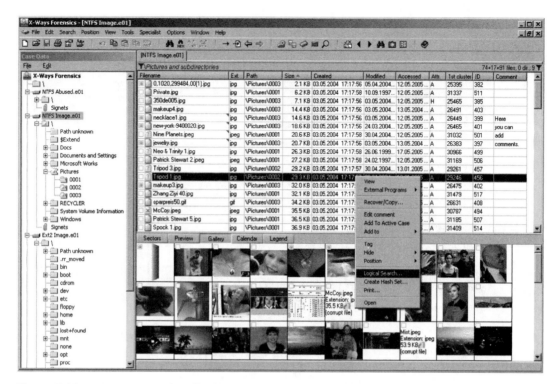

Figure 5-20   X-Ways Forensics allows an investigator to look at all graphics files on a system.

Tool: Traces Viewer

Traces Viewer allows an investigator to view all media files cached by Internet Explorer. It can also remove all Web traces made by Internet Explorer, including cookies, browsing history, and cache files (Figure 5-21).

Tool: PE Builder

PE Builder creates a bootable Windows CD-ROM that creates a BartPE (Bart Preinstalled Environment) that offers a complete Win32 environment with network support; a GUI; and FAT, NTFS, and CDFS support. An investigator can use this tool to perform analysis of a system that does not contain an operating system.

Tool: Ultimate Boot CD-ROM

The Ultimate Boot CD-ROM allows an investigator to run floppy-based diagnostic tools from CD-ROM drives without the need for an operating system. This tool has over 100 diagnostic and system management utilities. An investigator can modify NTFS volumes, restore deleted files, scan hard drives for viruses, create new NTFS volumes, and perform many other tasks.

The following are the types of tools included with the Ultimate Boot CD-ROM:

- CPU tester
- Memory tester
- Peripheral tools
- CPU information tools

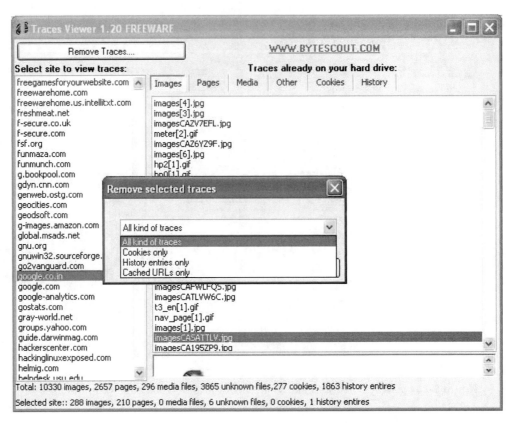

Figure 5-21 Traces Viewer can remove all Web traces, including cookies, history entries, and cached URLs.

- System information tools
- Benchmarking tools
- BIOS tools
- Hard disk installation tools
- Hard disk diagnostic tools
- Hard disk device management tools
- Hard disk wiping tools
- Hard disk cloning tools
- Hard disk low-level editing tools
- Hard disk partition tools
- Boot managers
- File tools
- NTFS tools
- Antivirus tools
- Network tools
- Boot disks

Figure 5-22 shows a screenshot from the Ultimate Boot CD-ROM.

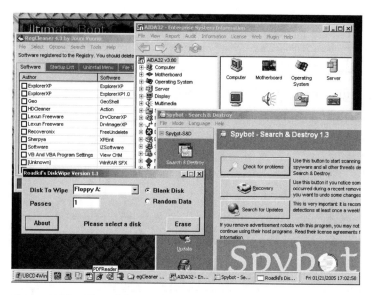

Figure 5-22   The Ultimate Boot CD-ROM includes many utilities that a forensic investigator may want to use.

Chapter Summary

- A DHCP server dynamically assigns IP addresses upon a client machine's request.
- Windows Firewall logs are stored in %SystemRoot%\pfirewall.log.
- Several registry values and settings could impact the forensic analysis.
- Modifications to audit policy are recorded as event ID 612 entries.
- The Application event log contains messages from the operating system and various programs.
- SAM files are located in the %SystemRoot%\System32\Config folder.
- Passwords are run through a specific hash algorithm and are stored as numeric values.

Review Questions

1. Describe the structure of the event log header.

_____

_____

2. Which fields are included in the IIS logs for a Web site but not for an FTP site?

_____

_____

3. What does an event ID 612 mean in regards to audit policy?

_____

_____

4. Describe the Kerberos authentication method.

_____

_____

5. Describe the functions of the Cain and Abel tools.

_____

_____

6. What is password cracking?

_____

_____

7. What types of event logs do domain controllers have that other systems do not?

_____

_____

8. What is the function of Word Extractor, and why would an attacker use this tool?

_____

_____

Hands-On Projects

1. Download the Helix tool SecReport and run it on your system to see the results.

2. Run Sigverif on your system and view the results.

3. Perform the following steps:

   - Navigate to Chapter 5 of the Student Resource Center.
   - Install and launch the Traces Viewer program.
   - Click on the **Images** tab (Figure 5-23).
   - Click on the **Pages** tab (Figure 5-24).
   - Click on the **Media** tab (Figure 5-25).
   - Click on the **Other** tab (Figure 5-26).
   - Click on the **Cookies** tab (Figure 5-27).

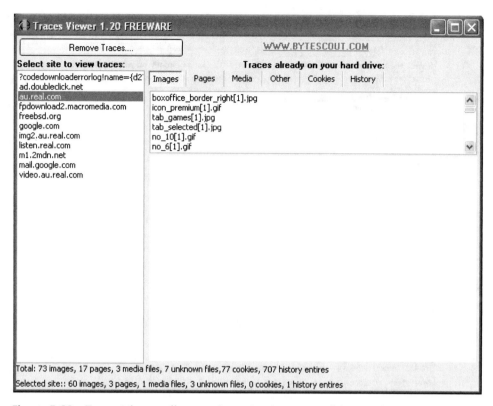

Figure 5-23 Traces Viewer allows an investigator to see all images included in the Web traces on a system.

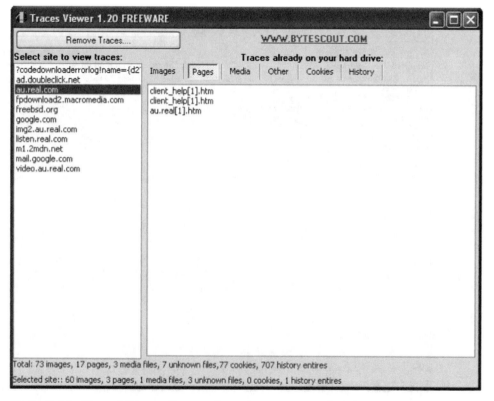

Figure 5-24 Traces Viewer allows an investigator to see all Web pages included in the Web traces on a system.

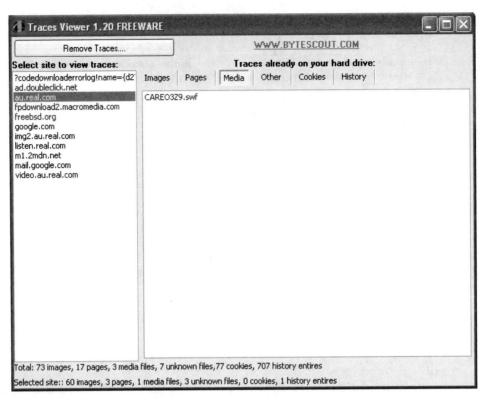

Figure 5-25 Traces Viewer allows an investigator to see all media included in the Web traces on a system.

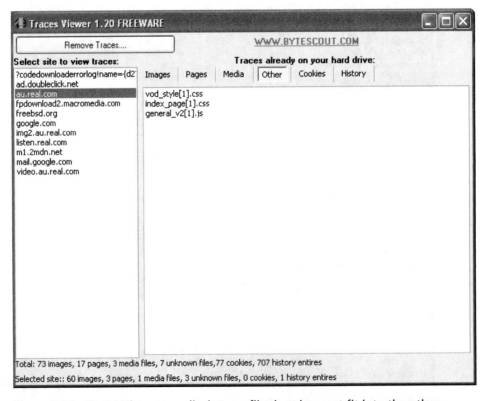

Figure 5-26 Traces Viewer can display any file that does not fit into the other categories.

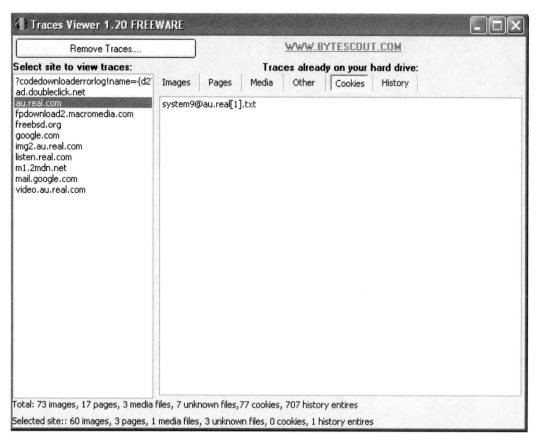

Figure 5-27   Traces Viewer allows an investigator to see all the cookies on a system.

Chapter 6

Linux Forensics

Objectives

After completing this chapter, you should be able to:

- Create a Linux forensic environment
- Analyze floppy disks
- Analyze hard disks
- Perform data collection using Toolkit
- Understand crash commands
- Take a step-by-step approach to a case
- Use Linux in forensics
- Describe Linux forensic tools

Key Terms

Live CD a bootable version of an operating system that is loaded directly into RAM and functions outside and independently of the target computer's operating system

Mounting the process of attaching a device to a directory

Mount point the directory where a device is attached

Introduction to Linux Forensics

Although not used as widely as Windows systems in forensic investigations, the Linux operating system can be very useful to a forensic investigator. This chapter will explain not only how to perform forensics with a Linux system as a target, but also why it can be beneficial to use a Linux system in other investigations.

Linux

Types of Linux Distributions

Linux is a free, UNIX-based, open-source operating system originally created by Linus Torvalds with the assistance of developers around the world. It comes in several different versions, called distributions, including Red Hat, SUSE, Debian, and Ubuntu. Each edition is unique, with its own particular strengths and weaknesses. There are three basic types of Linux distributions:

- Desktop distributions, which include a graphical interface and common applications, suitable for home use.
- Server or enterprise distributions that are used primarily for business applications, but can also be used as a home server.
- Live-CD distributions that are stored on bootable storage devices. A *Live CD* is a bootable version of an operating system that is loaded directly into RAM and functions outside and independently of the target computer's operating system.

Linux Boot Sequence

1. The first step in the bootup sequence for Linux is loading the kernel. The kernel image is usually contained in the /boot directory.
2. The soft link to the current kernel image is available in the /boot directory and is referenced by the Linux Loader (LILO) or, as has become more common, with GRUB. Details of the boot loader can be gained from LILO or GRUB using **more /etc/lilo.conf** or **more /etc/grub.conf**.
3. The third step is initialization. The file that controls initialization is /etc/inittab. The file that begins the process is /sbin/init. The run level and startup scripts are initialized, and the terminal process is controlled.

File System in Linux

Linux treats its devices as files, stored in /dev. Most Linux distributions share a basic directory structure, with files organized in the following directories:

- */bin*: Common commands
- */boot*: Files needed at boot time, including the kernel images that are pointed to by LILO or GRUB
- */usr*: Local software, libraries, games, etc.
- */var*: Logs and other variable files
- */dev*: Interface files that allow the kernel to interact with hardware and the file system
- */home*: Directories for each user on the system, containing user-specific personal and configuration files
- */mnt*: Mount points for external, remote, and removable file systems
- */etc*: Administrative configuration files and scripts
- */root*: The root-user home directory
- */sbin*: Administrative commands and process-control daemons
- */lib*: Basic system libraries
- */opt*: Optional and third-party software

In order to find system information, the following commands can be used:

- **uname -a**: returns the computer name and Linux version
- **ls -l**: returns the list of files in the current directory
- **ls -ul** [filename]: returns the access time of the file
- **netstat -s**: returns protocol information

UNIX and Linux use a tree, or hierarchical, structure for storing files and directories. In a UNIX disk structure, the topmost directory is the root directory and is denoted by a forward slash (/). A root directory has a number of directories, and these directories have subdirectories. A subdirectory is known as a child of the parent directory

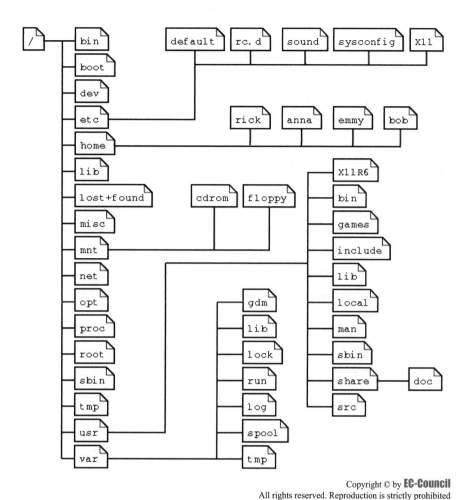

Figure 6-1   This is a typical Linux file structure.

from which it is branched. For example, in the directory /usr/game, /game is the child of /usr, and in turn, /usr is the parent of /game.

When a file system is created, a superblock is also created that keeps track of metadata including the type of file system, device block size, maximum file volume, name, and other information related to the file system. After the superblock, another important structure is the inode. An inode acts as an index of the file. Each node represents a file stored on the disk. Using the -I option with the ls command, a user can see the inode number of the file.

The second extended (ext2) file system is perhaps the most convenient Linux file system. It has improved algorithms and extra date stamps for last access, last inode modification, and last data modification. It can also track the state of the file system.

A typical Linux file system structure is shown in Figure 6-1.

Linux Forensics

Linux has a number of simple utilities for imaging and basic disk analysis, including the following:

- *dd*: Copies data from an input file or device to an output file or device
- *sfdisk* and *fdisk*: Determines the disk structure
- *grep*: Searches files for instances of an expression or pattern
- *md5sum* and *sha1sum*: Create and store an MD5 or SHA-1 hash of a file or list of files (including devices)
- *file*: Reads file header information in an attempt to ascertain its type, regardless of name or extension

- *xxd*: Command-line hex dump tool
- *ghex* and *khexedit*: Gnome and KDE (X Window interfaces) hex editors

Use of Linux as a Forensic Tool

Linux is often used in computer forensics for the following reasons:

- Greater control:
  - Treats every device as a file
  - Does not need a separate write blocker
- Flexibility:
  - Can be booted from a CD
  - Can recognize several file systems
- Power:
  - Distributions such as The Farmer's Boot CD and Sleuth make Linux a forensic tool in and of itself

Advantages of Linux in Forensics

There are several advantages of using Linux in forensic investigations, including the following:

- Software availability and accessibility:
  - Freely available software and source code
  - Tools can be closely analyzed
- Efficiency:
  - Allows for a good deal of automation and scripting
- Optimization and customization:
  - Software can be modified to fit special requirements
- Support:
  - Supports ad-hoc community
  - Uses open, published standards
  - Compatible across technologies and organizations

Disadvantages of Linux in Forensics

There are, of course, disadvantages to using Linux in forensics. Since the Linux operating system is very different from Windows or Mac OS, the investigator may need to be specially trained to use Linux. Also, because Linux is an open-source operating system, it is frequently updated. It takes time to implement these changes, which are never to be considered permanent or final.

Precautions During Investigation

During an investigation, an investigator has to be sure to follow these precautions:

- Avoid running programs on a compromised system.
- Do not run programs that will modify the metadata of files and directories.
- Write the results of the investigation to a remote location.
- Calculate the hash values of the data to avoid data alteration.

Recognizing Partitions in Linux

All file systems must be mounted before they can be used. Any file systems on partitions defined during installation are mounted automatically with each boot. Investigators should note that data can be written to devices, even when those devices are not mounted.

Simply mounting a file system does not protect it from being inadvertently changed, however. Linux recognizes storage peripherals as SCSI devices. If a standard IDE disk is being used, it will be referred to as *hda* if the disk is connected to the primary IDE controller as the master, and *hdb* if the disk is connected to the primary IDE controller as a slave device.

Similarly, IDE disks connected to the secondary IDE controller as master and slave will be referred to as *hdc* and *hdd*, respectively. To see a complete list of partitions available on a particular drive, the user can type **fdisk -l /dev/hd[a, b, c, or d]**.

Each partition is identified by its Linux name. The boot flag is indicated by an asterisk (*), and the output includes the beginning and ending cylinders for each partition. The number of blocks per partition is also displayed, as well as the partition ID and file system type.

Valid file types are displayed when fdisk is run with the -l option.

mount Command

Devices like floppies, CDs, and hard disk partitions must be attached to an existing directory on the system before being accessed. This process is called *mounting*, and the directory where the device is attached is called a *mount point*. After mounting the device, the files present on the device can be accessed by accessing the mount point. In order to remove the device, it must be unmounted before it is removed. During startup, the Linux operating system searches for the drives to be mounted, the privileges to be assigned to those drives, and the locations to mount them.

The mount command takes the device to be mounted, as well as the mounting point, as arguments. The mount point must be a directory that already exists on the system. For example, to mount the floppy drive a user enters the following command:

mount **/dev/fd0 /mnt/floppy**

When unmounting, the device must be specified to the unmount command as follows:

umount **/dev/fd0**

Another command to mount devices is **mount -t [type] [device] [directory]**, in which the kernel mounts the drive. For example, the following command mounts a USB drive:

mount **-t vfat /dev/ubb1 /home/user/pocketdrive**

Options with the mount command include the following:

- -a: Mounts all file systems in /etc/fstab (which do not contain the noauto option)
- -a **-t [type]**: Mounts all file systems of type [type] in /etc/fstab
- -a **-t no[type]**: Mounts all file systems except those of type [type] in /etc/fstab
- -a **-O [option]**: Mounts all file systems with option [option] specified in /etc/fstab
- -a **-O no[option]**: Mounts all file systems except those with option [option] specified in /etc/fstab
- -a **-F**: Mounts all file systems in /etc/fstab and forks a new mount instance for each
- -n: Does not write to /etc/mtab
- -f: Fake mount, performs everything but the actual mount; can be used to add /etc/mtab entries for devices previously mounted with the -n option
- -L **[label]**: Mounts the partition with label [label]
- -o **[option]**: Applies option [option]
- -r: Mounts file system read-only; same as -o ro
- -w: Mounts file system read-write; same as -o rw
- -l: Lists all mounted file systems
- -l **-t [type]**: Lists all mounted file systems of type [type]
- -v: Uses verbose mode
- -V: Shows version
- -h: Shows help
- --bind [dir] [newdir]: Mounts the device mounted on [dir] to [newdir] as well, making contents available from both locations
- --move [dir] [newdir]: Moves the file system mounted on [dir] to [newdir]

dd Command Options

The dd command is used to convert and copy a file. It reads the [InFile] parameter, converts it to the specified format and copies the data into the [OutFile] parameter. The syntax is as follows:

dd [bs=BlockSize] [cbs=BlockSize] [conv= [ascii | block | ebcdic | ibm | unblock] [lcase | ucase] [iblock] [noerror] [swab] [sync] [oblock] [notrunc] [count=InputBlocks] [files=InputFiles] [fskip=SkipEOFs] [ibs= InputBlockSize] [if=InFile] [obs=OutputBlockSize] [of=OutFile] [seek=RecordNumber] [skip=SkipInputBlocks] [span=yes|no]

Floppy Disk Analysis

When analyzing a floppy disk in Linux, an investigator should follow these steps:

1. Insert the floppy disk into the drive and obtain its SHA-1 hash.

2. Create an image of the floppy's contents.

   a. Use dd to create a forensic image and compare the SHA-1 hash of the image against that of the floppy by using the following commands:

      - dd if=/dev/fd0 of=/evidence/floppy1.img bs=512

      - sha1sum /evidence/floppy1.img >/evidence/floppy1img.sha1sum

      - cat /evidence/floppy1img.sha1sum

      - cat /evidence/floppy1.sha1sum

3. Identify the file system.

   a. Use the file utility to identify the file system of the floppy disk image by using the following command:

      - file /evidence/floppy1.img

4. Mount the image for analysis.

   a. Create a directory to mount the image.

   b. Use the mount utility to mount the image, using loopback, by using the following commands:

      - mkdir /mnt/analysis

      - mount -t vfat -o ro,noexec,loop /evidence/floppy1.img /mnt/analysis

      - umount /mnt/analysis

      - mount -o ro,noexec,loop /evidence/floppy1.img /mnt/analysis

5. Obtain an SHA-1 hash of the contents.

   a. Obtain an SHA-1 hash of each file on the floppy disk and check the files by using the following commands:

      - cd /mnt/analysis/mnt/analysis

      - find . -type f -exec sha1sum {}; >/evidence/floppy1img.sha1filehash /mnt/analysis

      - cat /evidence/floppy1img.sha1filehash
        da39a3ee5e6b4b0d3255bfef95601890afd80709 ./.ICEauthority
        9155df0f906411433388c335c902d0a7452c6a72 ./addressbook
        2406038ea5da9776c1f32ba3d7f0e84d0b3d2af9 ./crackdealers.d /mnt/analysis

6. View the file contents.

   a. Use the strings utility to extract raw text from a binary file by using the following command:

      - strings crackdealers.d | less

Hard Disk Analysis

To analyze a hard disk in Linux, an investigator should follow these steps:

1. Make an image of the hard disk using dd:

   - dd if=/dev/hda1 of=/var/case01.dd

2. Use md5sum to collect information about the system time and date:
   - **date > case01.evidence.seal**
   - **md5sum case01.dd > >case01.evidence.seal**
   - **gpg -clearsign case01.evidence.seal**

3. Mount the copy of the evidence into the file system:
   - **mount -o ro,loop,nodev,noexec case01.dd /mnt/evidence**

4. Capture the drive's forensic data:
   - **grave-robber -c /mnt/evidence -m -d /var/investigations/case01 -o LINUX2**

5. Extract deleted inode (modification/access/change) times:
   - **ils case01.dd | ils2mac > case01.ilsbody**

6. Combine evidence for timeline conversion:
   - **cat case01.ilsbody body > case01.evidence**

7. Generate timeline:
   - **mactime -p /mnt/evidence/etc/passwd -g /mnt/evidence/etc/group -b case01.evidence 11/28/2003 > case01.timeline**

Data Collection

Forensic Toolkit Preparation

Forensic investigators use their own forensic toolkit to find and collect any important data from a compromised system. The toolkit is a pack of tools such as nc, dd, datecat, pcat, Hunter.o, insmod, NetstatArproute, dmesg, and others. The investigator mounts the toolkit to a removable disk. It is safest to use the toolkit from a remote system in order to avoid changing the compromised system's metadata.

Data Collection Using the Toolkit

Using the toolkit, an investigator should follow these steps to collect data:

1. Media mounting:
   - Mount the toolkit on the external media:
   mount -n /mnt/cdrom
   - Calculate the hash value of the collected file:
   md5sum date_compromised > date_compromised.md5

2. Current date:
   - Collect the current date result, presented in UTC format:
   nc -l -p port > date_compromised
   /mnt/cdrom/date -u | /mnt/cdrom/nc <remote port>
   md5sum date_compromised > date_compromised.md5

3. Cache tables:
   - Collect the Mac address cache table:
   nc -l -p <port> > arp_compromised
   /mnt/cdrom/arp -an | /mnt/cdrom/nc <remote port>
   md5sum arp_compromised > arp_compromised.md5
   - Collect the kernel route cache table:
   nc -l -p <port> > route_compromised
   /mnt/cdrom/route -Cn | /mnt/cdrom/nc <remote port>
   md5sum route_compromised > route_compromised.md5

4. Current, pending connections and open TCP/UDP ports:
   - Collect information about current connections and open TCP/UDP ports:

     nc -l -p \<port> > connections_compromised

     /mnt/cdrom/netstat -an | /mnt/cdrom/nc \<remote port>

     md5sum connections_compromised > connections_compromised.md5

5. Physical memory image:
   - Access physical memory directly by copying the /dev/mem device or by copying the kcore file, located in the pseudo–file system mounted in the /proc directory:

     nc -l -p \<port> > kcore_compromised

     /mnt/cdrom/dd < /proc/kcore | /mnt/cdrom/nc \<remote port>

     md5sum kcore_compromised > kcore_compromised.md5

6. List modules loaded to kernel memory:
   - Check which modules are currently loaded into memory:

     nc -l -p \<port> > lkms_compromised

     /mnt/cdrom/cat /proc/modules | /mnt/cdrom/nc \<remote port>

     nc -l -p \<port> > lkms_compromised.md5

     /mnt/cdrom/md5sum /proc/modules | /mnt/cdrom/nc \<remote port>

   - Analyze the ksyms file to detect the presence of an intruder:

     nc -l -p \<port> > ksyms_compromised

     /mnt/cdrom/cat /proc/ksyms | /mnt/cdrom/nc \<remote port>

     nc -l -p \<port> > ksyms_compromised.md5

     /mnt/cdrom/md5sum /proc/ksyms | /mnt/cdrom/nc \<remote port>

7. List active processes:
   - Collect information about all processes, open ports, and files with the use of the lsof command:

     nc -l -p \<port> > lsof_compromised

     /mnt/cdrom/lsof -n -P -l | /mnt/cdrom/nc \<remote port>

     md5sum lsof_compromised > lsof_compromised.md5

Command	Description
/mnt/cdrom/cat /proc/version	Operating system version
/mnt/cdrom/cat /proc/sys/kernel/name	Host name
/mnt/cdrom/cat /proc/sys/kernel/domainame	Domain name
/mnt/cdrom/cat /proc/cpuinfo	Information about hardware
/mnt/cdrom/cat /proc/swaps	All swap partitions
mnt/cdrom/cat /proc/partitions	All local file systems
/mnt/cdrom/cat /proc/self/mounts	Mounted file systems
mnt/cdrom/cat /proc/uptime	Uptime

Table 6-1 An investigator can use these commands to collect information

8. Collect suspicious processes:
   - Copy the entire memory allocated by a process:

     nc -l -p <port> > proc_id_compromised

     /mnt/cdrom/pcat proc_id | /mnt/cdrom/nc <remote port>

     md5 proc_ip_compromised > proc_ip_compromised.md5

9. Collect information about the compromised system. Table 6-1 lists commands an investigator can use to find information.

10. Current time:
    - Gather information about the current time:

      nc -l -p <port> > end_time

      /mnt/cdrom/date | /mnt/cdrom/nc <remote port>

Keyword Searching

To search for signs of an intrusion, an investigator can use tools such as the following:

- **strings:**
  - Gathers all printable characters from image files
  - Use the -t switch to add an offset from the beginning of the file:

    strings -t d kcore > kcore_strings

    md5sum kcore_strings > kcore_strings.md5

- **grep:**
  - Gathers commands typed by an intruder, IP addresses, passwords, or even decrypted parts of malicious code

Linux Crash Utility: Commands

An investigator can use the crash command to extract artifacts from a memory sample. Figures 6-2 through 6-6 show the output of several crash commands:

Table 6-2 shows what various other crash commands show.

```
crash> ps
   PID    PPID   CPU     TASK     ST   %MEM     VSZ     RSS    COMM
>     0      0     0   c0660bc0   RU    0.0       0       0   [swapper]
      1      0     0   d1957aa0   IN    0.2    2032     672   init
      2      1     0   d1957550   IN    0.0       0       0   [migration/0]
      3      1     0   d1957000   IN    0.0       0       0   [ksoftirqd/0]
      4      1     0   d195eaa0   IN    0.0       0       0   [watchdog/0]
      5      1     0   d195e550   IN    0.0       0       0   [events/0]
      6      1     0   d195e000   IN    0.0       0       0   [khelper]
      7      1     0   d1ad2aa0   IN    0.0       0       0   [kthread]
     10      7     0   d1aafaa0   IN    0.0       0       0   [kblockd/0]
     11      7     0   d1aaf550   IN    0.0       0       0   [kacpid]
```

Figure 6-2   This is the output of **crash> ps**.

```
PID: 0        TASK: c0660bc0  CPU: 0    COMMAND: "swapper"
    RUN TIME: 00:56:51
  START TIME: 0
   USER TIME: 0
 SYSTEM TIME: 3097919

PID: 1        TASK: d1957aa0  CPU: 0    COMMAND: "init"
    RUN TIME: 00:56:51
  START TIME: 0
   USER TIME: 5
 SYSTEM TIME: 263

PID: 2        TASK: d1957550  CPU: 0    COMMAND: "migration/0"
    RUN TIME: 00:56:51
  START TIME: 0
   USER TIME: 0
 SYSTEM TIME: 0
```

Figure 6-3   This is the output of **crash> ps -t**.

```
crash> ps -a
PID: 0        TASK: c0660bc0  CPU: 0    COMMAND: "swapper"
ps: no user stack

PID: 1        TASK: d1957aa0  CPU: 0    COMMAND: "init"
ARG: init [5]
ENV: HOME=/
     TERM=linux

PID: 2        TASK: d1957550  CPU: 0    COMMAND: "migration/0"
ps: no user stack

PID: 3        TASK: d1957000  CPU: 0    COMMAND: "ksoftirqd/0"
ps: no user stack
```

Figure 6-4   This is the output of **crash> ps -a**.

```
PID: 0        TASK: c0660bc0   CPU: 0    COMMAND: "swapper"
ROOT: /     CWD: /
No open files

PID: 1        TASK: d1957aa0   CPU: 0    COMMAND: "init"
ROOT: /     CWD: /
 FD     FILE     DENTRY     INODE    TYPE  PATH
 10  d14eb080  c13b73c0  d16a75bc  FIFO  /dev/initctl

PID: 2        TASK: d1957550   CPU: 0    COMMAND: "migration/0"
ROOT: /     CWD: /
No open files
```

Figure 6-5   This is the output of **crash> foreach files**.

```
crash> foreach net
PID: 0       TASK: c0660bc0  CPU: 0    COMMAND: "swapper"
No open sockets.


PID: 1       TASK: d1957aa0  CPU: 0    COMMAND: "init"
No open sockets.


PID: 2       TASK: d1957550  CPU: 0    COMMAND: "migration/0"
No open sockets.


PID: 3       TASK: d1957000  CPU: 0    COMMAND: "ksoftirqd/0"
No open sockets.
```

Figure 6-6   This is the output of **crash> foreach net**.

Information	Command
Mounted file systems	**crash> mount**
Open files per file system	**crash> mount –f**
Kernel message buffer	**crash> log**
Swap information	**crash> swap**
Machine information	**crash> mach**
Loaded kernel modules	**crash> mod**
chrdevs and blkdevs arrays	**crash> dev**
PCI device data	**crash> dev –p**
I/O port/memory usage	**crash> dev –I**
Kernel memory usage	**crash> kmem –I**
Kernel vm_stat table	**crash> kmem -V**

Table 6-2   **An investigator can use these crash commands to extract system information**

Investigation Examples

Investigation Example I: Floppy Disk Forensics

Rebecca had filed a lawsuit against Good Company, Inc., for sexual harassment by one of its senior directors, Mr. Peter Samson. She claims that Mr. Samson used to send her explicit material through floppy disks marked as legitimate work, and she has submitted a floppy as evidence. An investigator has been called to investigate the case on behalf of Good Company, Inc.

How should the investigator proceed with the evidence?

Step-By-Step Approach to Investigation Example I

1. All processes must be documented. Documentation is critical for all investigations. Mishandling of documents or failure to maintain the chain of custody can destroy a case.

   a. To begin the investigation, the investigator should create a directory where all forensic activities can be done. For example, the investigator may choose to create a directory called "evidence." This can be achieved by issuing the command **mkdir evidence**.

   b. Investigators should not work directly on the evidence. This can cause unwanted modifications to the evidence, destroying its integrity. The evidence is usually imaged, and all work is then done on that image. In Linux, investigators can create a separate mount point to mount the image. For example, the investigator may choose to create a mount point called "investigation." This can be achieved by issuing the command: **mkdir /mnt/investigation**.

2. The disk structure should be determined. Linux has built-in tools that can be used for forensic investigation purposes, such as dd.

   a. The investigator can create an image of the disk using dd. For example, the investigator may choose to create an image of the disk by issuing the command **dd if=/dev/fd0 of=image.suspectdisk**.

   b. As previously mentioned, the investigation process should not alter the evidence. Because of this, the investigator may choose to change the read-write permissions of the image to read-only by issuing the command **chmod 444 image.suspectdisk**.

3. Once a separate mount point has been created, the investigator can proceed to mount the restored, imaged working copy and analyze the contents. For example, the investigator may choose to mount the newly created point investigations by issuing the command **mount -t vfat -o ro, noexec /dev/fd0 /mnt/investigations**. Alternatively, the investigator may choose to mount a point within the image file using the loop interface, rather than mounting the contents to another location. This can be done by issuing the command **mount -t vfat -o ro,noexec,loop image.suspectdisk /mnt/investigations**.

4. The integrity of the image file should be checked to be sure it is the same as the original. This can be done by checking the file hash using the command **md5sum /evidence/md5.image.suspectfile** or **sha1sum -c /evidence/SHA.image.suspectfile**.

5. The investigator can then list all files and directories in the image, including hidden files, by issuing the command **ls -alR**.

6. The handling date, file access, and alteration times should be noted. The investigator can make a list of all suspect files, along with access times, in the newly created directory by issuing the command **ls -laiRtu > /evidence/suspectfiles.list**.

7. The investigator can now search for likely evidence using grep. To search for the term [term] among the suspect file list, he or she can issue the command **grep -i [term] suspectfiles.list**.

8. In order to list unknown file extensions and changed file appearances, the investigator can issue the command **file [changedfile]**. These files can be viewed using strings, cat, more, or less.

9. Apart from searching suspect files, certain keywords from the entire file list can be searched for by issuing the command **cat /evidence/suspectfiles.list | grep [blackmailword]**.

   a. A systematic approach to searching for keywords would be to create a keyword list, saved in this example as /evidence/keywordlist.txt.

   b. Use grep on the files for the keywords and save it to a file:

      grep –aibf keywordlist.txt image.suspectdisk > results.txt

   c. View the results:

      cat results.txt

   d. Use the hex dump tool to analyze the files at each offset:

      xxd -s [offset] image.suspectdisk | less

Challenges in Disk Forensics with Linux

- Linux cannot identify the last sector on hard drives with an odd number of sectors.
- Most Linux tools are used at the command line and are more complicated than Windows or Mac tools.
- Devices can be written to, even if they are not mounted.
- Bugs in open-source tools can be used to question the credibility of the tools for forensic use.
- Original work, including the evidence, can be destroyed with a command-line typo, particularly when imaging.

Investigation Example II: Hard Drive Forensics

Mr. Jason Smith has been accused of storing illegal material on his company's system. An investigator has been called upon to examine the hard disk in question. How should the investigator proceed in extracting and preserving the evidence?

Step-By-Step Approach to Investigation Example II

1. As in the previous case, documentation plays a critical role. The investigator begins by noting the model information from the hard disk label and manufacturer's Web site, as well as the size and total number of sectors on the drive.

2. The investigator may then proceed to prepare an image of the hard disk. It may be wise to first wipe and format an image disk drive using the ext3 file system; this drive should have a capacity at least three times the size of the evidence. To ensure that all data has been erased from the drive, the disk should be filled with zeros. This can be achieved by issuing the command **dcfldd if=/dev/zero of=/dev/hda bs=4096 conv=noerror, sync**.

3. The next step is to partition the newly formatted disk and reboot. This can be achieved by issuing the command **fdisk /dev/had**.

4. The disk should then be formatted with the ext3 file system. This can be achieved by issuing the command **mkfs -t ext3 /dev/image.disk**.

5. The investigator then prepares the disk for imaging through the following steps:

   a. Mount the read-write image disk:

      mount /dev/hda /mnt/image.disk

   b. Create a directory for all documentation and analysis:

      mkdir /mnt/image.disk/case_no

   c. Create a subdirectory to hold the evidence image:

      mkdir /mnt/image.disk/case_no/evidence_no

   d. Document details of the investigation in a text file including the investigator's details, case background details, investigation dates, and other information.

   e. Document details of the disk media including:

      - the investigator's name and organization
      - case number
      - media evidence number
      - date and time of imaging
      - make, model, and serial number of computer and hard drive
      - source of hard drive
      - IP and system host name
      - scope of investigation

6. While imaging the disk, an investigator should keep the following in mind:

   a. Connect both the original evidence drive and drive to be imaged to the system.

   b. Verify all jumper settings related to the master and slave drives.

   c. Make sure the system will boot only from CD by checking the BIOS settings.

   d. Image the disk using dd:

      dd if=/dev/hdx of=image.disk conv=noerror,sync

      This will allow dd to try to ignore any errors (**conv=noerror**) and synchronize the output (**sync**) with the original.

7. Check for accuracy using md5sum.

8. Mount the disk and extract evidence. Images can be carved using dd or the hex dump tool xxd.

Linux Forensic Tools

The Sleuth Kit

The Sleuth Kit (TSK) is a collection of UNIX-based command-line file and volume system forensic analysis tools. The Sleuth Kit supports DOS partitions, BSD partitions (disk labels), Mac partitions, Sun slices (Volume Table of Contents), and GPT disks.

It analyzes raw (dd), Expert Witness (EnCase), and AFF file systems and disk images, supporting the NTFS, FAT, UFS 1, UFS 2, ext2, ext3, and ISO 9660 file systems (even when the host operating system does not support those file systems or has a different endian ordering).

Tools in The Sleuth Kit

- *File system layer tool*: This file system tools processes general file system data such as the layout, allocation structures, and boot blocks.
  - fsstat: Shows file system details and statistics including layout, sizes, and labels
- *Filename layer tools*: These file system tools process the filename structures, which are typically located in the parent directory.
  - ffind: Finds allocated and unallocated filenames that point to a given metadata structure
  - fls: Lists allocated and deleted filenames in a directory
- *Metadata layer tools*: These file system tools process the metadata structures, which store the details about a file. Examples of this structure include directory entries in FAT, MFT entries in NTFS, and inodes in extX and UFS.
  - icat: Extracts the data units of a file, which are specified by its metadata address (instead of the filename)
  - ifind: Finds the metadata structure that has a given filename pointing to it or the metadata structure that points to a given data unit
  - ils: Lists the metadata structures and their contents in a pipe-delimited format
  - istat: Displays the statistics and details about a given metadata structure in an easy-to-read format
- *Data-unit layer tools*: These file system tools process the data units where file content is stored. Examples of this layer include clusters in FAT and NTFS, and blocks and fragments in extX and UFS.
  - dcat: Extracts the contents of a given data unit
  - dls: Lists the details about data units and can extract the unallocated space of the file system
  - dstat: Displays the statistics about a given data unit in an easy-to-read format
  - dcalc: Calculates where data in the unallocated space image (from dls) exists in the original image; used when evidence is found in unallocated space
- *File system journal tools*: These file system tools process the journals that some file systems have. The journal records the metadata (and sometimes content) updates that are made. This could help recover recently deleted data. Examples of file systems with journals include ext3 and NTFS.
  - jcat: Display the contents of a specific journal block
  - jls: Lists the entries in the file system journal
- *Media management tool*: This tool takes a disk (or other media) image as input and analyzes its partition structures. Examples include DOS partitions, BSD disk labels, and the Sun Volume Table of Contents (VTOC). These can be used to find hidden data between partitions and to identify the file system offset for The Sleuth Kit tools.
  - mmls: This displays the layout of a disk, including the unallocated space. The output identifies the type of partition and its length, which makes it easy to use dd to extract the partitions. The output is sorted based on the starting sector so it is easy to identify gaps in the layout.
- *Image file tools*: This layer contains tools for the image file format.
  - img_stat: Shows the details of the image format
  - img_cat: Shows the raw contents of an image file
- *Disk tools*: These tools can be used to detect and remove a Host Protected Area (HPA) in an ATA disk. An HPA could be used to hide data so that it could not be copied during an acquisition.
  - disk_sreset: This tool will temporarily remove an HPA, if one exists. After the disk is reset the HPA will return.
  - disk_stat: This tool will show if an HPA exists

- Other tools:
  - hfind: Uses a binary sort algorithm to look up hashes in the NIST NSRL, HashKeeper, and custom hash databases created by md5sum
  - mactime: Takes input from the fls and ils tools to create a timeline of file activity
  - sorter: Sorts files based on their file type and performs extension checking and hash database lookups
  - sigfind: Searches for a binary value at a given offset; useful for recovering lost data structures

Autopsy

The Autopsy Forensic Browser is a graphical interface to The Sleuth Kit. Since Autopsy is HTML-based, the Autopsy server can be reached from any platform using an HTML browser. Autopsy provides a File Manager–like interface and shows details about deleted data and file system structures.

- Analysis modes:
  - A dead analysis occurs when a dedicated analysis system is used to examine the data from a suspect system. In this case, Autopsy and The Sleuth Kit are run in a trusted environment, typically a lab. Autopsy and TSK support raw, Expert Witness, and AFF file formats.
  - A live analysis occurs when the suspect system is being analyzed while it is running. In this case, Autopsy and The Sleuth Kit are run from a CD in an untrusted environment. This is frequently done during an incident response, while the incident is being confirmed. After it is confirmed, the investigator can acquire the system and perform a dead analysis.

- Evidence search techniques:
  - File listing (Figure 6-7): Analyze the files and directories, including the names of deleted files and files with Unicode-based names.
  - File content (Figure 6-8): The contents of files can be viewed in raw or hex format, or the ASCII strings can be extracted. When data is interpreted, Autopsy sanitizes it to prevent damage to the local analysis system. Autopsy does not use any client-side scripting languages.
  - Hash databases (Figure 6-9): An investigator can look up unknown files in a hash database to quickly identify them as good or bad. Autopsy uses the NIST National Software Reference Library (NSRL) as well as user-created databases of known good and bad files.

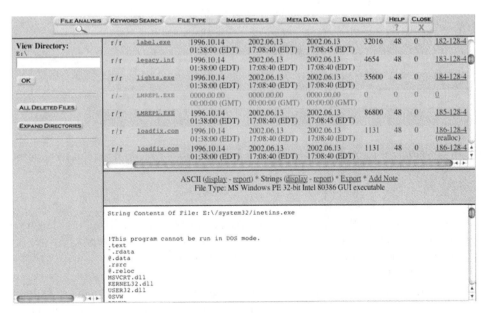

Figure 6-7 Autopsy allows an investigator to analyze files and directories.

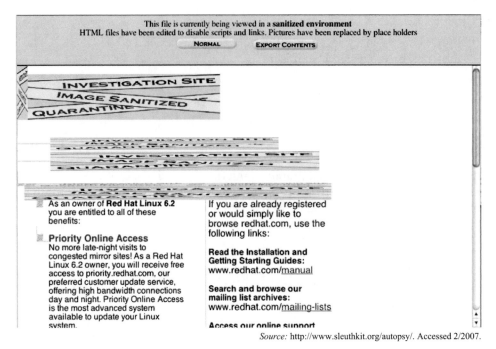

Source: http://www.sleuthkit.org/autopsy/. Accessed 2/2007.

Figure 6-8   Autopsy allows investigators to view file content.

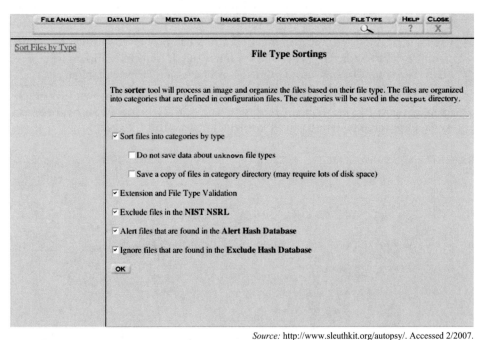

Source: http://www.sleuthkit.org/autopsy/. Accessed 2/2007.

Figure 6-9   Autopsy's hash databases allow an investigator to quickly determine if a file is good or bad.

- File type sorting (Figure 6-10): An investigator can sort files based on their internal signatures to identify files of a known type. Autopsy can also extract only graphic images (including thumbnails). The extension of the file will also be compared to the file type to identify files that may have had their extensions changed to hide them.

- Timeline of file activity (Figure 6-11): In some cases, having a timeline of file activity can help identify areas of a file system that may contain evidence. Autopsy can create timelines that contain entries for the modified, accessed, and changed (MAC) times of both allocated and unallocated files.

CREATE DATA FILE	CREATE TIMELINE	VIEW TIMELINE	VIEW NOTES	HELP	CLOSE

<- May 2002   Jul 2002 ->

Jun ▾ 2002   OK

Mon Jun 10 2002 19:33:10	3888	m..	-/-rwxrwxrwx	48	0	112-128-4	C:/system32/drivers/NTHANDLE.SYS
Thu Jun 13 2002 21:01:34	22299	.ac	-/-rwxrwxrwx	48	0	263-128-4	C:/system32/oemnadem.inf
Thu Jun 13 2002 21:01:35	20263	.ac	-/-rwxrwxrwx	48	0	270-128-4	C:/system32/oemnadlm.inf
	39386	..c	-/-rwxrwxrwx	48	0	193-128-4	C:/system32/mem.exe
	56	mac	d/drwxrwxrwx	48	0	49-144-7	C:/system32
	9488	..c	-/-rwxrwxrwx	48	0	191-128-4	C:/system32/lsass.exe
	9488	..c	-/-rwxrwxrwx	48	0	191-128-4	C:/system32/lsass.exe (deleted-realloc)
	33662	.ac	-/-rwxrwxrwx	48	0	268-128-4	C:/system32/oemnadin.inf
	86800	..c	-/-rwxrwxrwx	48	0	185-128-4	C:/system32/LMREPL.EXE
	25491	.ac	-/-rwxrwxrwx	48	0	269-128-4	C:/system32/oemnadlb.inf
	24391	.ac	-/-rwxrwxrwx	48	0	264-128-4	C:/system32/oemnaden.inf
	22297	.ac	-/-rwxrwxrwx	48	0	266-128-4	C:/system32/oemnadfd.inf
	85632	..c	-/-rwxrwxrwx	48	0	179-128-4	C:/system32/krnl386.exe
	22296	.ac	-/-rwxrwxrwx	48	0	267-128-4	C:/system32/oemnadim.inf
	32016	..c	-/-rwxrwxrwx	48	0	182-128-4	C:/system32/label.exe
	35225	.ac	-/-rwxrwxrwx	48	0	265-128-4	C:/system32/oemnadep.inf

Source: http://www.sleuthkit.org/autopsy/. Accessed 2/2007.

Figure 6-10   Autopsy allows an investigator to sort files based on their types, which is determined by their file signatures.

CREATE DATA FILE	CREATE TIMELINE	VIEW TIMELINE	VIEW NOTES	HELP	CLOSE

<- May 2002   Jul 2002 ->

Jun ▾ 2002   OK

Mon Jun 10 2002 19:33:10	3888	m..	-/-rwxrwxrwx	48	0	112-128-4	C:/system32/drivers/NTHANDLE.SYS
Thu Jun 13 2002 21:01:34	22299	.ac	-/-rwxrwxrwx	48	0	263-128-4	C:/system32/oemnadem.inf
Thu Jun 13 2002 21:01:35	20263	.ac	-/-rwxrwxrwx	48	0	270-128-4	C:/system32/oemnadlm.inf
	39386	.c	-/-rwxrwxrwx	48	0	193-128-4	C:/system32/mem.exe
	56	mac	d/drwxrwxrwx	48	0	49-144-7	C:/system32
	9488	.c	-/-rwxrwxrwx	48	0	191-128-4	C:/system32/lsass.exe
	9488	.c	-/-rwxrwxrwx	48	0	191-128-4	C:/system32/lsass.exe (deleted-realloc)
	33662	.ac	-/-rwxrwxrwx	48	0	268-128-4	C:/system32/oemnadin.inf
	86800	.c	-/-rwxrwxrwx	48	0	185-128-4	C:/system32/LMREPL.EXE
	25491	.ac	-/-rwxrwxrwx	48	0	269-128-4	C:/system32/oemnadlb.inf
	24391	.ac	-/-rwxrwxrwx	48	0	264-128-4	C:/system32/oemnaden.inf
	22297	.ac	-/-rwxrwxrwx	48	0	266-128-4	C:/system32/oemnadfd.inf
	85632	.c	-/-rwxrwxrwx	48	0	179-128-4	C:/system32/krnl386.exe
	22296	.ac	-/-rwxrwxrwx	48	0	267-128-4	C:/system32/oemnadim.inf
	32016	.c	-/-rwxrwxrwx	48	0	182-128-4	C:/system32/label.exe
	35225	.ac	-/-rwxrwxrwx	48	0	265-128-4	C:/system32/oemnadep.inf

Source: http://www.sleuthkit.org/autopsy/. Accessed 2/2007.

Figure 6-11   Autopsy establishes a timeline of file activity to assist an investigator in determining when files were modified, accessed, and changed.

- Keyword search (Figure 6-12): Keyword searches of the file system image can be performed using ASCII strings and regular expressions. Searches can be performed on either the full file system image or just the unallocated space. An index file can be created for faster searches. Strings that are frequently searched for can be easily configured into Autopsy for automated searching.

- Metadata analysis (Figure 6-13): Metadata structures contain details about files and directories. Autopsy allows investigators to view the details of any metadata structure in the file system. This is

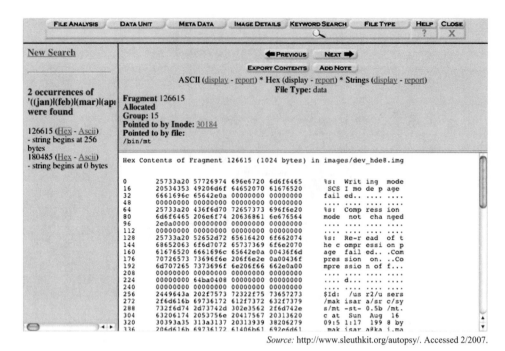

Source: http://www.sleuthkit.org/autopsy/. Accessed 2/2007.

Figure 6-12   Autopsy provides the ability to perform keyword searches.

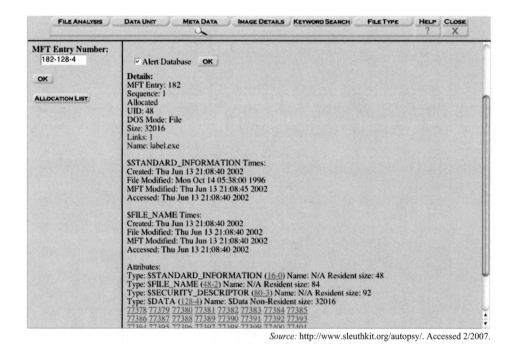

Source: http://www.sleuthkit.org/autopsy/. Accessed 2/2007.

Figure 6-13   Autopsy metadata analysis provides details about file metadata.

useful for recovering deleted content. Autopsy will search the directories to identify the full path of the file that has allocated the structure.

- Data-unit analysis (Figure 6-14): Data units are where file content is stored. Autopsy displays the contents of any data unit in a variety of formats. The file type is also given, and Autopsy will search the metadata structures to identify which has allocated the data unit.

- Image details (Figure 6-15): File system details can be viewed, including on-disk layout and times of activity. This mode provides information that is useful during data recovery.

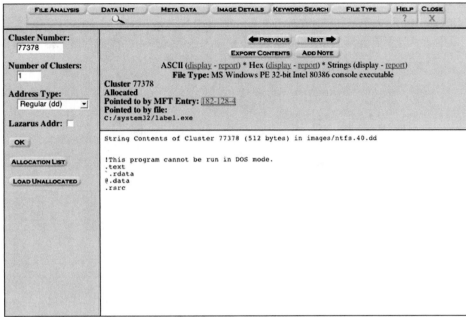

Figure 6-14   Autopsy analyzes data units to display file content.

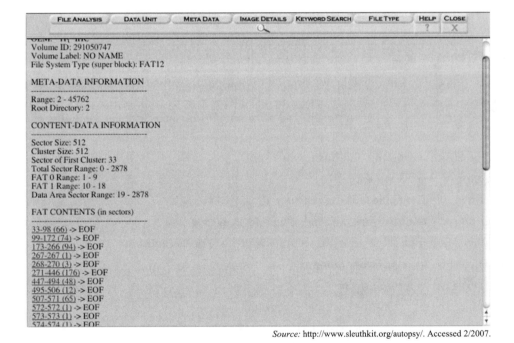

Figure 6-15   Autopsy displays file system details for an image.

SMART for Linux

SMART is a modular forensic tool. It supports plug-ins, is multithreaded, and can generate information on hashes. SMART can perform real authentication and verify the work of other forensic programs. It uses a graphical user interface, shown in Figure 5-16.

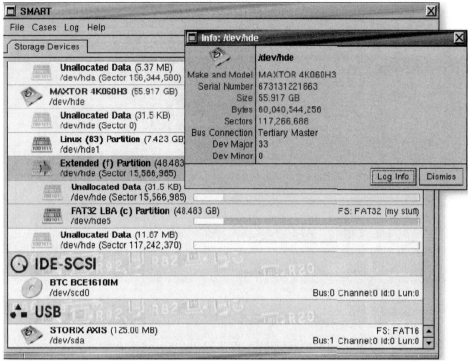

Source: http://www.logon-int.com/product.asp?sClassid=FORENSIC&sProdClassCode=ASR-P-0001. Accessed 2/2007.

Figure 6-16 SMART supports plug-ins for multiple uses.

Penguin Sleuth Kit

The Penguin Sleuth Kit is a bootable Linux distribution based on Knoppix. It collects several tools including The Coroner's Toolkit (TCT), Autopsy, and The Sleuth Kit, as well as penetration-testing and virus-scanning tools. It offers both a GUI environment and a command-line interface. The Penguin Sleuth Kit includes the following tools:

- The Sleuth Kit: Command-line forensic tools
- Autopsy: The Sleuth Kit GUI
- Foremost: Command-line data carving tool
- Glimpse: Command-line data indexing and searching tool
- Wipe: Command-line utility to securely wipe hard drives and files
- Etherape: Visual network monitor
- Fenris: Multipurpose tracer
- Honeyd: Command-line honeypot program
- Snort: Command-line network intrusion tool
- Dsniff: Command-line network auditing and penetration testing tools
- John the Ripper: Command-line password cracking tool
- Nikto: Web server scanner
- NBTScan: Command-line tool that scans for open NetBIOS name servers
- Xprobe: Command-line remote operating system fingerprinting tool
- Ngrep: Command-line network grep function
- Nemesis: Command-line network packet injector
- Fragroute: Command-line network intrusion testing tool

- Fping: Command-line multiple-host ping utility
- Tcptraceroute: Command-line tool for tracing routes taken by TCP packets
- Tcpreplay: Command-line utility that replays a TCP dump
- Nessus: Graphical security scanner
- Ethereal: Graphical network analyzer
- Netcat: Command-line tool to read and write over a network
- Tcpdump: Command-line tool that dumps network traffic
- Hping2: Command-line packet assembler/analyzer
- Ettercap: Command-line sniffer/interceptor/logger for Ethernet networks
- OpenSSH: Secure remote connection utility
- Kismet: Graphical wireless network sniffer
- AirSnort: Graphical wireless network intrusion tool
- GPG: Encryption utility
- OpenSSL: Secure remote connection utility
- Lsof: Command-line utility that lists all open files
- Hunt: Command-line TCP/IP exploit scanner
- Stunnel: SSL connection package
- Arpwatch: Command-line Ethernet monitor
- Dig: Command-line tool for querying domain name servers
- Chkrootkit: Tool that looks for signs of rootkits

The Farmer's Boot CD

The Farmer's Boot CD (FBCD) can safely and quickly preview systems (hard drives, thumb drives, digital music devices such as iPods, digital camera media, and more) directly from Linux. Its features include the following:

- Boot almost any x86 system
- Mount file systems in a forensically sound manner
- Preview data using a single, unified graphical user interface (GUI)
- Acquire media after it is previewed

The following are some of its advantages:

- Allows attaching digital cameras, previewing the contents of onboard memory, and dumping software information and graphics or video files
- Authenticates and acquires file systems or devices in simple point-and-click GUIs
- Generates a catalog of all hardware attached to the system, including serial numbers, make and model information, and settings and configuration information
- Dumps BIOS information of the system
- Easily obtains both hard drive and file system information
  - Hard drive information may include make and model, serial number, capacity, and partitioning schema.
  - File system information may include size, volume name, UUID, creation date, last mounted date, and other metadata information.
- Generates a list of deleted files for FAT12/16/32, NTFS, and ext2 file system types
- Captures network traffic (including HTTP, e-mail, and instant messenger traffic) and analyzes it with the provided tools

- Quickly previews all sessions found on multisession CDs
- Identifies data residing in file slack for supported file system types
- Analyzes the Windows registry
- Previews and analyzes e-mail stores, looking for attachments, decoding Base64, and searching for key terms
- Obtains file metadata for supported file types
- Easily identifies host protected areas (HPA) on ATA drives and soft-resets them for a full acquisition
- Can preview image files that contain file systems that start beyond 2 GB into the image file

Delve

The Farmer's Boot CD contains a forensic preview toolset called Delve. Delve's features are shown in Figures 6-17 through 6-25.

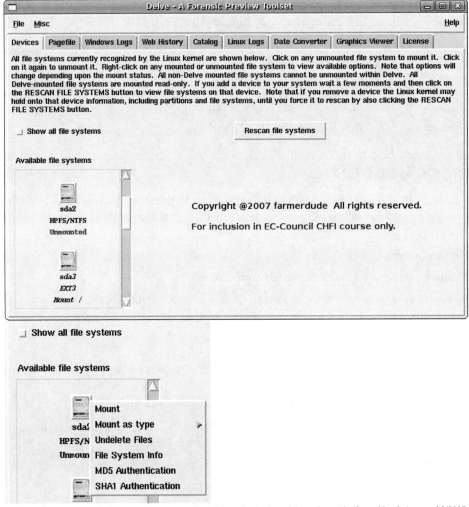

Figure 6-17   Delve's **Devices** tab mounts systems in a read-only manner. Right-click on any file system to view its available options.

Source: http://www.forensicbootcd.com/site/farmcd.html. Accessed 2/2007.

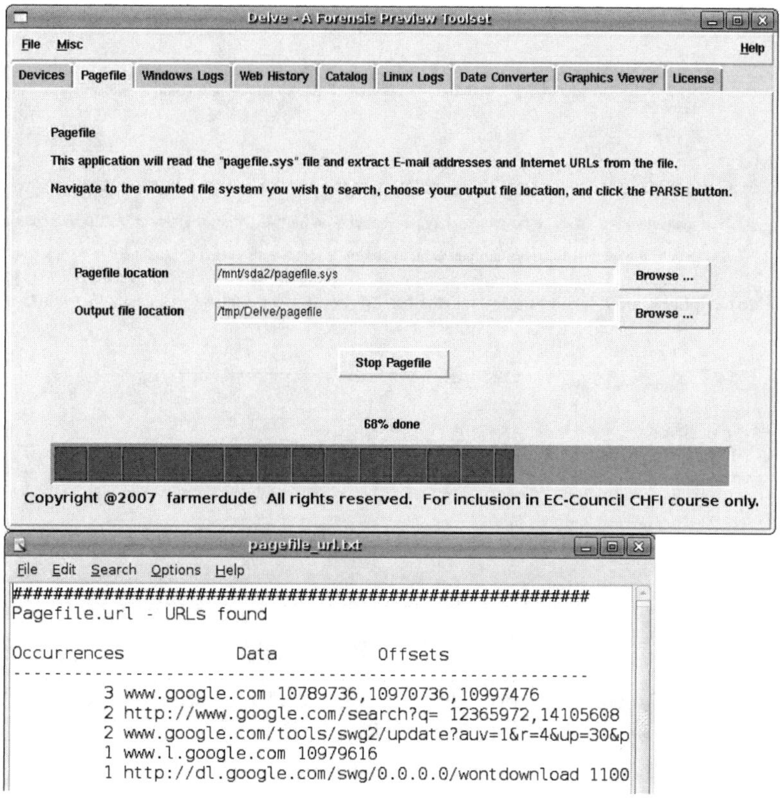

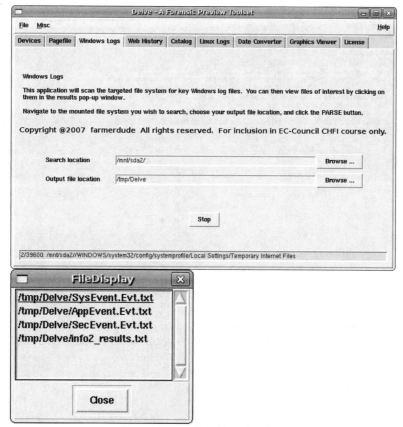

Figure 6-18 Delve's **Pagefile** tab is used to identify e-mail addresses and URLs in the Windows pagefile.sys file. URL output is shown to the right.

Source: http://www.forensicbootcd.com/site/farmcd.html. Accessed 2/2007.

Figure 6-19 The **Windows Logs** tab is used to identify key log files of interest on Windows systems and allow the user to view them.

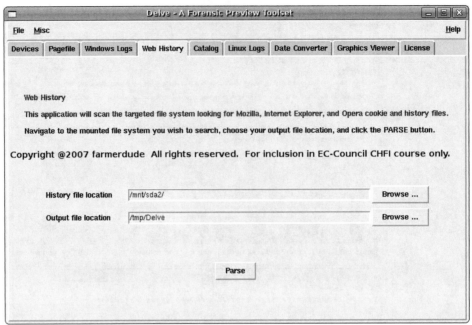

Figure 6-20 Delve's **Web History** tab is used to identify Web browser cache files and to extract cookie and history information.

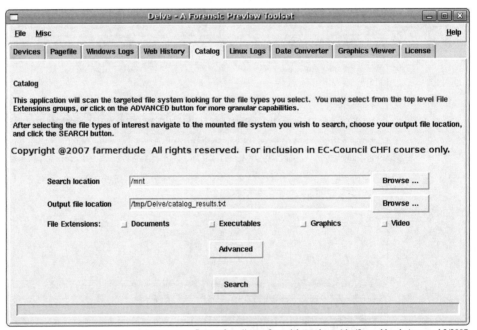

Figure 6-21 Delve's **Catalog** tab is used to identify and catalog files of interest by extension or header. Found files may be copied or opened, and a file list can be generated.

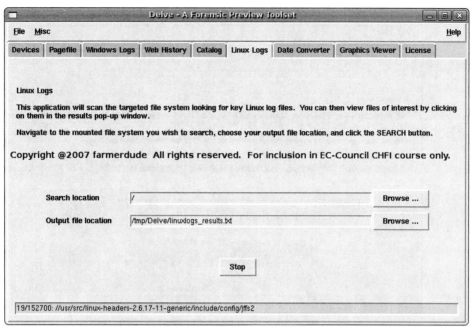

Figure 6-22 Delve's **Linux Logs** tab is used to identify key log files on Linux systems and allow the user to view them.

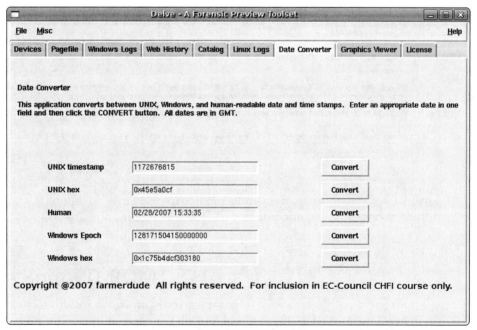

Figure 6-23 Delve's **Date Converter** tab is used to convert the date and time from one format to another.

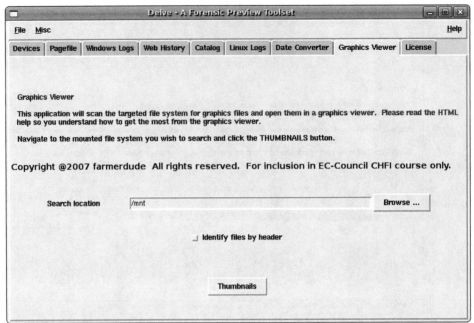

Figure 6-24 Delve's **Graphics Viewer** tab is used to identify graphics files and open a viewer for any found files.

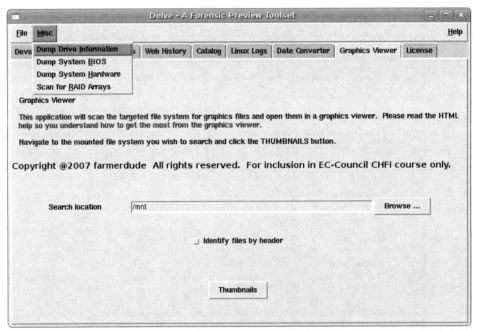

Figure 6-25 Delve's Misc menu provides miscellaneous utilities including dumping hard drive information, dumping the system BIOS tables, dumping an inventory of hardware, and scanning for RAID arrays.

Forensix

Forensix allows a system to be monitored so that in the event of a security compromise, it is easy to track the compromise back to its source and recover from it. Forensix performs a complete kernel-event audit on the target system and streams the high-definition audit trail to a back-end database that has been optimized for reconstruction queries.

Its functions include the following:

- Accurately replaying any and all system compromises
- Determining what specific data (such as credit card numbers) have been accessed on the system as a result of a compromise
- Automatically determining what modifications have been made to a system by an illicit user
- Selectively undoing system modifications

Maresware

Maresware provides tools for investigating computer records on an Intel-based Linux machine. It includes the following major programs:

- Bates_no: Adds identifying numbers to filenames in e-documents
- Catalog: Catalogs every file on a Linux file system and identifies headers
- Hash: Performs MD5, CRC, or SHA-1 hash of every file on a drive
- Hashcmp: Compares outputs of successive hash runs
- Md5: Calculates MD5 hash of a file
- Strsrch: Searches files for text strings
- U_to_A: Converts UNIX text to DOS text

Captain Nemo

Captain Nemo is a multiplatform file manager that enables access to any Linux drive from a Windows computer without requiring a network setup. To access a Linux drive, a user can connect it to a Windows machine with Captain Nemo running and it will mount the Linux partitions in Windows. It supports both ext2 and ext3, and can view the contents of most files, including some metadata. Captain Nemo's Windows interface is shown in Figure 6-26.

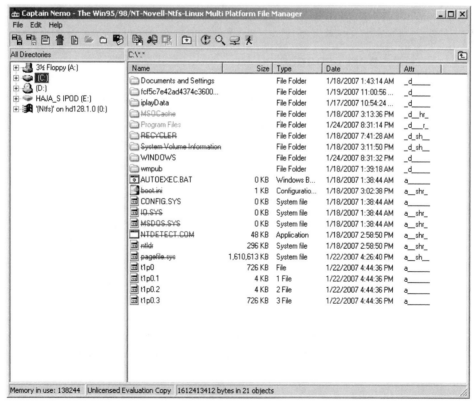

Source: http://www.forensicbootcd.com/site/farmcd.html. Accessed 2/2007.

Figure 6-26 Captain Nemo will mount Linux drives in Windows.

The Coroner's Toolkit (TCT)

The Coroner's Toolkit is a collection containing the following programs:

- The grave-robber tool captures digital information from the target system.
- The ils and mactime tools display access patterns of files.
- The unrm and lazarus tools recover deleted files.
- The findkey tool recovers cryptographic keys from a running process or from files.

FLAG

FLAG (Forensic Log Analysis GUI) is used for log file analysis and forensic investigations. It uses a database as a back end to assist in managing large volumes of data. FLAG is pictured in Figure 6-27, and its features include the following:

- Log analysis:
  - FLAG supports generic firewall logs.
  - It collects statistics about the logs and searches for suspicious activity.
- Network forensics:
  - It uses the dissected information to construct a knowledge base of different entities on the network.
- Disk forensics:
  - FLAG uses The Sleuth Kit tool to analyze dd images.

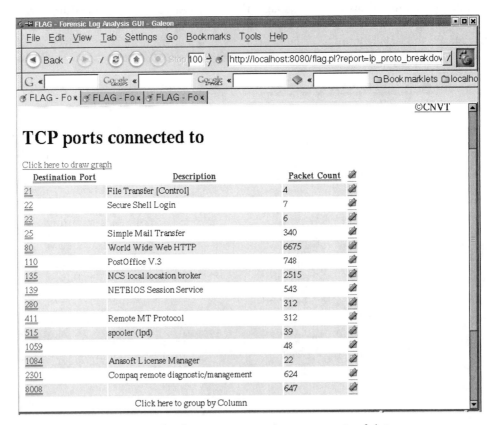

Figure 6-27   FLAG uses a database to manage large amounts of data.

md5deep

md5deep is a cross-platform set of programs used to compute MD5, SHA-1, SHA-256, Tiger, or Whirlpool message digests on an arbitrary number of files. Its features include the following:

- Recursive operation: md5deep is able to recursively examine an entire directory tree.
- Comparison mode: It computes the MD5 hash for every file in a directory and for every file in every subdirectory.
- Time estimation: It can produce a time estimate when processing very large files.

TestDisk

TestDisk helps recover lost partitions and make nonbooting disks bootable again. It can perform the following functions:

- Fix the partition table to recover deleted partitions
- Recover a FAT32 boot sector from its backup
- Rebuild a FAT12/FAT16/FAT32 boot sector
- Fix FAT tables
- Rebuild an NTFS boot sector
- Recover an NTFS boot sector from its backup
- Copy files from deleted FAT, NTFS, and ext2/ext3 partitions

Vinetto

Vinetto is a forensic tool used to examine Thumbs.db files. It extracts the related thumbnails to a directory and collects a metadata report on all nondeleted Thumbs.db files contained within a partition.

HELIX

HELIX from e-Fense is an incident response and computer forensic toolkit formerly based on Knoppix Live CD. There are numerous tools that can be used for forensic investigation on Windows and Linux systems. The HELIX Live CD is a bootable version that provides the OS and tools to audit and copy data from a suspect machine. Booting into HELIX provides a graphical menu for accessing forensic tools. The latest version, HELIX3, is no longer available as a free version and is based on Ubuntu. It contains updated and enhanced versions of the tools contained in previous versions. Figure 6-28 shows a screenshot from an older version of HELIX.

BackTrack

While a number of Live CD distributions exist, one stands out as a superlative, Swiss-Army-knife type of tool. BackTrack can be used as a bootable CD or bootable USB flash drive. It is also available as a VM appliance for use in a virtual environment. BackTrack provides over 300 different tools that can be used by security professionals or system administrators, including tools to perform penetration testing on systems, wireless cracking tools, network mapping tools, information gathering tools, vulnerability identification tools, forensic tools, and reverse engineering tools. Figure 6-29 shows a screenshot of the BackTrack GUI.

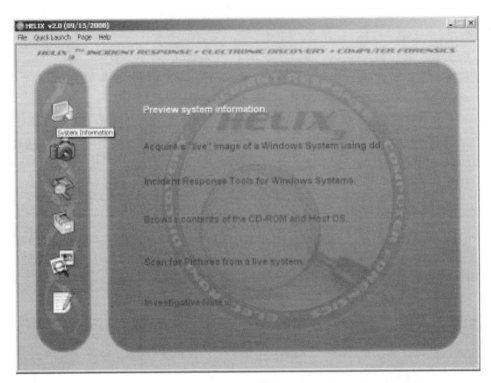

Figure 6-28 HELIX is a Live CD that provides a number of tools for forensic investigations.

Figure 6-29 BackTrack provides over 300 different tools.

Chapter Summary

- Linux imparts flexibility, power, and greater control as a forensic tool than other operating systems.
- Linux has a number of simple utilities that make imaging and basic analysis of suspect disks.
- There are several popular Linux toolkits that provide a GUI.

Review Questions

1. Describe the Linux file system.

_____

_____

2. What are the various data collection techniques for a live Linux system?

_____

_____

3. What is keyword searching?

_____

_____

4. Explain mounting an image file and timeline creation.

_____

_____

5. Explain evidence analysis techniques using Autopsy.

_____

_____

6. What are some precautions to take during an investigation?

_____

_____

7. List the Linux forensic tools.

_____

_____

8. List the tools included in the Penguin Sleuth Kit.

_____

_____

9. What is the Farmer's Boot CD?

_____

_____

Hand-On Projects

1. Use The Sleuth Kit for a Linux forensic investigation.

   ■ Boot your system using the Helix Bootable CD-ROM.

   ■ Click the **Helix** button, then **Forensics**, and then **Autopsy**. Your screen will look similar to Figure 6-30.

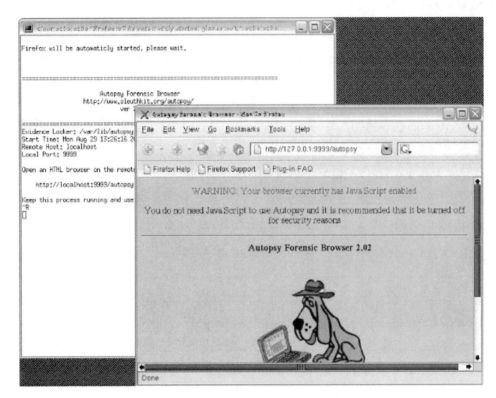

Figure 6-30   Start the Autopsy Forensic Browser.

   ■ Click the **New Case** button (Figure 6-31).

Figure 6-31   Click the **New Case** button to start a new case.

■ Fill out the form and click the **New Case** button (Figure 6-32).

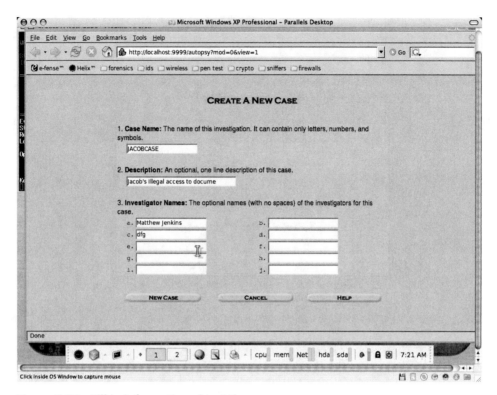

Figure 6-32 Fill in information about the case.

■ Click the **Add Host** button (Figure 6-33).

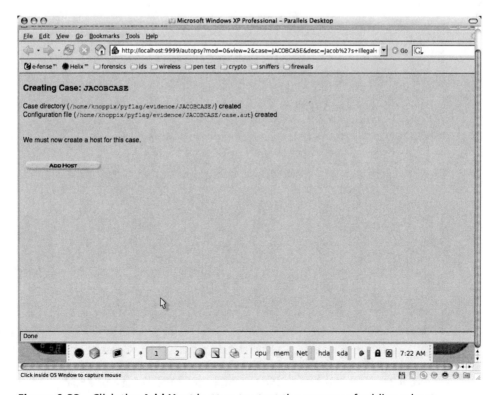

Figure 6-33 Click the **Add Host** button to start the process of adding a host.

▪ Fill out the form and click the **Add Host** button (Figure 6-34).

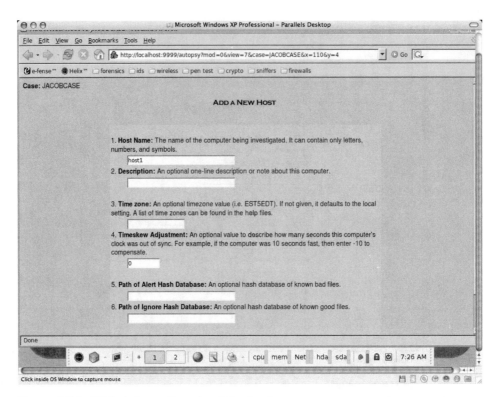

Figure 6-34 Fill in information about the host.

▪ Click the **Add Image** button (Figure 6-35).

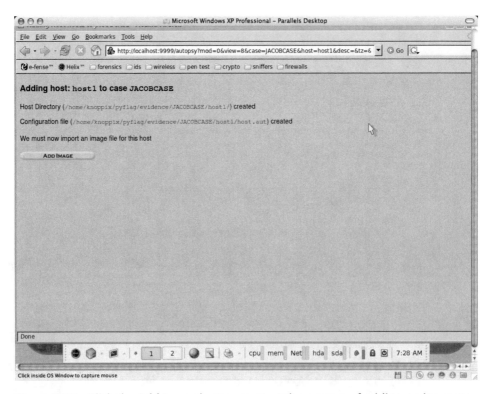

Figure 6-35 Click the **Add Image** button to start the process of adding an image to the case.

■ Click the **Add Image File** button (Figure 6-36).

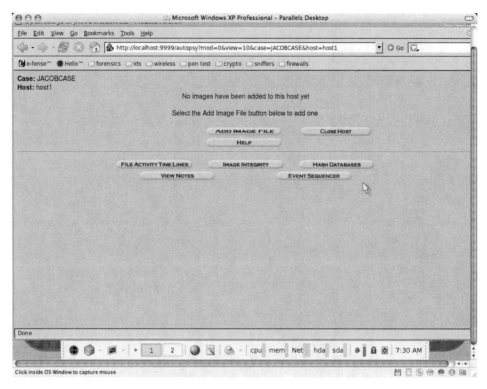

Figure 6-36   Click the **Add Image File** button to add an image file.

■ For the location, type **/dev/hda1** or **/dev/hda2**. Leave the other options as the defaults. Click the **Next** button (Figure 6-37).

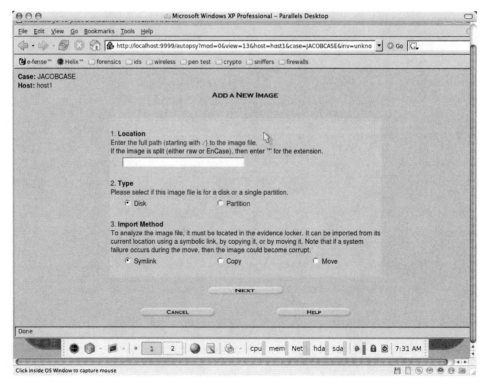

Figure 6-37   Fill in the location of the image file.

■ Select the correct volume type and then click the **OK** button (Figure 6-38).

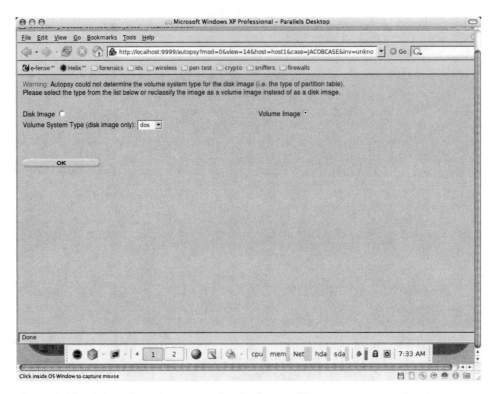

Figure 6-38   Select the volume type for the image file.

■ Click the **Add** button (Figure 6-39).

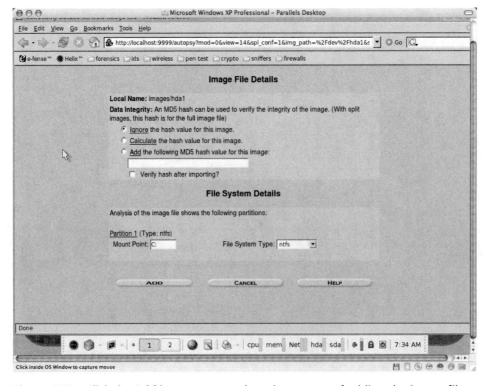

Figure 6-39   Click the **Add** button to complete the process of adding the image file.

■ Click the **OK** button (Figure 6-40).

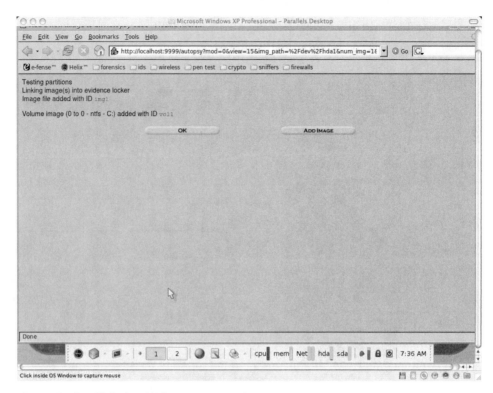

Figure 6-40   Click the **OK** button to continue.

■ Click the **Analyze** button (Figure 6-41).

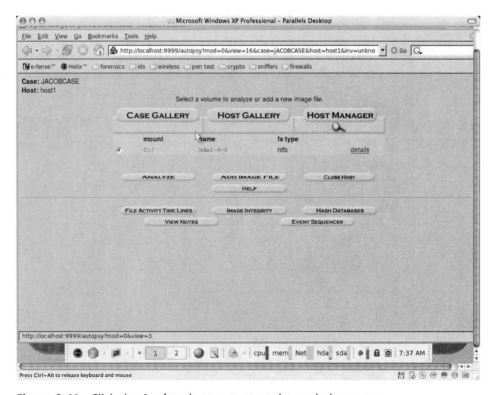

Figure 6-41   Click the **Analyze** button to start the analysis process.

2. Use Captain Nemo to access a Linux drive from a Windows computer.

 ▪ Navigate to Chapter 6 of the Student Resource Center.

 ▪ Install and launch the Captain Nemo program.

 ▪ Click the **Next** button (Figure 6-42).

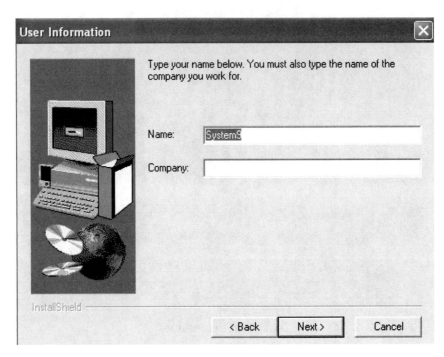

Figure 6-42 Click the **Next** button to continue.

 ▪ Click the **Finish** button (Figure 6-43).

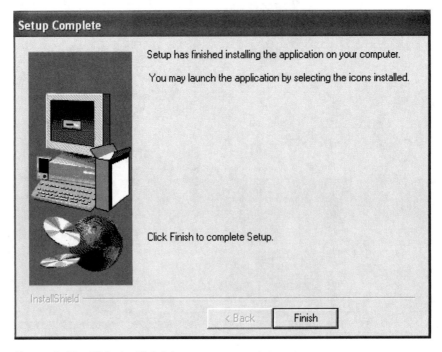

Figure 6-43 Click the **Finish** button to complete setup.

■ Explore the program's options (Figure 6-44).

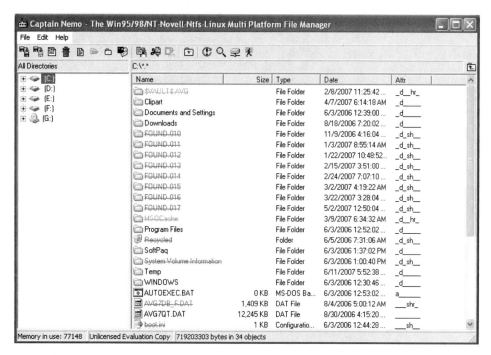

Figure 6-44 Explore the options in Captain Nemo to see how to access a Linux drive.

Chapter 7

Application Password Crackers

Objectives

After completing this chapter, you should be able to:

- Understand password terminology
- Use a password cracker
- Implement various cracking methods
- Perform system-level password cracking
- Perform application software password cracking
- Use default password databases
- Use password-cracking tools

Key Terms

Rainbow table   a table of password hashes created by hashing every possible password and variation thereof to be used in a rainbow attack to recover a plaintext password from a captured ciphertext

Introduction to Application Password Crackers

This chapter deals with password crackers and the tools used in password recovery. It covers concepts such as ways to bypass BIOS passwords, methods for removing CMOS batteries, and Windows XP/2000/NT keys. It also discusses BIOS password crackers and explains the Passware Kit, default password databases, and distributed network attacks.

Password Terminology

Passwords are the gateway to most computer systems. One of the easiest and most common ways to improve security is to adopt good password procedures. According to a survey conducted by an Information Week article in 2002, guessed passwords were found to be responsible for 22%

of all attacks. This indicates that the first step to secure a password is to choose one that cannot be easily guessed.

Passwords can be classified as weak or strong depending on how easy they are to guess or crack. The strength of passwords can be calculated mathematically by the length of time it would take for a brute force cracker to discover them. Strong passwords would take years to crack, while weak passwords could be broken in less than a second.

The strength of a password is not the only thing determining its quality. A good password must also be easy for the creator to remember, or it may need to be written down, which adds another vulnerability.

What Is a Password Cracker?

A *password cracker* is a program that is used to identify an unknown or forgotten password to a computer or network resource. It can also be used to obtain unauthorized access to resources.

Password crackers use two primary methods to discover passwords: brute force and dictionary searches. A brute force cracker runs through combinations of characters of a predetermined length until it finds a combination accepted by the system. When conducting a dictionary search, a password cracker searches each word in the dictionary for the correct password. Password dictionaries exist for a variety of topics, including politics, movies, and music groups.

Some password crackers search for hybrids of dictionary entries and numbers. For example, when a password cracker of this type reaches the word *ants* in its dictionary, it may search for *ants01*, *ants02*, *ants03*, and so on. This can be helpful when users have been advised to include numbers in their passwords.

A password cracker may also be able to identify encrypted passwords. After retrieving the password from the computer's memory, the program may be able to decrypt it. It could also use the same algorithm as the target system to create an encrypted version of the password that matches the original.

How Does a Password Cracker Work?

In order to understand how a password cracker works, it is important to understand how a password generator works. Most password generators use some form of cryptography to encrypt the passwords. For example, take a look at Figure 7-1.

In this table, below each letter is a corresponding number. Thus, A = 7, C = 2, and so forth. This is a code of sorts. But it can be easily decoded. Another example of cryptography is ROT-13, where each letter is replaced by a substitute letter. Moving 13 letters ahead derives the substitute letter (Figure 7-2).

This is, of course, fairly ineffective because there are programs that quickly identify this pattern. Software is available on the Internet that can create strong, difficult-to-crack passwords. In addition, users should change their passwords frequently.

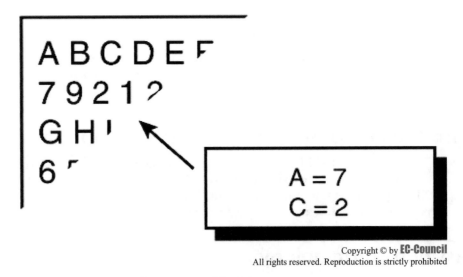

Figure 7-1 This is a simple cryptographic cipher.

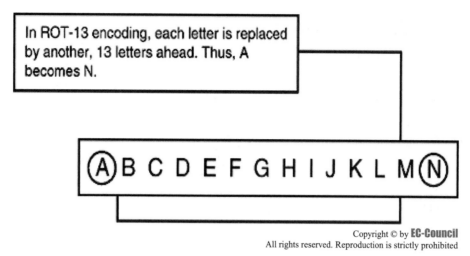

Figure 7-2 ROT-13 is another simple cryptography method.

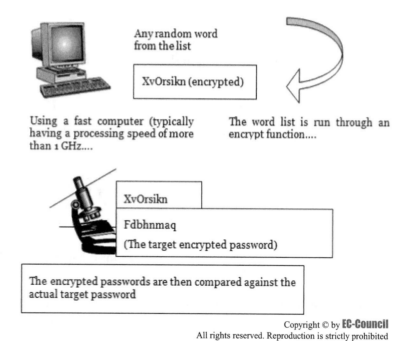

Figure 7-3 This shows how password cracking occurs.

Figure 7-3 shows how password cracking takes place.

The word list is sent through the encryption process, generally one word at a time. Rules are applied to the word and the word is again compared to the target password, which was encrypted using the same rules. If no match occurs, the next word is sent through the process. Some password crackers perform this task differently by taking the entire list of words, applying a rule, and from this, deriving their next list. This list is then encrypted and matched against the target password. The second technique is usually much faster. If a match occurs, the crack is successful. The plaintext word is then sent to a file for later use.

The majority of password-cracking utilities are not user friendly. In fact, when executed, some of them output nothing more than a cryptic message.

Password-Cracking Methods

Most password crackers use one or more of the following methods:

- Brute force attack
- Dictionary attack
- Syllable attack
- Rule-based attack
- Hybrid attack
- Password guessing
- Rainbow attack

Brute Force Attack

In a brute force attack, the attacker tries every possible combination of characters until the correct password is found. It is a slow method and takes a large amount of time against longer passwords.

The program will usually follow a sequence, such as the following:

1. aaaaa
2. aaaab
3. aaaac

The difficulty of a brute force attack depends on the following factors:

- How long can the password be?
- How many possible values can each component of the password have?
- How long will it take to attempt each password?

Dictionary Attack

In a dictionary attack, a dictionary file is loaded into the cracking application that runs against user accounts. The program uses every word present in the dictionary to find the password. Dictionary attacks can be considered more useful than brute force attacks, although they do not work against systems that use passphrases.

This attack can be applied under two situations:

1. In cryptanalysis, it is used to find out the decryption key for obtaining the plaintext from the ciphertext.
2. In computer security, it can be used to guess passwords.

In order to improve the success of a dictionary attack, the attacker may do the following:

- Use a number of dictionaries, such as technical dictionaries and foreign dictionaries
- Use string manipulation on the dictionary, meaning if a dictionary contains the word *system*, then the cracker would also try using *metsys* and other variations

Syllable Attack

A syllable attack is the combination of both a brute force attack and a dictionary attack. This is often used when the password is a nonexistent word. The attacker takes syllables from dictionary words and combines them in every possible way to try to crack the password.

Rule-Based Attack

This type of attack is used when an attacker already has some information about the password. He or she can then write a rule so that the password-cracking software will generate only passwords that meet this rule. For example, if the attacker knows that all passwords on a system consist of six letters and three numbers, he or she can craft a rule that generates only these types of passwords. This is considered the most powerful attack, because the cracker can narrow down the possibilities considerably. This technique combines brute force, dictionary, and syllable attacks.

Hybrid Attack

This type of attack is based on the dictionary attack. Often, people change their passwords by just adding numbers to their old passwords. In this attack, the program adds numbers and symbols to the words from the dictionary. For example, if the old password is "system", the user may have changed it to "system1" or "system2."

Password Guessing

Sometimes users set passwords that can be easily remembered, such as a relative's name, a pet's name, or an automobile license plate number. This can make the password easily guessed. Unlike other methods of password cracking, guessing requires only physical access or an open network path to a machine running a suitable service.

Common weak passwords include the following:

- Blank (none)
- The words *password*, *passcode*, *admin*, and their derivatives
- The user's name or login name
- A relative's name
- The user's birthplace or date of birth
- A pet's name
- Automobile license plate number
- A row of letters from the qwerty keyboard, such as "qwerty," "asdf," or "qwertyuiop"

Rainbow Attack

The rainbow attack is based on the cryptanalytic time-memory trade-off technique. Cryptanalytic time-memory trade-off is a method that requires less time for cryptanalysis. It uses already calculated information stored in memory to crack a code, such as a password. In a rainbow attack, a password hash table called a rainbow table is created in advance and stored into memory. This *rainbow table* is a table of password hashes created by hashing every possible password and variation thereof to be used in a rainbow attack to recover a plaintext password from a captured ciphertext.

During the recovery of the password, the cracker will simply look up the precalculated hash in the rainbow table to find the associated password. This attack reduces the time required to find complex passwords, but it will not work on all passwords.

Time Needed to Crack Passwords

Figure 7-4 shows how long a brute force attack will take under various circumstances. Notice how much more difficult it becomes to crack passwords by adding even one additional character.

System Password Cracking

Passwords for system software are created to prevent access to system files and other secured information that is used during a system's boot process. There are several ways to access a system by cracking these passwords, as discussed following.

Bypassing the BIOS Password

BIOS manufacturers provide a backup password that can be used to access the BIOS setup if the password is lost. The passwords that manufacturers provide are case sensitive. If a particular backdoor password does not work, then various case-sensitive combinations of the password should be tried.

The manufacturer's documentation must be read before trying the backdoor passwords, because BIOS combinations will lock the system completely if the password is typed wrong three times.

Table 7-1 shows various BIOS manufacturers and their backdoor passwords.

Copyright © by **EC-Council**

Figure 7-4 More complicated passwords take significantly longer to crack than simpler ones.

Manufacturer	Default Password
VOBIS & IBM	merlin
Dell	Dell
Biostar	Biostar
Compaq	Compaq
Enox	xo11nE
Epox	central
Freetech	Posterie

Table 7-1 This shows several BIOS manufacturers and their default passwords

Removing the CMOS Battery

A battery attached to the motherboard buffers the CMOS's settings. If the battery is removed and replaced after waiting 20 to 30 minutes, the password will reset itself. Some manufacturers back up the power to the CMOS chipset using a capacitor, so if removing and replacing the battery after 30 minutes does not work, replace the battery after at least 24 hours. Some CMOS batteries are soldered onto the motherboard; trying to remove a soldered CMOS battery may damage the motherboard and other components.

To clear the CMOS settings by removing the battery, follow these steps:

1. Shut down the computer and disconnect the power plug.
2. Locate the battery on the motherboard (approximately ½ inch in diameter).
3. Carefully lift it from the socket and place it aside.
4. Leave it for about 20 to 30 minutes.
5. Replace it in the socket.
6. Plug in and restart the computer.
7. As the computer begins its startup process, press the DEL, F10, or F1 key, depending on the specific computer, to get into BIOS/CMOS setup.

8. Look for the option to set the BIOS/CMOS to its default settings.

9. Check the settings of CPU, memory, and hard drive type and size.

10. Finalize all adjustments, save the settings, and restart the computer.

Jumper Settings

By adjusting the jumpers or dipswitches on a motherboard, all custom settings, including the BIOS passwords, will be cleared. The location of these jumpers or dipswitches on the motherboard varies, so refer to the system's documentation. If the documentation is not available, the jumpers and dipswitches can sometimes be found on the edge of the motherboard, next to the CMOS battery or near the processor. On a laptop computer, the dipswitches are usually found under the keyboard or in a compartment at the bottom of the laptop. Some manufacturers may label the jumpers and dipswitches as one of the following:

- CLEAR
- CLEAR CMOS
- CLR
- CLRPWD
- PASSWD
- PASSWORD
- PWD

To reset CMOS using jumpers or dipswitches, follow these steps:

1. Shut down the computer and disconnect the power plug.

2. Locate the jumpers or dipswitches to reset the BIOS/CMOS.

3. Make a note of the default positions of these jumpers/dipswitches.

4. Change them to the position to reset the BIOS/CMOS.

5. Leave the jumpers in place for 20 to 30 seconds.

6. Now change them back to their default positions.

7. As the computer begins its startup process, press the DEL, F10, or F1 key, depending on the specific computer, to get into BIOS/CMOS setup.

8. Look for the option to set the BIOS/CMOS to its default settings.

9. Check the settings of CPU, memory, and hard drive type and size.

10. Finalize all adjustments, save the settings, and restart the computer.

Tools for System Software Password Cracking

If there are no jumpers or dipswitches for resetting the system password and the battery cannot be removed, then either the BIOS/CMOS chip will have to be flashed by the user or the manufacturer, or tools such as those discussed following may be used to crack the password.

Tool: Windows XP/2000/NT Key Generator

The Windows XP/2000/NT Key Generator recovers most passwords and resets the domain administrator password for Active Directory domain controllers directly from a bootable CD-ROM. It also supports Windows 2003 Server.

Tool: CmosPwd

CmosPwd (Figure 7-5) decrypts passwords for the following BIOS types:

- ACER/IBM BIOS
- AMI BIOS
- AMI WinBIOS 2.5
- Award 4.5*x*/4.6*x*/6.0

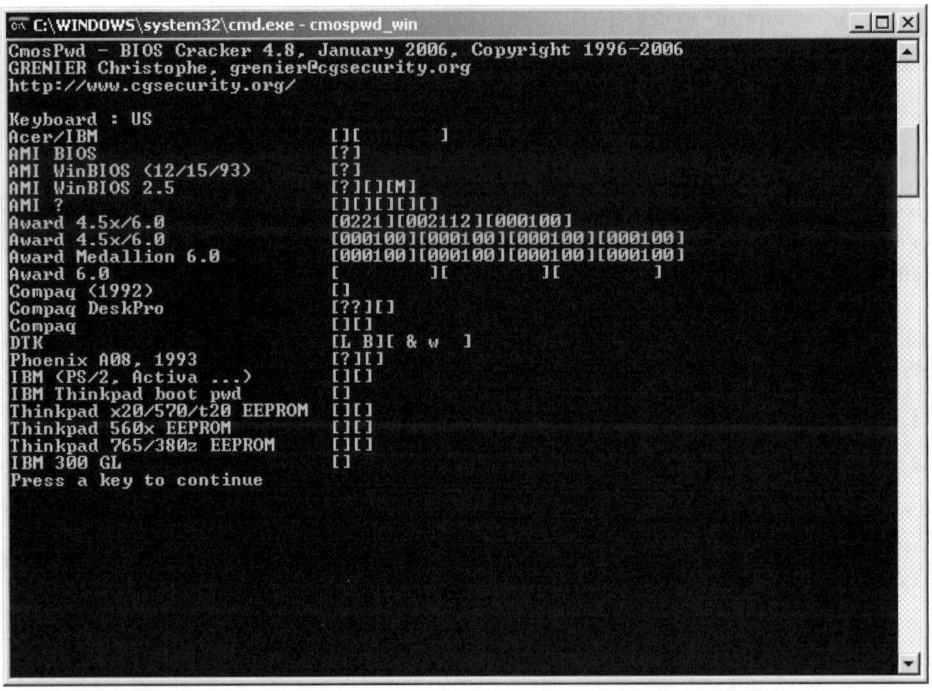

Figure 7-5 CmosPwd cracks several BIOS passwords.

- Compaq (1992)
- Compaq (new version)
- IBM (PS/2, Activa, Thinkpad)
- Packard Bell
- Phoenix 1.00.09.AC0 (1994), a486 1.03, 1.04, 1.10 A03, 4.05 rev 1.02.943, 4.06 rev 1.13.1107
- Phoenix 4 release 6 (User)
- Gateway Solo - Phoenix 4.0 release 6
- Toshiba
- Zenith AMI

Tool: ERD Commander

ERD Commander 2005 directly boots systems into a Windows-like repair environment from a CD, giving complete access to the system. It has network features allowing data to be accessed, and moved to and from the system. It is shown in Figure 7-6, and its features include the following:

- Boots directly from CD
- Has a Windows-like graphical user interface
- Uses Solution Wizard to help select the right tool
- Uses Crash Analyzer Wizard to pinpoint the cause of recent system crashes
- Allows complete disk sanitizing/data removal with Disk Wipe utility
- Includes the Locksmith utility to reset lost administrator passwords
- Includes FileRestore to quickly find and recover deleted files

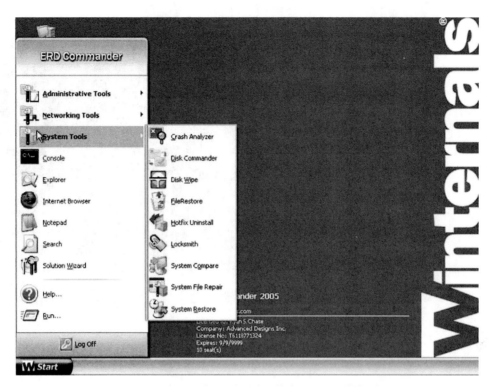

Figure 7-6   ERD Commander directly boots into a Windows-like interface.

- Provides access to XP restore points on unbootable Windows XP systems
- Detects malware and other applications that may be consuming system resources
- Compares key information on unbootable systems with that of a working system for diagnosis and troubleshooting
- Automatically identifies and replaces critical system files that have become corrupt
- Allows for formatting and partitioning of disks
- Provides emergency removal capability for faulty hotfixes
- Has a built-in network access to safely copy data to/from dead systems
- Has repair and diagnostic tools located on Start menu
- Includes repair tools System Restore, System File Repair, Service and Driver Manager, Hotfix Uninstall Wizard, Locksmith, Registry Editor, Explorer, Disk Management, and Command Prompt
- Includes data recovery tools Disk Commander and FileRestore
- Includes diagnostic tools Crash Analyzer Wizard, System Compare, Autoruns, Event Log Viewer, System Information, TCP/IP Configuration, and logical volumes utilities
- Is compatible with Windows NT, 2000, XP, and Server 2003

Tool: Active@ Password Changer

Active@ Password Changer is a DOS-based solution designed for resetting local administrator and user passwords on Windows XP/Vista/2003/2000/NT systems.

The software has a simple FDISK-like user interface (Figure 7-7). It supports multiple hard disk drives, detects several SAM databases (if multiple operating systems were installed on one volume), and provides the opportunity to pick the right SAM before starting the password recovery process.

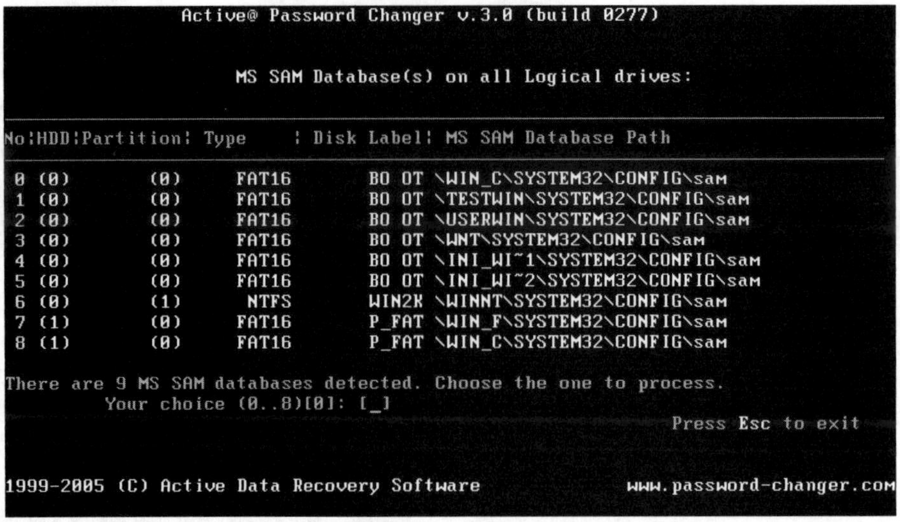

```
                    Active@ Password Changer v.3.0 (build 0277)

                    MS SAM Database(s) on all Logical drives:

No:HDD:Partition: Type    : Disk Label: MS SAM Database Path

  0 (0)      (0)     FAT16       BO OT \WIN_C\SYSTEM32\CONFIG\sam
  1 (0)      (0)     FAT16       BO OT \TESTWIN\SYSTEM32\CONFIG\sam
  2 (0)      (0)     FAT16       BO OT \USERWIN\SYSTEM32\CONFIG\sam
  3 (0)      (0)     FAT16       BO OT \WNT\SYSTEM32\CONFIG\sam
  4 (0)      (0)     FAT16       BO OT \INI_WI~1\SYSTEM32\CONFIG\sam
  5 (0)      (0)     FAT16       BO OT \INI_WI~2\SYSTEM32\CONFIG\sam
  6 (0)      (1)      NTFS      WIN2K \WINNT\SYSTEM32\CONFIG\sam
  7 (1)      (0)     FAT16      P_FAT \WIN_F\SYSTEM32\CONFIG\sam
  8 (1)      (0)     FAT16      P_FAT \WIN_C\SYSTEM32\CONFIG\sam

There are 9 MS SAM databases detected. Choose the one to process.
        Your choice (0..8)[0]: [_]
                                                  Press Esc to exit


1999-2005 (C) Active Data Recovery Software          www.password-changer.com
```

Figure 7-7   Active@ Password Changer resets user passwords.

Application Software Password Cracking

Tool: Advanced Office XP Password Recovery

Advanced Office XP Password Recovery uses brute force and dictionary attacks to recover passwords in the following Office applications:

- Microsoft Word
- Microsoft Excel
- Microsoft Access
- Microsoft Outlook

Tool: Word Password Recovery Master

Word Password Recovery Master cracks passwords on password-protected Microsoft Word documents, allowing them to be opened and edited. Word Password Recovery Master supports documents created in Microsoft Word 97/2000/XP/2003/2007 (Figure 7-8).

Tool: Office Password Recovery Toolbox

Office Password Recovery Toolbox is another tool for recovering passwords for Office documents, including Word, Excel, Outlook, and Access files. It uses an online decrypting server for password recovery (Figure 7-9).

Tool: Distributed Network Attack

Distributed Network Attack (DNA) utilizes the unused processing power of multiple machines across the network to decrypt passwords. In this attack, the DNA server is installed in a central location, where machines running the DNA client can access it over the network. The DNA server coordinates the attack, assigning small portions of the key search to machines distributed throughout the network. The DNA client will run in the background, only taking unused processor time. The DNA server is shown in Figure 7-10.

Tool: Passware Kit

Passware Kit combines more than 25 password recovery programs into one single package, including crackers for Office, Windows 2003/XP/2000/NT (both local and domain administrator accounts), Lotus Notes, WinRAR, WinZip, Access, Outlook, Acrobat, Quicken, QuickBooks, WordPerfect, VBA, and more. Passware Kit is shown in Figure 7-11.

Figure 7-8   Word Password Recovery Master can crack the passwords on Word files.

Figure 7-9   Office Password Recovery Toolbox uses a powerful online server to crack Office passwords.

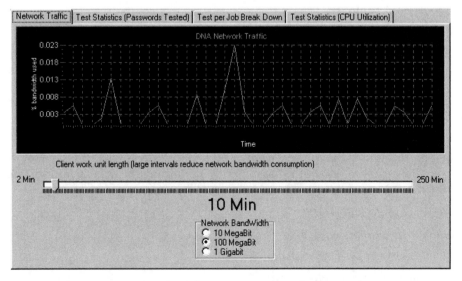

Figure 7-10   DNA uses distributed computing to crack passwords.

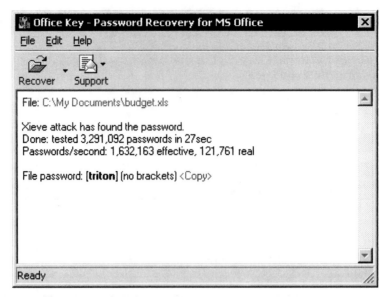

Figure 7-11 Passware Kit combines over 25 password recovery programs.

Tool: Accent Keyword Extractor

Accent Keyword Extractor compiles dictionaries from words that it can find on the Web and then uses these for a dictionary attack. After loading a Web page, it will make a list of words on that page and then follow all links on the page to look for more words. It is an especially powerful tool because it can be used to create dictionaries for any language. The application can sort the words from a Web site in alphabetical order or by the length of the word.

Tool: Advanced ZIP Password Recovery

Advanced ZIP Password Recovery cracks passwords for ZIP files, including self-extracting archives. It is a brute force cracker that can check 15 million passwords per second. For rule-based attacks, Advanced ZIP Password Recovery can be customized according to password length, character set, and various other options.

The user can interrupt the program at any point and later resume the process from the same point. Application ZIP Password Recovery works in the background using idle CPU power (Figure 7-12).

PDF Password Crackers

CrackPDF, Abcom PDF Password Cracker, and Advanced PDF Password Recovery can all be used to access password-protected Adobe PDF files. CrackPDF and Abcom PDF Password Cracker use brute force attacks to discover the passwords, while Advanced PDF Password Recovery simply removes the password protection entirely.

Default Password Databases

A default password database provides a list of vendors and information related to their products' default settings, such as protocols used, usernames, passwords, levels of access, and validation of the passwords. Some of the databases allow users to add to the databases by submitting the default information for their equipment. Some of these databases can be found at the following Web sites:

- *http://phenoelit.darklab.org/*
- *http://www.defaultpassword.com/*
- *http://www.cirt.net/cgi-bin/passwd.pl*
- *http://www.virus.org/default-password/*

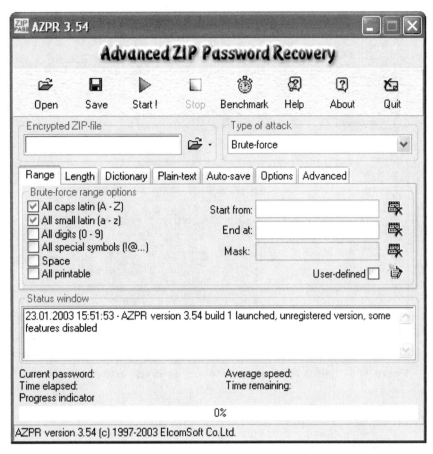

Figure 7-12   Advanced ZIP Password Recovery uses idle CPU time to crack ZIP passwords by brute force.

Password-Cracking Tools

Tool: Cain & Abel

Cain & Abel recovers network-stored passwords using various techniques, such as network packet sniffing, dictionary attacks, brute force attacks, and cryptanalysis attacks. Cain & Abel (Figure 7-13) includes the following features:

- Recovers passwords from VNC profiles, SQL Server Enterprise Manager, remote desktop connections, and wireless connections
- Records VoIP conversations
- Decodes scrambled passwords
- Calculates hashes
- Sniffs traffic and recovers passwords transmitted using most popular protocols, including FTP, SMTP, POP3, HTTP, MySQL, ICQ, Telnet, and others
- Reveals password boxes
- Uncovers cached passwords
- Dumps protected storage passwords

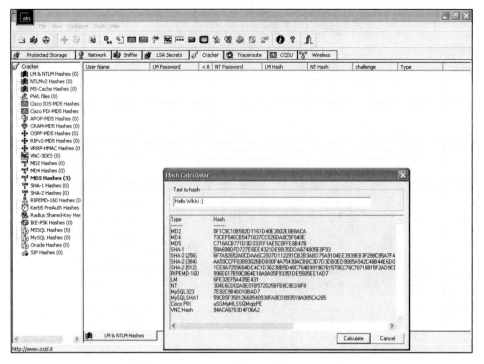

Figure 7-13   Cain & Abel recovers network-stored passwords.

Tool: LCP

LCP audits and recovers user account passwords in Windows NT/2000/XP/2003. It searches for attacks in the operating system, and fixes and recovers forgotten passwords. LCP can import account information from the following sources:

- Local computer
- Remote computer
- .SAM file
- .LC file
- .LCS file
- PwDump file
- Sniff file

LCP can recover passwords using dictionary attacks, brute force attacks, or hybrid attacks (Figure 7-14).

Tool: SID&User

The SID&User tool (Figure 7-15) can recover the SID for a given username, or vice versa, for Windows NT/2000/XP/2003 systems.

Tool: ophcrack

ophcrack is a Windows password cracker that uses rainbow tables and runs on Windows, Mac OS X (Intel CPU), and Linux. It dumps password hashes in the following three ways:

1. Encrypted SAM, in which it dumps the hashes from the SAM (the Security Accounts Manager that manages the database of usernames, passwords, and permissions) and system files retrieved from a Windows machine while booting on another disk

2. Local SAM, in which it dumps the hashes from the Windows machine

3. Remote SAM, in which it dumps the hashes of a remote Windows machine, but requires the username and password of an administrator and the name of the share

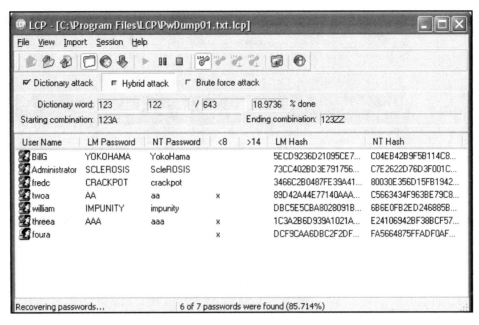

Figure 7-14   LCP recovers user account passwords in Windows.

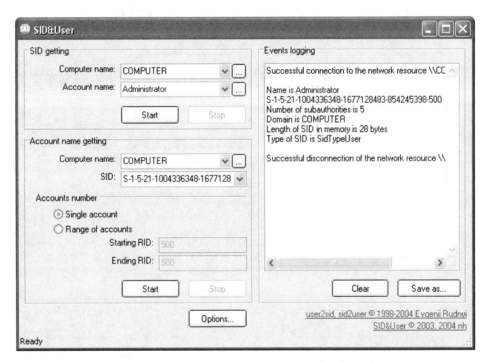

Figure 7-15   SID&User can determine the SID associated with a username.

ophcrack's GUI is shown in Figure 7-16. It is able to successfully crack the following:

- Ninety-nine percent of passwords of six or less characters from this set:
  - 0123456789abcdefghijklmnopqrstuvwxyzABCDEFGHIJKLMNOPQRSTUVWXYZ!"#$%&' ()*+,-
    ./:;&<=>?@[\]^_`{|}~ (including the space character)
- 99% of seven-character uppercase and lowercase alphanumeric passwords
- 99% of eight-character lowercase alphanumeric passwords

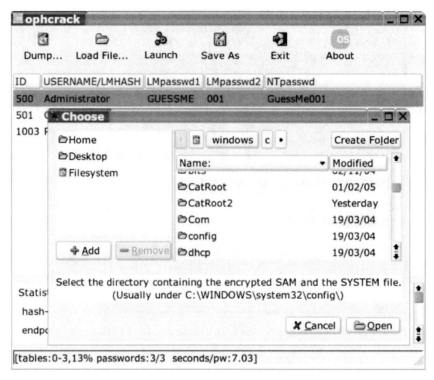

Figure 7-16 Ophcrack uses rainbow tables to quickly crack weaker passwords.

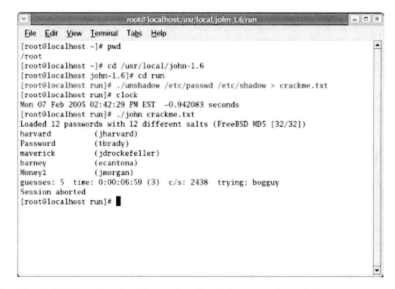

Figure 7-17 John the Ripper is a free, fast, open-source password cracker.

Tool: John the Ripper

John the Ripper is a fast and free password-cracking and auditing tool available for UNIX, Windows, DOS, BeOS, and OpenVMS. It is shown in Figure 7-17 and can quickly identify user accounts with weak passwords.

Tool: DJohn

DJohn, or Distributed John, uses distributed computing on Linux x86, FreeBSD, and Solaris systems to crack passwords using brute force. The DJohn server divides the possible passwords into units and assigns them to clients, which try them and report the result. DJohn should be run on a closed network for added security.

Tool: Crack

Crack is a UNIX password-guessing tool designed to crack weak passwords. It uses very little memory and runs in the background, using the brute force method. Its API allows for easy integration with arbitrary password formats, and it has been tested on Solaris, Linux, FreeBSD, NetBSD, OSF, and Ultrix systems.

Tool: Brutus

Brutus is a brute-force password cracker that can find passwords of HTTP, POP3, FTP, and Telnet servers. It builds 60 connections at a time and is available for Windows operating systems. Its features include the following:

- Facilitates dictionary-based user/password attacks against various network applications
- Recovers valid access tokens like username and password for a given target system, such as an FTP server, a password-protected Web page, or a router console POP3 server
- Has a multistage authentication engine using 60 simultaneous target connections
- No username, single username, and multiple username modes
- Password list, combo (user/password) list, and configurable brute force modes
- Highly customizable authentication sequences
- Loads and resumes position
- Imports and exports custom authentication types as BAD files seamlessly
- SOCKS proxy support for all authentication types
- HTML form/CGI authentication types

Brutus is shown in Figure 7-18.

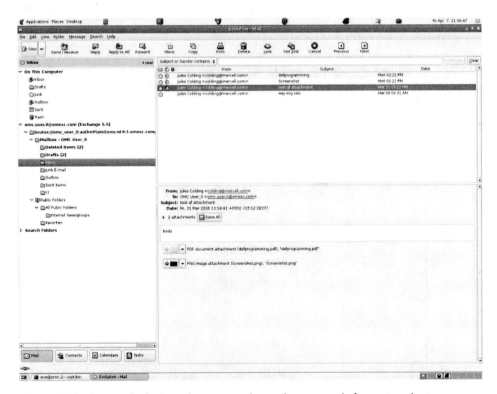

Figure 7-18   Brutus is designed to remotely crack passwords for network servers.

Tool: Access PassView

Access PassView reveals passwords of protected MDB files, including those created with Microsoft Access 95/97/2000/XP or Jet Database Engine. It can be run either as a command-line tool or a drag-and-drop GUI (Figure 7-19). Access PassView can recover main database passwords of up to 18 characters, but it cannot recover user-level passwords.

Tool: RockXP

RockXP retrieves or changes the product keys from Windows XP installations and other Microsoft products. It can also save the product activation information to a file and recover usernames and passwords for Windows Secure Storage, MSN logins, and Internet connection parameters. RockXP as shown in Figure 7-20.

Tool: Magical Jelly Bean Keyfinder

The Magical Jelly Bean Keyfinder (Figure 7-21), is another way to retrieve the product keys for Microsoft products.

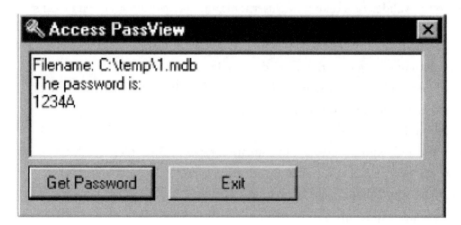

Figure 7-19   Access PassView can determine the passwords of MDB files.

Figure 7-20   RockXP can change the product keys for Microsoft products.

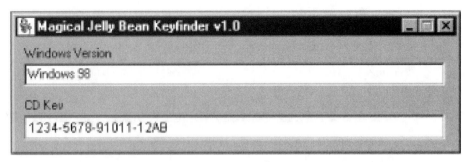

Figure 7-21   Magical Jelly Bean Keyfinder retrieves Microsoft product keys.

Filename	Encryption	Version	CRC Value	Password 1	Password 2	Password 3	Full P:
Copy of 1.pst	Best	14	0x2dfd2d88	bt7FL4	Pvjs27	VNrljI	F:\Do
Copy (2) of 1.pst	Best	14	0x8b1b92b8	SU48Y6	Q8SGl7	WMfeYA	F:\Do
2.pst	Best	14	0xa1a5248e	gr5q9	0EeBW3	LVA5c4	F:\Do
3.pst	Best	14	0x586a0425	2222	YUTqJB	hkMkvE	F:\Do
0000.pst	None	14	0xa52a526a	EfsT04	TWYw76	yk1Qr9	F:\Do
abcd.pst	Best	23	0xccc6120d	abcd	sph9t0	mRSGU1	F:\Do
Copy of abcd.pst	Best	23	0xccc6120d	abcd	sph9t0	mRSGU1	F:\Do
Outlook.pst	Compressible	23	0x00000000				F:\Do
6.pst	Compressible	14	0xcfba9599	6	yZUzCC	YUfCxF	F:\Do
nir1.pst	Compressible	14	0xd0286bd1	nir1	lsCm61	SBEG68	F:\Do
1.pst	Best	14	0xd7e37b41	4YCyv	bi5gh4	1f3tA5	F:\Do
1234.pst	Compressible	14	0xbaa73fbf	1234	yZdHpA	hkNkwC	F:\Do
5.pst	Compressible	14	0x00000000				F:\Do

16 pst file(s), 1 Selected

Figure 7-22   PstPassword provides possible passwords for Outlook PST files.

Tool: PstPassword

PstPassword recovers lost passwords of PST files in Outlook 97, Outlook 2000, Outlook XP, and Outlook 2003. It provides three different passwords for each password-protected PST file. It's possible that one of them will be the original password, or none of them will, but they will all work. PstPassword is shown in Figure 7-22.

Tool: Protected Storage PassView

Protected Storage PassView is a small utility that reveals the passwords stored by Internet Explorer, Outlook Express, and MSN Explorer by reading information in Windows Protected Storage. It works on Windows 95/98/ME/NT/2000/XP. As shown in Figure 7-23, this tool can extract passwords that the user has chosen to save, as well as AutoComplete forms in Internet Explorer.

Tool: Network Password Recovery

The Network Password Recovery tool recovers all network passwords stored for the current user. This utility (Figure 7-24) can extract the following types of passwords:

- Login passwords of remote computers on the LAN
- Passwords of mail accounts on the Exchange server
- Passwords of MSN Messenger accounts
- Passwords of password-protected Web sites

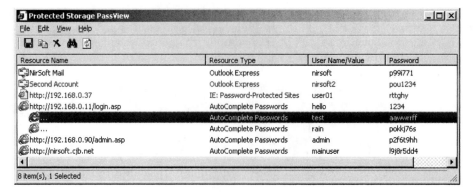

Figure 7-23 ProtectedStorage PassView shows passwords that the user has chosen to have various Windows programs remember.

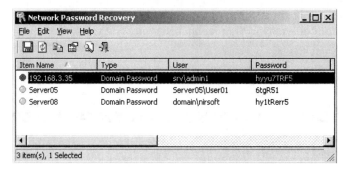

Figure 7-24 Network Password Recovery can recover saved passwords to LAN computers.

Tool: Mail PassView

Mail PassView is a password-recovery tool that reveals the passwords and other account details for the following e-mail clients:

- Outlook Express
- Microsoft Outlook 2000 (POP3 and SMTP accounts only)
- Microsoft Outlook 2002/2003 (POP3, IMAP, HTTP, and SMTP accounts)
- IncrediMail
- Eudora
- Netscape 6.*x*/7.*x*
- Mozilla Thunderbird
- Group Mail Free
- Yahoo! Mail (if the password is saved in Yahoo! Messenger application)
- Hotmail/MSN mail (if the password is saved in MSN Messenger application)
- Gmail (if the password is saved by Gmail Notifier application or by Google Talk)

For each e-mail account, the following information is displayed:

- Account name
- Application
- E-mail

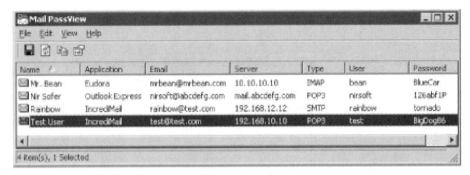

Figure 7-25   Mail PassView recovers passwords for several e-mail clients.

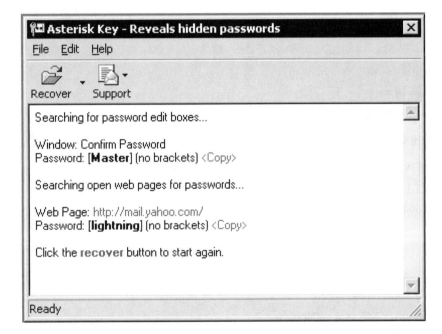

Figure 7-26   Asterisk Key shows the passwords hidden under asterisks.

- Server
- Server type (POP3/IMAP/SMTP)
- Username
- Password

Mail PassView is a standalone executable (Figure 7-25).

Tool: Asterisk Key

The Asterisk Key utility (Figure 7-26) instantly reveals passwords that are hidden under asterisks. After clicking the program's **Recover** button, all passwords obscured by asterisks in opened windows are shown.

Tool: Messenger Key

Messenger Key (Figure 7-27) instantly recovers passwords for instant messaging programs, including the following:

- ICQ
- ICQ Lite

Figure 7-27 Messenger Key recovers passwords for instant messaging programs.

- MSN Messenger
- Google Talk
- Yahoo! Messenger

Tool: MessenPass

MessenPass is another password recovery tool for instant messaging programs, including the following:

- MSN Messenger
- Windows Messenger (in Windows XP)
- Yahoo! Messenger (versions 5.*x* and 6.*x*)
- Google Talk
- ICQ Lite 4.*x*/2003
- AOL Instant Messenger
- AOL Instant Messenger/Netscape 7
- Trillian
- Miranda
- GAIM

MessenPass is shown in Figure 7-28. It is used to recover the passwords for the current user, and only works if the user knows the password for one of the other programs listed above. A user cannot use this program to get other users' passwords. The program will detect instant messenger applications installed on the computer, decrypt the stored passwords, and display all username/password pairs that it finds. The ones that it finds are only those that are in the current user's profile.

Tool: Password Spectator

Password Spectator shows passwords hidden behind asterisks in Windows. The program will always stay on top of other windows, displaying passwords in fields where the cursor moves, as demonstrated in Figure 7-29.

Tool: SniffPass

SniffPass listens on the network, captures the passwords that pass through the network adapter, and displays them on the screen instantly. On any 32-bit Windows operating system, it captures passwords that use the following protocols:

- POP3
- IMAP4

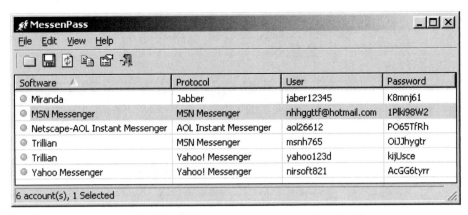

Figure 7-28   MessenPass recovers passwords for the current user's IM software.

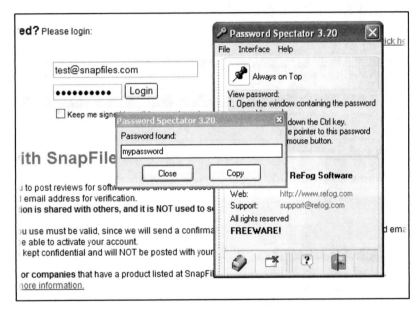

Figure 7-29   Move the mouse over a password field and Password Spectator will show the stored password.

- SMTP
- FTP
- HTTP (basic authentication passwords)

SniffPass is shown in Figure 7-30.

Tool: Asterisk Logger

Asterisk Logger is another tool that reveals the passwords stored behind the asterisks in standard password text boxes under Windows 9*x*, Windows ME, Windows 2000, and Windows XP. Asterisk Logger can also display additional information about the revealed password, such as the date and time on which password was revealed, the name of the application that contains the revealed password box, and the executable file of the application. It does not work with Internet Explorer Web pages, however.

Asterisk Logger can save its results in HTML format (Figure 7-31).

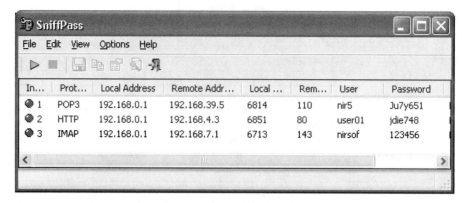

Figure 7-30 SniffPass listens to the network adapter for any passwords that go through it.

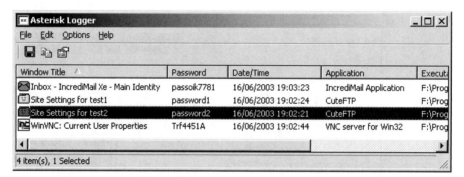

Figure 7-31 Asterisk Logger displays passwords stored under asterisks.

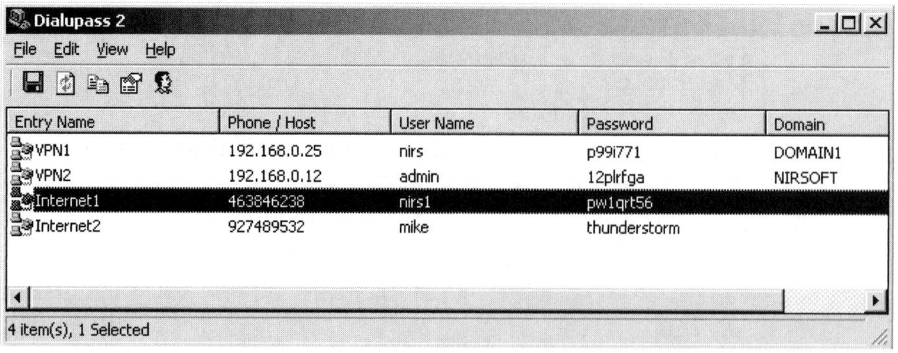

Figure 7-32 Dialupass retrieves passwords for Windows dial-up networking.

Tool: Dialupass

Dialupass enumerates all dial-up entries on the computer and reveals their stored logon details, including username, password, and domain. This program works on Windows 95, Windows 98, Windows ME, Windows NT, Windows 2000, and Windows XP. On Windows 2000 and Windows XP, Dialupass only reveals dial-up passwords when the user is logged on with administrator privileges. Dialupass works only if the user has chosen to save the logon information (Figure 7-32).

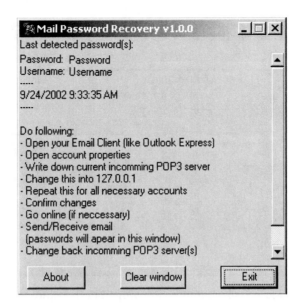

Figure 7-33 Mail Password Recovery can recover the password for any POP3 server, regardless of the e-mail client.

Tool: Mail Password Recovery

Mail Password Recovery allows users to recover e-mail passwords for any POP3 account, as long as it is stored in an e-mail program on the computer. It only works with POP servers, so it will not work for Web-based e-mail services. In order to use the program, follow these steps:

1. Open the e-mail client (such as Outlook or Thunderbird).
2. Open the account properties.
3. Write down the current incoming POP3 server.
4. Change this server to 127.0.0.1.
5. Repeat this for all necessary accounts.
6. Confirm the changes.
7. Tell the e-mail client to check for new messages.
8. The e-mail passwords should appear in Mail Password Recovery.
9. Change the incoming POP3 servers to their original values.

Mail Password Recovery is shown in Figure 7-33.

Tool: Database Password Sleuth

Database Password Sleuth (Figure 7-34) instantly recovers passwords for Microsoft Access 95/97/2000/2002 databases.

Tool: CHAOS Generator

CHAOS Generator creates a password of any length and character content, and then copies that password to the clipboard. It works on all Windows operating systems (Figure 7-35).

Tool: PicoZip Recovery

The PicoZip Recovery tool uses brute force and dictionary attacks to recover passwords from ZIP files. It supports both ZIP archives and self-extracting ZIP files, and can pause and resume the attack at any time. PicoZip Recovery supports Windows 95/98/NT/2000/XP (Figure 7-36).

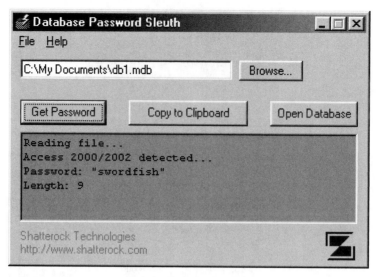

Figure 7-34 Database Password Sleuth instantly recovers Microsoft Access passwords.

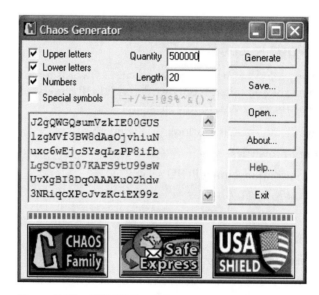

Figure 7-35 CHAOS Generator generates passwords of any length, using any characters.

Tool: Netscapass

Netscapass reveals the stored mail password (POP3 server password) for Netscape Communicator 4.*x*, Netscape 6.*x*, and Netscape 7. It also reveals the stored passwords for Web sites in Netscape 6.*x* and Netscape 7. It does, however, have the following limitations:

- Netscape 6.*x*/7.*x* passwords cannot be recovered if they were encrypted with a password by using the password manager.

- If Netscape 6.*x*/7.*x* is installed on Windows NT/2000/XP, the utility can show only the passwords of the current logged-on user.

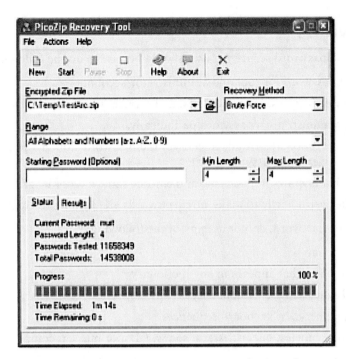

Figure 7-36 PicoZip Recovery uses brute force and dictionary attacks to unlock ZIP files.

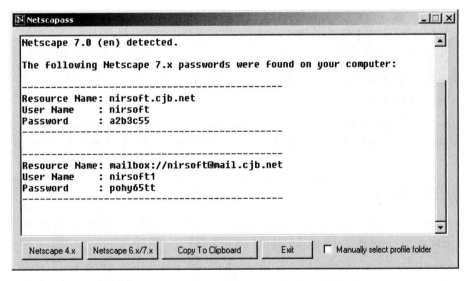

Figure 7-37 Netscapass recovers e-mail passwords from Netscape.

- Netscape Versions 4.5 and above save the profile's information in a special file named nsreg.dat instead of using the registry as in earlier versions. If Netscapass is unable to find the passwords, use the **Manually select profile folder** option, and select the profile folder manually.

To use Netscapass, load the program and click the button corresponding to the version of Netscape currently being used (Figure 7-37).

Securing Passwords

In order to improve password security, a user should be sure to do the following:

- Use a strong password for root and administrator accounts.
- Stop unrequired services, buggy services, and services not protected by a well-configured firewall.
- Change the administrator's password periodically.
- Use strong encryption algorithms to encrypt the password storage files, such as the SAM (Security Account Manager) and passwd.conf file.
- Use a filter that operates in real time, and enforce some level of length and complexity of passwords.
- Run a cracker periodically to make sure passwords are difficult to crack.

When selecting a password, do not use any of the following:

- The account name
- Any word or name that appears in any dictionary
- Phrases and slang with or without spaces
- Alphabetic, numeric, or keyboard sequences
- Titles of books, movies, poems, essays, songs, CDs, or musical compositions
- Any personal information
- Any combination of characters resembling a vanity license plate
- Any character repeated more than once in a row

A strong password should have the following characteristics:

- Contain at least eight characters
- Include a digit or punctuation
- Use uppercase and lowercase letters
- Be easy to remember
- Have words separated by a symbol
- Include special characters

Always use different passwords on different machines, and be sure to change them periodically. When changing to a new password, make it a completely new one and not just a minor variation of an older password.

Chapter Summary

- A password is a secret series of characters created to secure important files from unauthorized access.
- A password cracker is a program that can decrypt passwords.
- Password crackers are used for both legitimate and illegitimate purposes. Users can recover lost or forgotten password using password crackers, and hackers can use them to break into systems.
- Crackers use various cracking methods such as brute force, dictionary attack, syllable attack, rule-based attack, distributed network attack, and guessing.
- Password-cracking software is classified as system software password cracking and application software password cracking.

Review Questions

1. What is a password cracker?

   _____

   _____

2. How does a password cracker work?

   _____

   _____

3. Why is a rule-based attack considered more powerful than other password-cracking methods?

   _____

   _____

4. How is password-cracking software classified?

   _____

   _____

5. What is system-level password cracking?

   _____

   _____

6. Describe Distributed Network Attack (DNA).

   _____

   _____

7. What are rainbow attacks?

   _____

   _____

8. Differentiate between syllable, rule-based, and hybrid password attacks.

   _____

   _____

9. What is a default password database?

   _____

   _____

10. Describe the features of a secure password.

    _____

    _____

Hands-On Projects

1. Use Advanced PDF Password Recovery.

   - Download and run the Advanced PDF Password Recovery tool from *www.forensics-intl. com/breakers.html*.

   - Load a password-protected PDF file into the program.

   - Remove the password.

2. Use Word Password Recovery Master.

   ▪ Download and run the Word Password Recovery Master tool from *www.rixler.com/ word_password_recovery.htm*.

   ▪ Load a password-protected Word file into the program.

   ▪ Discover the password.

3. Browse a default password list.

   ▪ Visit *www.defaultpassword.com*.

   ▪ Browse the list of default passwords.

4. Run the Cain & Abel tool to recover your network-stored passwords.

Index